Thoughts on th

"They won the Super Bowl with a waiver-wire team. No one has done anything like that before."

—Ex-Packers GM Ron Wolf, March 17, 2002

"Robert Kraft, who owns the New England Patriots, has proven conventional wisdom wrong on two counts since buying the franchise in 1994: dynasties are not possible in the NFL in this age of salary caps (the team will be going for its third Super Bowl in four seasons this year) and you cannot finance a new stadium without significant taxpayer money (Gillette Stadium was financed by private debt backed by revenue from the new stadium)."

—*Forbes* magazine, September 2004

"Under the circumstances as they are now, we may never see another coach win three Super Bowls in our lifetime."

—Bears GM Jerry Angelo, September 28, 2005

## Praise for *The Blueprint*

"Price's level of research is evident. His chronicles of the checkered past of the team to its current power are thorough and his sources varied as he draws on the experience of everyone from former players to season ticket holders to fellow beat writers."

—*New Hampshire Union Leader*

"Price . . . delivers a brisk narrative of the snakebit early years of the Patriots and a thorough examination of the personnel deals and philosophy that have lately brought in the players who won Super Bowls for them. . . . He's done enough to make me return to the couch on Sunday."

—Jay Jennings, *The New York Times Book Review*

# THE
# BLUEPRINT

# THE
# BLUEPRINT

### HOW THE **NEW ENGLAND PATRIOTS**
### BEAT THE SYSTEM TO CREATE THE
### LAST GREAT NFL SUPERPOWER

## CHRISTOPHER PRICE

THOMAS DUNNE BOOKS

St. Martin's Griffin ≋ New York

THOMAS DUNNE BOOKS.
An imprint of St. Martin's Press.

THE BLUEPRINT. Copyright © 2007 by Christopher Price. All rights
reserved. Printed in the United States of America. For information,
address St. Martin's Press, 175 Fifth Avenue, New York, N.Y. 10010.

www.thomasdunnebooks.com
www.stmartins.com

*Book design by Michael Collica*

Library of Congress Cataloging-in-Publication Data

Price, Christopher.
    The blueprint : how the New England Patriots beat the system to
create the last great NFL superpower / Christopher Price. — 1st St.
Martin's Griffin ed.
        p.   cm.
    ISBN-13: 978-0-312-38485-2
    ISBN-10: 0-312-38485-8
    1. New England Patriots (Football team)   I. Title.

    GV956.N36 P74 2007
    796.332'640974461—dc22                        2007022083

First St. Martin's Griffin Edition: September 2008

10 9 8 7 6 5 4 3 2 1

*Kate. Without you, none of this would be possible.*

# CONTENTS

# ACKNOWLEDGMENTS

I am a Natural-born Sportswriter. I have a knack for it, a God-given talent. After I first learned that it was possible to sleep late and go to work at Two in the afternoon, and still get Paid for it, I never did anything else.

—*HUNTER S. THOMPSON*

I loved writing both versions of this book, but this is perhaps my favorite part of the whole process—thanking those people who helped make it all possible. Many folks were thanked the first time around, but there are a select few who deserve another set of thank-you's, like the folks at St. Martin's—Pete Wolverton, Katie Gilligan, Elizabeth Byrne, and Joe Rinaldi—who all played a major role in the success of *The Blueprint*. Thank you. And the indefatigable team of Greg Dinkin and Frank Scatoni at Venture Literary are the best pair of agents you could hope for.

Setting aside the many unbelievable on-field aspects of the 2007 Patriots' season, there were plenty of colleagues who made it a fun year, most of whom I managed to thank in the first version. But there *were* folks I forgot on the first one who deserve a mention here, people like Hector Longo, Mike Lowe, Doug Flynn, Dave Brown, Russ Charpentier, John Tomase, Michael Felger, Karen

Guregian, and Christopher Gasper. In addition, a special shout-out goes out to Charlie Pierce—his book *Moving the Chains: Tom Brady and the Pursuit of Everything* is an excellent read for anyone wanting to get inside the head of the Patriots' quarterback. (Here's hoping we see you in the third row of the Gillette Stadium press box sooner rather than later, sir.) And Kevin Winter, Adam Jones, and Chris Curtis carried me through a season of football analysis on ESPN 890. You are all professionals, in the truest sense of the word.

There were several good folks who have passed through the halls at Metro over the last year who were great friends and colleagues, but who were not mentioned in the hardcover edition but deserve a sincere thank-you here: Stuart Layne, Matt Killorin, Jason Notte, Neda Ahanin, Marissa Berenson, Nathan Fried-Lipski, and Meghan Healy are all tremendous. And Jordan Raanan and Dave Sandora are two great colleagues: a big thanks to you all. And another round of thanks goes to Jeff Howe, who continues to do a fantastic job. You're the best, Jeff, even if you did go to UMass.

Friends remain a constant in my life, and while many of them were thanked in the first edition, there are others who deserve an extra set of thanks. Julie Cornell put in overtime while proofreading the paperback. Mac Constantine is one of the biggest Patriots fans I know, and always makes sure I keep my eyes on the prize. (Brighton Center is a great place to be a football fan—if you're ever in the neighborhood, stop by Jim's Deli for lunch, and then go see Mac at 3 Scoops for some good food and good football talk. Tell them Chris sent you.) I owe each one of my friends a healthy commission—they were some of the best salespeople around when it came to spreading the gospel of *The Blueprint*. I also want to thank any one of the hundreds of folks who came out to one of the many book signings throughout New England over the course of the fall and the winter, e-mailed me with kind words, or simply bought a copy, liked it, and recommended it to a friend.

In the end, none of this happens without my family. Every bit of success I have ever achieved I owe to them. And again, I couldn't have done any of this without my wife, Kate. She remains, as always, the best wife a sportswriter could ever hope for. She—along with our faithful cat, Stretch, helps make our house the best home-field advantage I could ever hope for. Thank you for being you.

—Christopher Price
June 2008

## INTRODUCTION

# THE TRIUMPH OF SMART FOOTBALL

> We are building a big, strong, fast, smart, tough, and disciplined
> football team that consistently competes for championships.
> —*MISSION STATEMENT, NEW ENGLAND PATRIOTS*

I wish I could tell you that I knew something big was going to happen. Back in the summer of 2001, I wish I could say, "Yep, I knew that these Patriots were going to be something special. I knew they had what it takes to not only win the Super Bowl that year, but to go on and win three of the next four."

But I didn't. Truth was, no one thought that, and if any football writers say they did, they're lying. When I started covering the team that July for Boston Metro, I thought I knew a little something about the game of football, but truth be told, I had no idea that Bill Belichick and the Patriots were on to something. In fact, as summer became fall, I distinctly remember feeling vaguely disappointed, that I had shown up late to a party that had gone on throughout the mid-1990s. I had missed the good times, the craziness and the electricity that came along with the Bill Parcells era. As it started to fade into memory, the tales from the older reporters became taller, and the legend of the Tuna grew. *I was here when he held his introductory press conference—he answered all of*

1

*the questions in ancient Aramaic. . . . Did you know that the Rat Pack thought he was so funny that they asked him to open for Sinatra at the Sands? . . . I once saw him coach a game against the Oilers using just eight guys—including a kicker—and he still found a way to beat them!*

And more important, I had missed all the feuds between the coach and owner, battles that had dominated the New England sports pages when Parcells had left in a huff for New York four years before. I had missed the playoff football. I had missed the big games. And maybe, most importantly, I missed all the great quotes. *She's coming along. I reserve the right to change my mind. If they want you to cook the dinner, they should at least let you shop for some of the groceries.* Now, all that was left were a few holdovers like Drew Bledsoe, Tedy Bruschi and Willie McGinest, as well as a few others who could still spin a tale or two about life with Parcells. And there was Bill Belichick, a dour man who was famous for his sleep-inducing press conferences. There was no more show. There was no more razzle-dazzle. There was no promise. All that was left was a nondescript team of fairly anonymous players who suited up every Sunday in one of the worst stadiums in the National Football League.

(Of course, it didn't help matters that in the old stadium, the Patriots held press conferences in Super Box A, a large room that offered a magnificent view of the playing field, but, on a clear day, would attract all sorts of sunlight, which would heat the room an extra ten to fifteen degrees. The warmth, combined with Belichick's delivery, could knock out a weary reporter in a matter of minutes, leaving him snoozing in the back row of the press room like a college freshman sitting through a lecture on physics.)

But slowly, something started to happen, something dramatic. Through the fall of 2001, the puzzle pieces started to come together . . . and everyone gradually started seeing what exactly was going on. After Bledsoe went down, he was replaced by Tom Brady, Troy Brown kept catching passes, Adam Vinatieri kept kicking game-winning field goals, and the season kept going, on and on, far past the point where any of us in the press believed it was going to reach. There was the six-game win streak to close out the regular season. There was the Snow Bowl in January, when the Patriots beat Oakland on a pair of Vinatieri field goals and knocked off the Steelers to reach Super Bowl XXXVI.

Along the way, Belichick's pet phrases—"The strength of the wolf is the pack" or "It's not about collecting talent, it's about assembling a team" were two favorites—started to become more than just empty sayings you might find on a business motivational poster. They had helped give life to this unassuming, ragtag team that was somehow standing on the cusp of history that Sunday night in New Orleans.

I don't think I fully comprehended what was going to happen until there was less than a minute left in Super Bowl XXXVI. I was sitting and typing an early story for Boston Metro in a press room underneath the stands at the Superdome when I looked up at the television. Brady had just led the Patriots on the drive of his life, and Vinatieri was lining up for the kick that would give the Patriots their first title in the forty-two-year history of the franchise. "What Tom Brady just did," said John Madden as Vinatieri came onto the field, "gave me goose bumps."

That's when it hit me. I turned to my friend Mike Parente, who was covering the game for the *Woonsocket Call*, and said, "The Patriots are going to win the Super Bowl." Growing up as a sports fan in New England through the 1970s and 1980s, there were some safe bets: The Celtics would always find a way to win it, the Red Sox would always find a way to blow it, and the Patriots would always find some way to embarrass you. The words "Patriots" and "Super Bowl" had as much business being in the same sentence as "Carrot Top" and "Academy Award." As someone who had grown up in New England—and had followed the Patriots since I was old enough to know what football was—it was a phrase I never thought I'd hear. For years, the Patriots were a laughingstock, not only throughout New England, but in the sports world in general. And now, they were going to win the Super Bowl. It was as if the mom-and-pop store down the street, the one that had been run into the ground by a crazy uncle and nearly forced to close up shop half a million times, had suddenly gotten its act together and was set to announce a takeover of IBM.

Hours later, after the game was over and the postgame interviews had concluded and the stories had been filed, I grabbed a beer as I was leaving the press room and stepped out onto the floor of the Superdome. I collected a handful of red, white, and blue confetti for a friend who was a colossal Patriots fan and stuffed it in my bag. I wanted to make sure I remembered the moment. After all, the Patriots winning the Super Bowl? It would almost certainly be a once-in-a-lifetime thing.

But somewhere along the way, the franchise became the gold standard for the rest of the league. Brady, David Patten, and the rest of the Cinderellas did not turn into pumpkins after Super Bowl XXXVI. Richard Seymour evolved into one of the best defensive linemen in the league. And it all played out against the backdrop of brand new Gillette Stadium, a state-of-the-art venue that opened in February 2002.

Visitors who gained access to the inner hallways at Gillette saw a series of giant billboards that lined the walls with motivational phrases from people like John Wooden and Magic Johnson. Placed there to inspire employees, they ostensibly contained the secrets of building a successful franchise—and some believed them to be the guideposts to the sudden success of the Patriots. But the real secrets to their success aren't located on the walls of Gillette Stadium, but tucked away in a filing cabinet in the front office. They are a very simple set of core beliefs when it comes to team-building that has managed to make the Patriots the last NFL superpower.

---

*New England has approached the salary cap era in a manner differ-ent than most.* Since the mid-1980s, most of the great teams either mortgaged their future on a handful of players, depended too heavily on one player, or simply allowed their teams to grow old together. The 49ers of the late 1980s and early 1990s were at the end of one of the best runs in the history of the game, and, with multiple Hall of Famers, were a franchise at the peak of its power after defeating the Chargers in Super Bowl XXIX. But the onset of age and some highly questionable contracts made it clear they were woefully unprepared for life in the salary cap era. As a result, their mismanagement during a key stretch has doomed them to failure for most of the last ten years. The Cowboys of the early 1990s wagered on a trio of young offensive stars—Troy Aikman, Emmitt Smith, and Michael Irvin—and it paid off with three titles in four years. But they also were unable to plan for life in the salary cap era, so when the trio retired, so did the Cowboys' chances at Super Bowl glory. The team is just now starting to make a serious return to championship contention. And the Den-ver teams of the late 1990s placed most of their eggs in one basket, creating an entire team around quarterback John Elway, a formula that paid off with back-to-back titles in the late 1990s. However, de-spite a steady stream of Pro Bowl running backs and offensive line-men since then, as well as one of the most highly regarded coaches in the game, they have won just two playoff games since Elway's retirement after the 1998 season.

Ultimately, these were teams that believed they could only gain success in the short term. In the NFL, the conventional wisdom when it came to dealing with the new NFL economy went some-thing like this: *With the salary cap, balanced scheduling, the onset of free agency and planned parity, there's no way anyone will be able to maintain a high level of success over an extended period of time.* So teams threw money at stars, mortgaging their future by maxing out their budgets on a handful of talented players who could help them rise above the pack for a two- to four-year period. They knew they had a relatively small window of opportunity, and they believed the best way to take advantage of the situation was to strike while the iron was hot, finances be damned.

But that short-term glory ultimately came at a heavy price. Instead of planning for real long-term success—and maybe passing on a high-level player here and there in the name of seeing an even bigger picture—those teams lived for the present, settling for short-term gain by overpaying big-name players and not watching their bottom line. As a result, they have been consigned to salary cap hell.

In direct contrast, the Patriots did not make a mad rush toward the free agent buffet. After Belichick and Scott Pioli took control in 2000, the Patriots signed a collection of mostly bargain-basement free agents who could fit into the system that Belichick was working with. He knew his signees weren't always the kind of player who was the most talented at their position. But quite often they were above-average players—and to put it simply, no one had found the proper way to utilize their talents. Linebacker Mike Vrabel was going nowhere in a Pittsburgh system. Wide receiver David Patten was thought of as nothing more than a nice complementary player, someone who could provide depth at receiver. Defensive back Otis Smith was thought of the same way on the other side of the football. Ditto for veterans like Mike Compton and Bryan Cox, both of them veterans who simply couldn't fit in in other locales.

In New England, they inked contracts with the Patriots that had a low impact on the salary cap, but ultimately brought sizable returns on New England's investment because they were able to find a place in Belichick's system, a system that valued versatility and the strength of the team over the success of the individual. Vrabel quickly became a bedrock at linebacker for the Patriots, playing a major role after he arrived prior to the 2001 season. Patten made his mark as one of the most dependable receivers in the game; during his time in New England, no receiver caught more touchdown passes from Tom Brady than he did. And Smith, Compton, and Cox all brought a veteran's toughness that became the hallmark of the 2001 Patriots.

And while there have been some free agents busts—wide receiver Donald Hayes, defensive lineman Steve Martin, and linebacker Monty Beisel are three notable examples of deals gone bad—the Patriots have stuck to their philosophy, often passing on the flashiest player in favor of one who will do a better job of fitting into their scheme, both financially and otherwise. In recent years, defensive lineman Ted Washington, tight end Christian Fauria, and safety Rodney Harrison are three examples of relatively low-cost, high-impact free agents who have become key players in the Patriots' run. It all comes back to the bottom line: Sometimes, you're better off avoiding the supremely talented player who may or may not fit into your scheme and choosing an above-average player who wants to sacrifice everything in the name of becoming part of something special, something bigger than himself.

*If you want to win in the NFL, there is zero room for sentimentality.* Good character or no, contracts are awarded based on the possibility of future performance, not past performances. As a result, under Belichick and Pioli, popular players have been shipped out without hesitation. After the 2001 season, quarterback Drew Bledsoe was traded to a divisional rival for a draft pick, while safety Lawyer Milloy was flat out released days before the start of the 2003 season. There is a coldness there, a Machiavellian approach that some personnel men and coaches simply don't have the stomach for. There are no lifetime achievement awards for a longtime veteran looking to coast into retirement with a fat contract. And you can't afford to have emotion color your analysis of a player, especially at the bargaining table, where a bad contract can hamstring a franchise for a generation. In New England, many times, a player is looked at simply as a commodity, and when that commodity isn't worth what the owner is paying for it, he is let go.

Unlike some other sports, there is a bottom line for winning in the NFL—a darker side—and the Patriots are well aware of it.

The Milloy incident is the most striking. The safety was one of the key figures in New England's unlikely run to the title in 2001, a popular and hard-hitting player who had managed to build a reputation as one of the better defenders in the league. In addition, it was clear that he and Belichick were tight. All you had to do was look at the NFL Films presentation of the Patriots' celebration in the moments following their improbable win over the Rams in Super Bowl XXXVI. After Adam Vinatieri's game-winning kick sailed through the uprights, Belichick throws his arms in the air. The first person to hug him was his daughter, Amanda. The second person to join him in celebration was Milloy. But prior to the start of the 2003 season, Belichick and the rest of the New England coaching staff clearly believed the cost of keeping Milloy around far outweighed what they were getting on the field. After a brief give-and-take between the Patriots and Milloy's agents, New England decided to cut him loose. Around the NFL, the move was widely construed as a mistake. Milloy was a well-established player, familiar with the Belichick system and immensely popular with his teammates, including golden boy quarterback Tom Brady. Most of the thirty-one other teams believed the easy move would have been to buckle to the contract demands and give Milloy the dollars he was looking for, salary cap be damned. *He's a popular veteran, he's put in plenty of time with the team, and he helped them win a Super Bowl. Why not take the cap hit? He deserves the reward.*

But the Patriots are not most teams. With an eye on the bottom line, they decided to release him. The move looked even worse when, in the days before the season opener against Buffalo, he signed with the Bills, and helped Buffalo deliver a 31–0 smackdown of the Patriots. It was a short-term nightmare for New England, but Belichick and New England were proven right in the end. Without Milloy, the 2003 Patriots would go down as one of the great teams in NFL history, putting together a fifteen-game win streak and rolling to their second title in three years. If they had signed Milloy to the deal he wanted, they knew the cap hit they were going to take would have long-term ramifications on their financial situation. Instead, they ultimately traded a week of bad press for a spot in the NFL record books.

*The ownership has placed its complete trust in the front office.* Currently, Carolina's Jerry Richardson is the only former pro football player who owns an NFL team. But that doesn't prevent many owners from acting as if they know just as much about the game of pro football as any general manager, coach, scout, or player—or maybe more. Instead of standing back and letting their football men run the show, these meddlesome owners can send a team spiraling in the wrong direction for years with their hands-on approach.

For the Patriots, this was very nearly the case in the mid-1990s. In 1996, owner Robert Kraft and head coach Bill Parcells engaged in a notable spat over who the team should take with its first-round pick in the draft. Parcells preferred a defensive lineman—reportedly, Cedric Jones, Duane Clemons, or Tony Brackens—while Kraft was pushing for a wide receiver, specifically Terry Glenn. Kraft won out, and according to several media members, he later boasted: "Well, there's a new sheriff in town." It was a dispute that was the first of a long line of squabbles between the coach and the owner, one that led to Parcells leaving at the end of the season. Kraft later told reporters: "I had it up to here with that guy. . . . It just isn't any fun to go down there. [What happens with Parcells] is my decision. I own the team. He works for me. With me, it's a matter of respect. We give him everything he wants, and still he shows no respect for me." At his farewell press conference, Parcells uttered one of the great sound bites in the history of sports media, one he believed summed up his relationship with Kraft. "If they want you to cook the meal, they should at least let you shop for some of the groceries."

Obviously scarred by the relationship, Kraft hired Belichick in

2000 and retreated mostly to the shadows. There's quite a difference when you compare the present situation to the fight for control that marked the previous years in Foxboro, and a stark contrast to many teams around football whose owners think they have the acumen to make personnel suggestions. In Foxborough, it's clear who makes the moves: Belichick and Pioli.

"I trust Bill's judgment to do things that are right for the team," Kraft said shortly after the team released Milloy before the start of the 2003 season. "He explained to me what he was doing and we supported him. Did I feel bad as a fan? Absolutely."

That level of trust has paid off for Kraft: Over the last five years, the team has become one of the most lucrative sports franchises in the world. In 2005, the Patriots joined the exclusive billion-dollar club. The Forbes 2005 National Football League team value rankings put New England at No. 3, at $1 billion, trailing only the Redskins and the Cowboys. Elsewhere in sports, only Manchester United, the famed United Kingdom soccer team, carries a billion-dollar price tag.

"When I bought the team, I was a kid with peach fuzz who hadn't shaved. And I got nicks and scrapes," said Kraft, years after his experience with Parcells. "You have to get knocked around and see for yourself firsthand. It's an intoxicating business, and you can get seduced by it. . . . My involvement in the trenches was something I would change."

"I'm thankful Robert allows us to do what we do," Pioli said. "He understands what we have going here. We've got an owner that asks questions—but doesn't question us."

*It's not about collecting talent. It's about assembling a team.* In Foxborough, it's an oft-repeated phrase that cuts to the heart of the Patriots' team-building approach. Every team wants a Pro Bowler at each position, but it's a far-fetched concept. Instead of trying to shoot for the moon with every signing, you augment your true superstars at the key spots with as many above-average players as possible—preferably players who are willing to put the goals of the team ahead of their personal goals and share the same big-picture concept with management.

In 2001, the Patriots were roundly ridiculed for passing on heralded Michigan wide receiver David Terrell. New England had an offense that had finished near the bottom of the league in receiving yards, and, on paper, appeared to clearly need some help when it came to stretching the field. Instead, they settled on defensive lineman Richard Seymour out of Georgia. The move was made after the Patriots had a chance to sit down with Seymour to discover not only what sort of player he was, but the kind of person he is. "I know what kind of player Bill wants in his system," Pioli has said. "The word we use is 'makeup.' We're very concerned about a player's makeup. My job is to find players who are compatible with their head coach."

That doesn't mean the Patriots haven't signed big-ticket free agents. They were able to agree on a deal with premier pass-rushing linebacker Rosevelt Colvin after the 2002 season, and did the same after the 2006 season, inking Adalius Thomas to a similar contract. It just means that if that particular player isn't likely to fit into their system, they'll take a pass, no matter how talented that player might be. "What Scott [Pioli] and I have always believed in, and continue to believe in, is to try to add quality people and quality players to this football team," Belichick said in 2002.

But the secret to their success goes beyond talking points. As the years have gone on, it's clear the Patriots draft smart and look for talent on places it wouldn't normally occur the other thirty-one teams to look. They work the free agent market like an expert trader, knowing when to buy (Vrabel, Harrison, Colvin) and when to sell (Milloy, Bledsoe). They think differently than their competitors, seeking out football opinions from people outside the game—like Ivy League economists and statisticians. And despite their great level of success, they stayed motivated, using a series of slights (some of them real, some of them only perceived) from all corners of the football world to remain hungry.

As a result of their success over the next few years, a late January trip to some exotic far-off location—like Houston or Jacksonville— for the Super Bowl has almost became part of my annual itinerary, the same way a trip to the in-laws for Thanksgiving is automatically penciled onto the calendar at the start of every year. *Schedule flight. Book hotel room. Pick up rental car. Observe and write about Super Bowl victory. Grab commemorative confetti for friend. Fly home. Repeat the following season.* It was only after the third trip— after the Patriots beat the Eagles to win Super Bowl XXXIX, their third title in four years—did I start to think that maybe there would be a book here.

At first, the idea for the project would be modest in size, something along the lines of "A Year with a Champion." But the project started to evolve, to become bigger in scope. It was clear there was more at work here. It was a friend who made the ultimate suggestion: Why not take a look at the Patriots in the same manner Michael Lewis approached *Moneyball*? While the concept was slightly different—the Oakland A's operated on a fixed income against teams that had unlimited budgets, while New England operated with the same budgetary restraints as the rest of the NFL, all having to deal with a salary cap—the general idea was the same. In a league where there are so many forces operating to bring a team back to the middle, how does one break free? With free agency, a salary cap, and balanced scheduling working to hinder all thirty-two teams in their aspirations to become a dynasty, how does a team go about building a champion? And more important, how does it sustain that championship level over an extended period of time?

Along the way, I discovered some new truths about the team I grew up pitying. The Patriots have hit upon a convergence—really, the NFL's perfect storm. The ownership hired the proper people to run their football operations, adding people like Belichick and Pi-oli, men who had a singular vision of what it would take to build a successful program over a long term. Belichick, having learned from his previous experience as a head coach in Cleveland, placed the right people in the right places, hiring talented and forward-thinking assistants and coordinators who would help lay the foundation for success—and who could serve as his eyes and ears when he was unable to judge.

When it came to a rebuilding plan, those decision makers had some leeway with a fan base that didn't expect a whole lot from a franchise that had spent the better part of forty years doing nothing but frustrate them. When it came to ownership, Robert Kraft put the lessons into place he had learned while wrestling with former head coach Bill Parcells; this time, he stood back and gave complete control of the franchise to a group that had a clear and distinct plan for success. That ownership gave them the final say about who to draft or trade and about any moves needed to bring a championship. And the decision makers were able to find the sort of talent that could fit into the system—smart and savvy men who knew that the price of a title is often subordinating your own interests to a greater good. In the end, it has added up to a business model that has delivered the unlikeliest dynasty in the history of the NFL.

CHAPTER ONE

# THE PUNCHLINE

I knew the Boston media was going to be tough, but this is ridiculous.

*—PATRIOTS HEAD COACH CLIVE RUSH, AT ONE OF HIS INTRODUCTORY PRESS CONFERENCES WITH NEW ENGLAND, JANUARY 30, 1969. RUSH HAD JUST INTRODUCED HIS NEW GENERAL MANAGER, AND WENT TO GRAB THE MICROPHONE—WHICH WAS UNGROUNDED—AND LET OUT A PIERCING SCREAM. SOMEONE REALIZED WHAT WAS HAPPENING, AND PULLED THE PLUG FROM THE SOCKET.*

**A**t the end of the 1950s, there were few American institutions as well established as the National Football League. Under Commissioner Bert Bell, the league had a stable hand at the rudder. Bell had guided it through a difficult stretch that included a challenge from the All-American Football Conference, as well as a period of unprecedented growth that had made a motley collection of owners who were teetering on the brink of financial ruin into a unified group of wealthy individuals. By 1959, they were able to stand side by side with Major League Baseball as a viable professional entity.

And why not? They had more money than most third-world countries. They had owners who were willing to pour cash into their product. They had larger-than-life coaches like Vince Lombardi and Paul Brown, square-jawed Midwestern men of honor who put team above everything in the quest for a title. And it had the stars needed to rival baseball: Johnny Unitas, Sam Huff, Paul Hornung, and Jim Brown; all joined the league within a four-year span in the late 1950s and went on to become authentic American pop culture archetypes, larger-than-life characters who loomed over the sports landscape.

And most importantly, the owners had television. While baseball was distrustful of television, the NFL embraced it. In 1950, the Los Angeles Rams and Washington Redskins had all their games televised, while other teams were able to strike separate deals that would ensure at least some of their games were on television. The following year, the DuMont Network paid the league $75,000 to televise the 1951 NFL Championship Game nationally. The ratings were enough to draw attention from other networks, and NBC upped the ante in 1955, becoming the official televised home of the NFL Championship Game—and paying $100,000 to the league for the privilege. But the league entered a new realm on December 28, 1958, when a nationwide audience watched the NFL Championship Game at Yankee Stadium between the Baltimore Colts and New York Giants. In a game that went into sudden-death overtime, Johnny Unitas, Alan Ameche, Roy Berry, Sam Huff, and Frank Gifford became household names. Known since as the Greatest Game Ever Played, the images from that game—Unitas masterfully leading his team down the field, the physical charisma of Huff, the heroics of Ameche—built a passion for the game that would grow throughout the rest of the century. "Three days later, Castro's forces would overthrow Cuba. But on December 28, 1958, America witnessed the beginning of its own revolution—and this one would be televised," said Michael MacCambridge in *America's Game: The Epic Story of How Pro Football Captured a Nation*. "Like a rebel army seizing the seat of power, pro football had announced its insurgency with an epic football game at the most hallowed ground in baseball, the House That Ruth Built."

Into this climate came a rich young Texan by the name of Lamar Hunt. Hunt had watched the 1958 title game, and like the rest of the American sporting populace, he was transfixed. He had petitioned the NFL for a team, but had been turned down. Despite their level of success, the thinking among NFL executives was that the league must be careful not to "oversaturate" the market by expanding too quickly.

In response, Hunt decided to start his own league—the American Football League, or AFL. Hunt's new league boasted all kinds of cash. He was the heir to a fortune built on Texas oil—in 1948, *Fortune* magazine said his father, H. L. Hunt, was the richest man in world—and would never have to work a day in his life if he didn't want to. In New York, he got the support of Barron Hilton of the Hilton hotel chain. Houston's Bud Adams, the wealthy scion of another Texas oil family, was also part of the group. These were men with deep, deep pockets. Many others who were soon involved weren't as wealthy as those men, but they at least owned their own stadium, like Denver's Bob Howsam. Hunt quickly found like-minded millionaires who were interested in replicating the success of the NFL, inking deals in New York and Los Angeles. By the end of the summer of 1959, they had six teams, two shy of their goal to start a new league.

That's when Boston entered the picture.

Pro football and New England never seemed to fit. It started in the early stages of the twentieth century, when the Boston Redskins began playing in 1932 at Braves Field. Owner George Marshall was the man at the controls of the Redskins—who were originally named the Braves, because they shared Braves Field with their baseball brethren. They moved their base of operations to Fenway in 1933, and were a perfectly pedestrian 15–15–4 over their first three seasons. As a result, the city's sports fans paid relatively little attention. For Marshall, the final straw came in 1936, when Boston won its last three regular season games to vault into the NFL Championship Game—and only 4,813 showed up for the regular-season finale. Despite the fact that Fenway was to host the NFL Championship, an enraged Marshall moved the game to the Polo Grounds in New York, where the Redskins were handed a 21–6 loss by the Green Bay Packers. Marshall soon gave up on Boston, as the Redskins moved to Washington a year later.

In 1944, pro football gave Boston another shot with the Boston Yanks. Ted Collins—known as the manager for singer Kate Smith—tried to get a team in New York, but had to settle for Boston. The Yanks merged with Brooklyn in 1945 and joined the All-America Football Conference a year later. But no series of moves could help the troubled franchise, which would go 9–24 over three years before moving to New York.

As the world of professional football continued to grow throughout the 1950s, Boston sports fans were left on the sidelines, content to watch a budding Celtics dynasty and the final act of Red Sox legend Ted Williams. Instead, they adopted the Giants as their football team. New York games were broadcast throughout New England, and generations of football fans were raised on stories of Huff, Gifford, and Charlie Connerly.

But that wasn't going to stop Billy Sullivan. The Boston business-man and former Notre Dame public relations man spent the better part of the 1950s trying to obtain an NFL franchise for the city. He had a grand vision of a pro football team in Boston, complete stadium having a retractable roof and plenty of luxury boxes. After all, Boston was the biggest city in the country lacking a football team. *Why shouldn't Bostonians be able to watch football?* Throughout the decade, he had a team squarely in his sights: the lowly Chicago Cardinals. The Cardinals had lost more than a hundred games and roughly $1 million in the 1950s, thanks in large part to the Bears, who ruled the hearts and minds of the Chicago football fans. Sullivan, as well as a small group of Boston-area businessmen, believed they could attract the Cardinals to New England.

But while Sullivan was long on charm and guile, he was short on cash—at least, the kind of cash needed to land an NFL team. "Billy Sullivan was a great character," said sportswriter Leigh Montville, who covered the team for *The Boston Globe* for almost twenty years as a beat writer and columnist. "I've always felt he was like Frank Skeffington in *The Last Hurrah*. You know, the ultimate Boston Irish bullshitter."

Sullivan loved football, but was in way over his head when it came to raising the kind of dough needed to support a professional football team. And there were several other people—many of whom had deeper pockets than Sullivan and his investors—who were interested in the Cardinals. Ultimately, he lost out to St. Louis. He then turned his attention to Hunt and the AFL. And after some creative politicking—he fended off last-minute attempts to put a team in Philadelphia or Atlanta, and helped sway the other AFL owners with testimonials from former Notre Dame coach Frank Leahy—and even though he had to borrow $17,000 of the $25,000 entry fee, Hunt and the boys allowed him to join what they had started calling the Foolish Club on November 17, 1959. There was no money, no stadium, no head coach, and no general manager, and the first league draft was in six days. But just like that, Boston was officially in the business of professional football. Sullivan had almost single-handedly won over the AFL with charm and guile. In retrospect, Hunt was a bit bemused by the whole thing.

"We talked to people from anywhere and everywhere, including Atlanta, but none of them were very good because, obviously, we would have taken somebody good in another city that had a stadium before we would have taken a city without a stadium. It shows how desperate we were to take a man we'd never met and who had no money and no stadium," Hunt said in *The New England Patriots: Triumph and Tragedy*.

"Boston probably had the most unusual beginnings of any franchise in history; in fact, I'd call them very improbable, especially from the standpoint of how we do things today: all the research that goes into the people, the city, the Stanford Research Institute reports, all that kind of thing," he would add. "But I guess there never would have been an American Football League if we'd had enough sense to do those things."

There was little time to pat each other on the back, however, as the front office had to get to work quickly: Forty-one players were taken by the Patriots in that first draft, with the top pick being Ron Burton, an All-American running back out of Northwestern. In addition, Syracuse halfback Gerhardt Schwedes was the first player taken by Boston in the territorial draft. Shortly afterward, the Patriots announced that Mike Holovak was the director of player personnel, while Ed McKeever was tapped to be the first general manager. The team immediately began adding players, with Clemson quarterback Harvey White becoming the first to sign a contract with the Patriots. And on February 8, 1960, Lou Saban was named head coach.

Now, all they needed were some team colors and a mascot. Sullivan had a letter from artist Walter Pingree which he liked that read:

Dear Mr. Sullivan,

As a rapid [*sic*] football fan and delighted with our new Boston Patriot's [*sic*], Pro-football team, I would respectfully like to submit my original idea for the Patriot's [*sic*] uniforms. Red, white, and blue colors are a symbol for patriotism. I believe this uniform to be unique and colorful, and indeed worthy of the fine team I know we will have here in Boston. I am looking forward the the [*sic*] coming season with eagerness and much enthusiasm and you can count on

me as one who will be there to root the team on, win, lose,
or draw.

> Sincerely,
> Walter J. Pingree

Sullivan quickly responded in kind, sending Pingree a letter dated April 7, 1960. On a letterhead bearing the Metropolitan Coal and Oil Company—of which Sullivan was president—he replied with the good news:

> Dear Mr. Pingree:
> I can't begin to tell you how much we appreciate your
> thoughtfulness in reference to the uniform. I am sure it will
> please you to learn that we are planning to adopt it, and, as
> the first step, we are having a uniform designed along the
> lines of that which you suggested. A couple of changes have
> been made, but they are relatively slight. I think you will be
> happy to learn that *The Boston Globe* is taking a color pic-
> ture of one of our players wearing the new uniform, and it
> will appear before long in that fine publication. I will look
> forward to meeting you in the near future, but meanwhile, I
> do want you to know that we are very grateful for your
> thoughtfulness.
>
> > Sincerely,
> > William H. Sullivan

The local entry was named the Boston Patriots, and there was cause for real optimism as they began their first season. From 1962 through 1964, Mike Holovak guided them to 26 wins in 42 games, and they did make an appearance in the 1963 AFL title game. They were part of a new and exciting league, a wide-open counterpart to the three-yards-and-a-cloud-of-dust conservatism that domi-nated the buttoned-up world of the NFL. It was the league that de-livered mavericks like Al Davis to the world of professional football and appealed to younger fans by offering a flashier alternative to the more conservative NFL. Team uniforms were bright and colorful. Wide-open offenses were commonplace, led by talented quarterbacks like John Hadl, Daryle Lamonica, and Len Dawson, all of whom led deep passing attacks. It certainly caught the eye of a Maryland teenager named Bill Belichick. "It was kind of exciting," Belichick would recall years later. "You had some guys there like [Hank] Stram, and the two-point play and [Joe] Namath, and there seemed to be something that was a little bit different than the NFL. . . . It seemed like there was less defense. A lot of high-scoring games. There were a lot of exciting players in that league—maybe it was because there wasn't much defense, I don't know. It seemed like there was a lot of 41–38, some of those kinds of games. It was entertaining. It really was."

In Boston, they were able to boast an impressive offense of their own. That talented team included running back Jim Nance, who won a pair of AFL rushing championships. Quarterback Vito "Babe" Parilli was the starting signal caller for seven years, leading the offense throughout the 1960s and making three AFL All-Star teams. On defense, the Patriots also boasted a nucleus of talented young players. Linebacker Nick Buoniconti made five consecutive AFL All-Star Games over the course of his career with the Patriots. The pass rush was manned by Bob Dee, who became one of the most dependable players in franchise history, never missing a game from 1960 through 1967. He was joined by defensive tackle Jim Lee Hunt, who had twenty-nine sacks in his career. But the best-known star of the 1960s was Gino Cappelletti, the team's placekicker and ace wide receiver. The Minnesota product, who was working as a bartender when he tried out with the team, became the AFL's all-time high scorer with 1,100 points. He was a five-time AFL All-Star, and one of only three players to play in every game in the AFL's ten-year history.

But as the 1960s wore on, it was clear that there would be more cases of low comedy than high drama. That was first evident during a late season game at Boston University in 1961, when the Patriots were involved in a tight contest in front of their first home sellout, and the overflow crowd had surged forward onto the sidelines in anticipation of a Boston win. Down the stretch, the Patriots held a 28–21 lead and were desperately trying to hold off the Texans as the clock ticked down. Dallas wide receiver Chris Burford shook clear in the end zone and appeared to have a game-tying touchdown pass from quarterback Cotton Davidson well within his sights. But a man in a London Fog trench coat burst from the sidelines, knocking down the pass. The officials never saw the play—despite the protestations of Burford—and Texas officials only realized what had happened after they watched the game film later that week.

In 1968, in hopes of trying to increase media interest in the team, the franchise invited reporters to sit in with them during the college draft. Head coach Mike Holovak, general manager Ed McKeever and the rest of the assistants were with them as they prepared to draft defensive lineman Dennis Byrd of North Carolina State. Holovak told reporters he was going to give Byrd a call at home to let him know he has been taken by the Patriots. The writers in the room listened in on the conference call, which, by all accounts, went something like this:

HOLOVAK: "Is Dennis there, please?"
ANSWER: "He's not."
HOLOVAK: "This is Mike Holovak, the coach of the Boston
    Patriots, and I'd like to get in touch with him. Do you
    know where I can reach him?"
ANSWER: "The hospital."
HOLOVAK: "Hospital? What's he doing in the hospital?"
ANSWER: "He's just had a knee operation."

All in all, it was a less than memorable draft for Boston. Later in the day, the team came close to drafting a wide receiver . . . who had been killed in an accident a month earlier.

23

In 1969, the franchise introduced Clive Rush as vice president and head coach. Rush was nearly killed in one of his introductory press conferences when he grabbed an ungrounded microphone. And in his first season with the Patriots, he was caught short-handed before a game when starting defensive back John Charles was getting his ankles taped. Sullivan burst in with a contract in an attempt to get him signed. Charles refused the deal, and was released on the spot. Moments later, sitting in the stands, Bob Gladieux—who had been cut by the team ten days earlier—told his friends he was going to get a hot dog. Gladieux then heard his name over the public-address system, asking him to report to the locker room. When his friends saw him thirty minutes later, he was in a Patriots uniform making the tackle on the opening kick-off. (Gladieux would later tell reporters he had drunk too much earlier in the day and came to the sidelines after the tackle and got sick.)

Later in 1969—after the Patriots lost their first seven games—Rush decided on a new plan of attack. Prior to the eighth game of the season, against Houston, reporters would later reveal that Rush came up with the idea for the Black Power Defense. He told his team he'll be the first coach in the history of the NFL to put eleven black players on the field at the same time. However, Rush failed to see the error in his logic—he didn't have eleven black players on defense at the time. As a result, he was forced to convert a handful of offensive players to defense. After Houston quarterback Don Trull was sacked midway through the first half, forcing the Oilers into a third-and-long situation, the Black Power Defense made its one appearance on the field—and Trull fired a pass down the middle for an easy first down.

"The whole Clive Rush era was amazing. He just did a bunch of goofy things," recalled Montville. "Every day when you went in to talk to him, he had a big glass of scotch, and he'd be drinking scotch with the big bottle right on the desk. I was new, I thought, 'Hey, maybe all these guys drink scotch.'

"You'd come in there as a reporter, and he'd say, 'What are you, fact or flair?' I thought it over, and said, 'I'm probably more flair,'" Montville said. "He said things like, 'You know who you should talk to? [Legendary Oklahoma football coach] Bud Wilkinson. Here, I'll get him on the phone.' And he'd call up Bud Wilkinson and Bud Wilkinson wouldn't know what to say and I wouldn't know what to say."

It wasn't just the coaches who were colorful. In 1973, linebacker Steve Kiner managed to write his name in franchise infamy. According to a Will McDonough story in 1999, Houston ran a pass play early in a game against the Patriots, and Kiner never moved. "Throughout the play, he stands with his hands on his shell pads in a two-point stance, and simply watches," recalled McDonough. "Fellow linebacker Edgar Chandler asks him what he is doing. Kiner says he doesn't know, and adds, 'I think I better leave the field now.'"

(Kiner was unique. McDonough recounted another incident that took place the year before, while Kiner was driving a rental car in Tennessee, when he was stopped by a sheriff. "The sheriff had questions about Kiner's license and registration, so he told Kiner to follow him to town," wrote McDonough. "Which he did. The sheriff stopped at the police station, but Kiner kept going, out the other side of town. The sheriff chased him down and said, 'Didn't I tell you to follow me to the station?' Kiner replied, 'But you didn't say anything about stopping.'")

However, despite the occasionally odd antics coming from their Boston franchise, the AFL not only survived, it thrived. Most expansion leagues that sprang up throughout the United States in the 1960s and 1970s were fly-by-night operations that struggled to get from one year to the next, let alone gain any sort of footing with the American sporting public. In 1974, the World Football

League mounted a brief challenge to the NFL. The teams signed some sixty NFL stars and regulars by June of that year, including Larry Csonka, Jim Kiick, and Paul Warfield. But the cash ran out quickly, and the league barely made it through two seasons before folding. The same thing happened in pro hockey with the World Hockey Association and in pro basketball with the American Basketball Association. In each case, it was a lack of funds that did them in. The American Football League was the lone exception. The AFL remains the only league in North American pro sports ever to have merged with a major league and have *all* its teams continue to exist.

At the start, the AFL owners were not only extremely wealthy, but extremely savvy. They endorsed the idea of revenue sharing, which meant each one of the AFL teams would get an equal share of the television revenue money paid by ABC. As a result, each of the eight teams in the AFL entered the 1960 season guaranteed to earn more in television revenues than five of the established franchises in the NFL, instantly making them financially viable. (On June 9, 1960, the league signed a five-year television contract worth $8.5 million with ABC, which brought each team roughly $170,000. And in 1965, the league signed a lucrative $36 million television contract with NBC.) As a result, the AFL did not lose any teams after its first year of operation. In fact, the only major change was the relocation of the Chargers from Los Angeles to San Diego.

For all of the instant stability the AFL provided, the Patriots were clearly the exception to the rule. They appeared to spend most of the latter half of the 1960s stuck in their own theater of the absurd. After a strong start, they began sliding back in the mid-1960s. After moving from site to site throughout the decade, they began the 1969 season at Boston College's Alumni Stadium—returning to the field that had hosted their home games in 1963—and played their home games the following year at Harvard's home field. Hunt's concerns about the Patriots were coming true.

No stadium meant no stability. And that was a big headache for the league, both from a public relations and a financial standpoint. The moving from venue to venue wasn't easy on the franchise: Each time the team was forced to move into a new home, it was forced to pony up some cash for new amenities. In both Harvard and Boston College's case, that meant money for a new playing surface. At BC, the team also paid for the building of a new parking lot. At Harvard, the university allowed them to use just one locker room, which the Patriots allowed the visiting teams to use. As a result, the Patriots were forced to dress at a nearby motel and meet underneath the stands for pregame and halftime.

During a preseason game on August 16, 1970, at Boston College, Patriots fans were forced from the stands by a fire that ignited under the bleachers. (Radio broadcaster Gil Santos later confessed to feeling like the radio operator of the *Titanic;* he continued to broadcast the game as the flames drew closer.) Midway through the 1970 season, Rush suffered a breakdown. He was fired and replaced by John Mazur, who spent most of the next year feuding bitterly with his general manager, who spent most of *his* time battling with Sullivan over personnel issues and money problems. The franchise had gone through three coaches and four home fields in its first ten years of existence.

However, all that was in the past as they prepared to open Schaefer Stadium. In the eyes of Billy Sullivan, it was the final step in a long and laborious quest to legitimize pro football in New England. Sullivan had been getting plenty of pressure from the league to get a suitable venue, one with at least 55,000 seats. After all, this wasn't the Foolish Club anymore. The league was heading into a new era. The AFL-NFL merger was completed in 1970, and things became more uniform. There were significant upgrades in all facets of the game. New stadiums were going up around the country. Beginning in late 1966, St. Louis, Atlanta, Pittsburgh, Philadelphia, and Cincinnati all opened new multisport stadiums within four years of one another. Film exchanges between the teams became mandatory. Each thirteen-team conference was divided into three divisions, with the best record among the division nonchampions receiving a wild-card berth into the playoffs with the division winners. And *Monday Night Football* made its debut in 1970, bringing professional football into prime time. The league had dramatically changed since Sullivan and the Patriots joined the party ten years earlier.

And so New England stepped into the modern era of pro football with a new venue of its own. It was a long time in coming. After traipsing from Boston University to Fenway Park to Harvard to Boston College, Sullivan had exhausted all local possibilities as well as a few outside the state. (Over the years, he made a series of threats to move the team to any number of cities, including Tampa, Seattle, Toronto, and Memphis.)

In the late 1960s, Sullivan talked with city and state officials about finding some funding to build a beautiful new home for his football team. However, no one on Beacon Hill was interested in rolling out the cash for a new stadium, so he was one of the first owners in professional sports to exploit the idea of naming rights. (It was a plan first tried by baseball's St. Louis Cardinals, who, in 1966, as a franchise owned at the time by Anheuser-Busch, proposed naming their then-new ballpark Budweiser Stadium. When this idea was nixed by the commissioner of baseball, they then proposed the title Busch Memorial Stadium after one of the company's founders. The name was readily approved; Anheuser-Busch then immediately afterward released a product called Busch Bavarian beer—now known as Busch beer. The name would later be shortened to Busch Stadium.)

If the Cardinals found funding with Anheuser-Busch, Sullivan could do the same. He inked a deal with New York–based Schaefer Brewing Company for a cool $1 million. In return, the NFL got its first taste of naming rights. Sullivan also raised money through the sale of 400,000 shares in Stadium Realty Trust. And after a sizable donation of land from the Foxboro Raceway, Sullivan and the Foxborough town fathers announced on April 4, 1970, that the team would build a 60,000-seat stadium in Foxborough for a cost of just over $6.5 million. In March of 1971, to reflect the geographic change, the team officially changed its name from the Boston Patriots to the Bay State Patriots—which lasted for about two weeks, until Sullivan and the rest of the franchise realized in horror that headlines throughout the state would refer to the BS Patriots. Suitably chagrined, they settled on New England Patriots. The official groundbreaking for the stadium took place on September 23, 1971, and less than a year later it was completed.

In the 1972 preseason opener against the New York Giants, 60,423 fans showed up. On the field, things worked out perfectly: Quarterback Jim Plunkett, the Heisman Trophy winner out of Stanford, was taken first in the draft that spring by the Patriots and looked like he could be the sort of player you could build a franchise around. In addition, Cappelletti booted a thirty-six-yard field goal for the first points in the new stadium as New England went on to post a 20–14 victory.

But the stadium and surroundings were clearly a mess. Wide receiver Randy Vataha told *The Boston Globe* that the first time he went into the bathrooms, he got quite a surprise. "The bottom of the urinal was higher than my bellybutton," he said. "They had to guess how high to place them, and must have thought all pro football players were giants. They got them right a couple of weeks later." Out on Route 1, things weren't any better. Thousands of fans were late due to a horrific traffic jam. Thousands more didn't get to the game at all. Those who did show up had to deal with overflowing toilets everywhere in the stadium.

"It was awful. It was like hanging in your mother's basement," said former season ticket holder Dan Pires, who would go on to cover the team. "That was about it. There was a sense of home, but it wasn't really where you wanted to be."

Then-GM Upton Bell recalled in a story later published in *Boston* magazine: "Getting the stadium ready took us to the last moment, down to installing the goalposts. The smiles were short-lived. Sixty thousand fans were in the stands, with a commensurate number of cars in the parking lots, something neither the traffic engineers nor the state police had apparently considered. Hundreds, maybe thousands, of ticket holders never even made it to the game. And, afterward, the mother of all traffic jams unfolded. Cars caught fire or were abandoned. Many people didn't get home until three or four in the morning.

"The next day we got a call from the Department of Public Works. Change all the night games to day games, we were told, or we could not use our brand-new stadium. Sullivan agreed, but all the opponents had to be on board, which they soon were—except the Los Angeles Rams. After all, the Rams said, it was hotter in the daytime. The players would suffer. All that suffering had to be worth something, the Rams figured—like, for instance, a discreet draft choice. So that's what they got—in exchange for moving one game from night to day.

"The Board of Health was next to come calling—the day before the season opener against the Raiders. Engineers had discovered a small problem with the sewer system—namely, faulty plumbing. No toilets, no football. When in the colorful history of pro football had anybody ever seen a team's front office, including the president, poised over every single toilet in a stadium, ready to flush in unison on a countdown over the PA system?

"The toilets flushed. The game was on."

Many of the problems with the new stadium had to do with the plumbing. On the day of the first regular-season home game—September 16, 1971, a 20–6 win over the Raiders—a pipe burst after the game, dumping raw sewage on the Oakland players; it appeared to be the ultimate instance of adding insult to injury. It was later discovered that some allegedly unhappy union workers had found out that nonunion guys had been employed during construction of the stadium and tossed some planks and boulders into the new pipes before they were sealed up.

The story remains difficult to believe, but those who were there swear it happened. It's just one of many hard-to-believe stories about the stadium that have arisen over the years. For roughly thirty years, Schaefer Stadium—renamed Sullivan Stadium, and later Foxboro Stadium—was much more than a home for the New England Patriots. It was a metaphor for professional football in New England. When you compared it to other venues around the league, you started to understand why. The frozen tundra of Lambeau Field inspired thoughts of Vince Lombardi, Bart Starr, and Ray Nietschke and stoked memories of the great Packers teams of days gone by. Toughened by the whipping winds that come blustering off the Ohio, the Allegheny, and Monongahela rivers, Three Rivers Stadium was the symbol of the great Steelers teams of the 1970s. San Francisco's Candlestick Park provided the backdrop for the most enduring image of the 49ers legacy—Dwight Clark, etched in stark relief against the skyline, reaching for Joe Montana's touchdown catch that ended up being the difference in the 1982 NFC Championship Game against Dallas. And the home of the Cowboys—Texas Stadium—was like the state itself, bold and loud, providing the larger-than-life Dallas teams with the impressive backdrop needed to dominate the 1990s.

And then there was Schaefer Stadium. Figuratively, it was stuck in the middle of nowhere. Foxborough is a small New England town that sits halfway between Boston and Providence. Neither city wanted to build them a stadium, so the franchise chose an out-of-the-way suburb along Route 1 next to an old racetrack. And the roads in and out of town were not built to sustain the apocalyptic traffic jams that plagued the city eight Sundays a year.

While it remained a place that most football fans would turn up their nose at, many Patriots players and fans were simply excited to have a place to call home.

"As we drove up Route 1, up that slight hill toward Schaefer Stadium, I thought it was the Taj Mahal," said tight end Russ Francis, recalling the first time he got a look at the place. "I had seen pictures of the Taj Mahal, and it looked more beautiful to me than that.

"So people can say what they want about the traffic problems and the restroom problems—of course, we [players] didn't have to deal with much of those issues—but it was a grand old stadium and one that was my home for the eight years I played for the team."

"Everyone knocked the hell out of it, but I didn't think it was that terrible," said Jack Grinold, a season ticket holder from 1960 until 1982. "When it was being built for $6.7 million, they were renovating Yankee Stadium for $120 million. That's a pretty good deal, a good example of some *real* Yankee ingenuity."

The stadium wasn't the only place where the Sullivans cut corners. The franchise quickly got a reputation as cheap: Players were told not to turn down the sheets in their rooms during road trips for fear of a steeper hotel bill. Bedsheets *were* used, mostly as a projection screen for game films. And the on-field product wasn't much better. The Patriots won just eleven games from 1970 through 1972, and remained a distant fourth in the hearts and minds of the New England sporting public. After 1967, the Red Sox had undoubtedly become the top sports ticket in town, and were in the hunt for a title throughout the latter stages of the 1960s and into the early 1970s. With Bobby Orr, Phil Esposito, Gerry Cheevers, and the rest of the Big, Bad Bruins of the 1970s, Boston was the class of the NHL, taking home Stanley Cup titles in 1970 and 1972. And after taking home eight consecutive titles and eleven in thirteen years throughout the 1950s and '60s, the Celtics—led by JoJo White and Dave Cowens—were undergoing another renaissance in the early 1970s, winning titles in 1974 and 1976.

But after spending just over ten years making a series of wrong moves, the Patriots finally made the right one. On January 26, 1973, the franchise hired Chuck Fairbanks as its new head coach. Fairbanks had guided powerful Oklahoma University to a 49–18–1 record over five years, and was considered a rising young star. He wasn't Sullivan's first choice (the owner later confessed privately the Patriots had also pursued Penn State head coach Joe Paterno and Southern California head coach John McKay), but he proved more than up to the task of guiding the franchise through one of their most prosperous eras. Days after hiring Fairbanks, New England had one of the greatest drafts in the history of the franchise: They selected future Hall of Fame offensive lineman John Hannah fourth overall, fullback Sam Cunningham eleventh, and wide receiver Darryl Stingley nineteenth overall. In 1974, linebacker Steve Nelson was taken in the second round, while 1975 saw the selections of tight end Russ Francis and quarterback Steve Grogan. And the trade of Plunkett to the 49ers prior to the 1976 season would produce four important draft picks. Defensive back Mike Haynes, another future Hall of Famer, and center Pete Brock were selected as a result of the Plunkett deal in 1976, and defensive back Raymond Clayborn and running back Horace Ivory were taken with the other two picks in 1977. It was a group that would go on to form the nucleus of a talented team that made a serious play for the Super Bowl in 1976.

The centerpiece was Grogan, an emotional young star out of Kansas State who wouldn't back down from anyone. "Quarterbacks are supposed to be these guys with these California attitudes. Not Steve, man. He would get fired up," Hannah said with a smile. "He believed that quarterbacks should be football players and not wear a skirt."

"I was a second-year guy [who was] as happy as could be to be a starting quarterback in the NFL," Grogan said of the 1976 season, his first full year as a starter. "I didn't know I was supposed to be scared, or I couldn't do the things they were asking me to do, so I just went out and had fun and played hard, and things just kind of fell into place."

The 1976 season began with next to no expectations: New England had finished 3–11 in 1975 as a young team struggled to find its footing. In a conference that included the defending Super Bowl champions from Pittsburgh, as well as always tough Miami and Oakland, it was figured the Patriots would finish no better than .500 as young talent like Grogan (in his first full year as a starter), Cunningham, Francis, and Stingley continued to mature. And after a 27–13 loss to the Colts to open the season, it appeared it would be more of the same. But back-to-back wins over the Steelers and Dolphins were followed by a 48–17 thrashing of the Raiders, and the collective football world began to sit up and take notice. The Patriots buzzed through the rest of the regular season, running up an 11–3 record (and a six-game winning streak to end the season) and serving notice to the rest of the NFL that New England was a team to be taken seriously.

"I personally thought it was our year, because it was 1976, it was the Bicentennial and we were the Patriots. I thought destiny was going to take us all the way in there," defensive lineman Ray Hamilton told NFL Films. "The Patriots had been bad as long as you can remember, and the team had been losing for so, so long. What happened was amazing. It was the biggest turnaround I had ever seen in the NFL, in coaching and in playing."

Behind an offensive line that boasted Hannah and the equally talented Leon Gray, the Patriots ground game posted an astounding 2,948 rushing yards on the season. On the strength of their punishing ground game, New England qualified for a wild-card berth and traveled to Oakland.

"The Raiders knew going into their 1976 playoff game with the Patriots that, after having been thrashed back in Foxborough during the regular season, they were going to have to pull out every dirty trick they had. And they had an arsenal, I promise you," Francis said. "One particular play, I was running down the middle, and right through my facemask comes this elbow. I went to put my hand on my nose, and there was nothing there. It was just flat. I was searching for it. I found it on my cheek."

The vaunted Raiders had suffered just one loss all season (a

48–17 defeat to the Patriots), and with home field advantage appeared to have a clear path to postseason glory. But no one bothered to tell the Patriots, as New England charged to a 21–10 lead after three quarters. A fourth-quarter score by the Raiders made it 21–17, but referee Ben Dreith made a controversial roughing-the-passer call on Patriots lineman Ray Hamilton, giving the Raiders the ball on the Patriots' 13-yard line, complete with a fresh set of downs.

"Richard Bishop was at right tackle, I was at left tackle, and we decided to run a tackle twist. And Stabler was there with the ball, and I went up with my hands, tipped the ball and tackled him," Hamilton recalled, years later in an interview with NFL Films. "Then, I looked around, and there was a flag on the ground—I thought it was for holding, maybe.

"They said the infraction was for roughing the passer, which was bull."

Given new life, Stabler made the most of it, eventually plunging in from the one-yard-line with ten seconds left for what proved to be the game-winning touchdown. "It wasn't a late hit," Stabler would tell NFL Films years later. "It was controversial, because I do think it was a silly rule. But it gave us another opportunity to get the ball in, and we did."

The call would gain Dreith a small measure of infamy with Patriots fans everywhere, so much so that he wouldn't work another New England home game for the rest of his career. "After that, Ben Dreith never came to Foxborough again to do another game. He only did one other game after that, but we never saw him at any Patriots [home] games anymore," Hamilton said.

The Raiders would go on to easy wins over the Steelers in the AFC title game and the Vikings in the Super Bowl. The Patriots went home, wondering what might have been. "People here in Boston talk about Bucky Dent's home run to beat the Red Sox in the playoff back in the late 1970s. The other one was the call that was made against Ray Hamilton against the Raiders in the 1976 playoff game," Grogan later recalled. "I think in 1976, we could have very easily won it all because there were so many great young players on that team, and a great coaching staff, that if we had won it all, we might have gotten several more."

While New England believed the playoff loss would be the start of something big, it signaled the beginning of the end for Fairbanks. After helping pave the way for a record-breaking season for the New England ground game, offensive linemen Gray and Hannah were seeking more money. Reportedly, agent Howard Slusher met with Fairbanks and Bill's son Chuck, the team's legal advisor, at Fairbanks's house. (However, Sullivan sat in the bedroom while the other two were in the kitchen. Sullivan reportedly refused to be in the same room with Slusher.) According to reports, Fairbanks struck a deal, which was later nixed by Chuck. "I go tell Chuck and he starts blubbering in my bedroom," Fairbanks told reporters years later. "He says I'm going to break his father. I told him to stop blubbering because we had a deal. So he goes off and convinces his dad to take them to arbitration."

As a result, the agent told the Pro Bowl offensive linemen to walk out on the eve of the 1977 season, and the duo eventually missed three games. After they returned, the Patriots were able to run off a pair of four-game win streaks and end up with 9–5 record, but it wouldn't be enough, as they missed out on the postseason by a game.

According to many of the players, Chuck Sullivan was the source of many of the problems the franchise had throughout the 1970s.

"There was just one guy who kind of goofed it up on that side of things, and that was his son Chuck," Francis said. "[He] may have meant to do what was best for his father, but sure didn't. I think without belaboring the point or taking anything away from Billy Sullivan's name, because I hold him in the highest regard, [but] that became an issue. With the way that Chuck Sullivan dealt with the players, dealt with Chuck Fairbanks, the head coach who was

supposed to be running the team and Chuck Sullivan clearly interfered with that. That was the beginning of the end.

"The team he interfered with . . . would have gone on to win Super Bowl championships," he added. "But that is water under the
bridge, or under the dam in that case. A raging torrent of miscues
on his part. We can look back and say, 'Woulda, coulda, shoulda,'
but . . . players and coaches alike look back and say that from the
bottom of our hearts. Mainly because of the fact that we felt the
fans deserved the best we could give them. They were the reason
we were there. It had nothing to do with money at the time. It had
everything to do with pride of being on that team. There was a
great chemistry on that team, and we felt that opportunity had not
slipped away from us, but was taken away from us."

The rest of the 1970s were marked with moments of high comedy and dark tragedy, with the unquestioned low point in the history of the franchise coming in a preseason game against Oakland
on August 12, 1978. A talented first-round pick out of Purdue in
1973, wide receiver Darryl Stingley was coming off the finest season of his career, finishing the 1977 season with a career-best 39
catches for 657 yards and 5 touchdowns. But coming over the
middle on a crossing pattern, Stingley took a savage, but legal, hit
from Oakland defensive back Jack Tatum. The hit broke Stingley's
neck, making him a quadraplegic for life. He died in 2007.

Though Sullivan had got his start in media relations, he didn't always do a great job dealing with the media. He didn't care much
for a skit that Montville and radio broadcaster Gil Santos performed at a football writers dinner, and, the next day at a media
golf outing, he let Montville know exactly how he felt about it.

"We get done, and I'm going to take a shower and Billy Sullivan
is in there," Montville said. "He starts yelling and screaming at me

because of the skit. He says, 'If you were an older man, I'd come over and kick you in the balls.' And [former *Globe* sportswriter] Ray Fitzgerald, he always had a short fuse, he stood up and said, 'Well, I'm older, Billy. Why don't you come over and do it to me?' Here's this fucking media relations guy, and he's telling me he's going to come over and kick me in the balls."

In 1978, as the New England sporting populace watched the Red Sox complete the most infamous collapse in team history, the Patriots were running off a seven-game win streak and vaulting to the top of the AFC East. A dramatic 34-yard field goal by David Posey with eight seconds remaining helped beat Buffalo, giving New England its first division title in fifteen years.

But even as Patriots fans were celebrating the division crown, trouble was brewing. Fairbanks was clearly still angry the Sullivans had undermined him in the Gray-Hannah negotiations, later saying the failed negotiations were "the start of it." As a result, he had secretly decided take the head coaching job at the University of Colorado at the end of the season, and the story leaked to the press just hours before the season finale, a Monday night game against the Dolphins in Miami. An enraged Sullivan found out what was going on and suspended Fairbanks before the game, saying, "You cannot serve two masters two thousand miles apart," and leaving offensive coordinator Ron Erhardt and defensive coordinator Hank Bullough in charge of the team. Even by the Patriots' standards, the New England locker room was a surreal place before the Dolphins game. As Erhardt and Bullough each gave a pregame pep talk, Fairbanks sat silently in the corner on a trunk. "He shook hands with us as we went out," defensive lineman Ray Hamilton told reporters. "We didn't know who to believe. We were trying to forget about it and just go out and play, but obviously that didn't work."

New England ended up with a 23–3 loss, but was still coming home to face the Houston Oilers for the first playoff game in the history of Schaefer Stadium. After some legal wrangling, it was determined that Fairbanks would be the one who would lead the team into the postseason. But New England, rattled by the Fairbanks decision, was trounced by the Oilers, 31–14. As Fairbanks left the field, he was showered with boos. Fans mockingly sang: "Goodbye, Chucky. Goodbye, Chucky. Oh, goodbye, Chucky. We hate to see you go."

The next season, with Fairbanks in Colorado and Erhardt the new head coach, it was more low comedy. The most famous incident came in September when *Boston Globe* writer Will McDonough and defensive back Raymond Clayborn engaged in a legendary locker room throwdown. It began when McDonough was trying to interview wide receiver Harold Jackson after a 56–3 win over the Jets. McDonough was standing too close to Clayborn's locker, and the two began to exchange words. Clayborn was pointing his finger at the *Globe* writer and accidentally got him in the eye. McDonough then popped Clayborn, knocking him down. McDonough then landed a second shot to the forehead, and surrounding writers and players were caught in a scrum. In the fray, owner Billy Sullivan was pushed into a canvas laundry bin.

"Clayborn's number was 27, and Harold Jackson was number 28, and Harold Jackson had a really good game, and all the sportswriters were around Harold Jackson's locker," Montville recalled. "Clayborn came out of the shower, and had trouble getting to his locker and started yelling and screaming and pushing his way through people. McDonough kind of said something to him like, 'Straighten up and don't be an idiot,' or something like that, and Clayborn started talking to McDonough, and he meant to put his finger in McDonough's chest, and it slipped and went into McDonough's eye. McDonough then just grabbed him and threw him into a locker."

The on-field slide toward mediocrity embittered the fans even further, and they struck back whenever they got the opportunity. Games in Schaefer Stadium always had the potential to get ugly; in an October 18, 1976, contest against the Jets, several fans ran onto the field, and there were dozens of arrests made for drunk and disorderly conduct. (The low point was an incident where a drunken fan was discovered urinating on an emergency medical technician who was trying to revive a heart attack victim.) Paul Perillo, who would go on to cover the team for *Patriots Football Weekly*, was at his first game that night.

"All the stories you hear about Foxboro Stadium and the rowdiness," Perillo said, "are all one thousand percent true.

"I went to the game with my father, my grandfather, and my uncle, and I remember them truly being concerned walking back to the car through the parking lot at the end of the game," he said. "At the old stadium, they had a chain-link fence around the outside, and there had to be fifteen or twenty guys handcuffed to the fence—one arm handcuffed to the fence. There were guys getting arrested left and right. I didn't know what was going on, but I saw all these guys who were handcuffed, but I can kind of remember my family being somewhat concerned: 'What the hell are we doing taking an eight-year-old kid to a Monday night game in Foxborough?'"

But on September 29, 1980, a *Monday Night Football* game was the unquestioned low point. After spending most of the afternoon drinking in the dirt parking lots around the stadium, almost one hundred fans were arrested for a variety of offenses, ranging from drunk and disorderly conduct to assaulting a police officer. (Foxborough selectmen later proposed a ban on *Monday Night* games, a ban that lasted nearly fifteen years.) And late in the 1985 season, after a late-season win over Cincinnati assured the Patriots a playoff berth as a wild-card team, glory-starved fans celebrated by tearing down the goal posts. As they paraded down Route 1 with their trophy, a section of the metal posts brushed up against a 13,200-volt wire. Five of the fans suffered burns and were taken to the hospital.

Throughout the early 1980s, the celebrations were few and far between, as it was a slow and steady slide back to mediocrity for the Patriots, first under Erhardt, who had taken over after Fair-banks left, and then Ron Meyer. But midway through the 1984 sea-son, New England fired tough-guy Meyer and replaced him with the laconic Raymond Berry. In his first full season at the helm, Berry guided New England to an 11–5 regular season mark and a wild-card berth. An opportunistic bunch, that team suddenly caught fire and became the first franchise in league history to win three playoff games on the road, the last of which came in Miami against the hated Dolphins, ending New England's eighteen-game unbeaten streak at the Orange Bowl and propelling the team into its first Super Bowl.

But even as they were making history, there was still a sense that these were the same old Patriots. In a postseason win over the Raiders, GM Pat Sullivan spent the game on the New England side-line, taunting several Raiders players, including Howie Long. After the game, Sullivan confronted Long on the field. Raiders line-backer Matt Millen intervened and attacked Sullivan with his hel-met. Sullivan staggered away with a split forehead. And in the week leading up to the Miami game, there was an incident involving wide receiver Irving Fryar, who missed the team flight to Miami on the Wednesday before the AFC title game. He explained to re-porters he had sliced his right pinkie at his home the night before while putting away a kitchen knife. The injury was severe enough to keep him out of the game. But the Friday before the game, Fryar changed his story. He and his wife, Jacqueline, had argued in the parking lot outside a Boston restaurant, he said. Fryar allegedly struck his wife, who was five months pregnant, and she retaliated by attacking him with a knife. Fryar, who was in Miami when he confessed, was sent home to deal with his marital problems.

Almost predictably, the Patriots were hammered in Super Bowl XX, suffering a 46–10 loss to the Bears. (At the time, it was the worst defeat in Super Bowl history.) New England was steam-rolled by Jim McMahon, Walter Payton, and an unstoppable Chicago defense that drove starting quarterback Tony Eason from the game early in the first half and allowed the Patriots just seven yards rushing. Compounding matters was a report in *The Boston Globe* that appeared days after the game in which the team admitted that there were several drug users on the team. The *Globe* identified six players as drug abusers: Fryar, Clayborn, Tony Collins, Stephen Starring, Kenneth Sims, and Roland James. It was the culmination of a ten-year run of lunacy that would have made any franchise blush.

"You would never see a team that would have more bad luck," Perillo said. "From the time they lost that playoff game in 1976 they had no business losing—it was stolen away from them with some ridiculously bad officiating. In 1978, they have another team that's as good as any in football, and the owner is so cheap that the head coach decides to leave and take a college job and it rips the team apart as they're preparing for the playoffs. They're preparing to play in their first Super Bowl, and they get hit with a drug scandal. No matter what happens. Every time they took a step forward, they got slammed by a truck."

The NFL enjoyed an unsurpassed era of growth in the late 1970s and early 1980s, becoming a billon-dollar industry. But it became clear that as the 1980s wore on, the Sullivans were getting deeper and deeper over their heads financially. They had lost millions when the players went out on strike in 1982, but they were hit hardest a few years later when they went into business with legendary promoter Don King on the Jacksons' "Victory Tour." On the surface, it seemed like a sound financial decision, one that could make the Sullivan family millions: Fronted by their world-famous brother Michael (who was just coming off the success of the album *Thriller*), the Jackson Family would tour America together for the first time in over a decade. But the family didn't take into account the cost of fronting such a massive undertaking—the

Jacksons were using the largest stage in music history, one so huge that it took reconstruction of many of the concert venues just to get the staging inside the stadiums. And they were clearly out of their league when it came to negotiating with King. (When King sat down with Patriots vice president Chuck Sullivan, he referred to the younger Sullivan as "Charlie the Tuna.") Sullivan later estimated in court that the tour ended up costing the Sullivan family between $6 million and $8 million, while King made money on the venture. (Estimates from court records indicate it was anywhere between $500,000 and $3 million.) In addition, court records also indicated that the family lost $14 million on Sullivan's licensing of T-shirts and other memorabilia from the tour, for a total of roughly $20 million to $22 million in losses for the family. The collateral for loans for the licensing agreement was Stadium Management Corp. and Sullivan Stadium itself, which Chuck Sullivan owned and managed. It all added to the idea that Chuck and his family were in over their heads financially. King himself would later tell a story about Chuck. "You know, in all my years, I haven't been in awe of many institutions in American society. But the one place I've always looked upon with great reverence was Harvard University," King said. "To me, it was the school on the hill, the light of knowledge. And then I met Chuck Sullivan, and I said, *'This* motherfucker went to *Harvard?'*"

Several potential buyers lined up to take a look at the team, including famed real estate developer Donald Trump and former U.S. postmaster general Robert Tisch. But in the end, it was Victor Kiam who bought the team in October 1988. He kept the Sullivans on board: Billy, the family's seventy-three-year-old patriarch, remained the team president, while his sons, Pat and Chuck, also stayed on, with Pat as general manager. But for all intents and purposes, the sale marked the unofficial end of the Sullivan era.

Sullivan, relieved to be out from under a mountain of debt, had a big smile when he left Foxborough after signing over his team for $85 million to Kiam and local businessman Fran Murray. "I have never felt better," he said. "I won't need an airline ticket to fly back to Boston. I'm on Cloud Nine."

In the Sullivan family, New England football fans had a well-meaning collection of relatives who ran the show, but were oftentimes hamstrung because of money. From the moment they had to borrow almost two-thirds of the entry fee to join the AFL, the Sullivans were always operating on thin ice when it came to their football team. Whether it was building the stadium, cutting corners on salary, or saving money at concessions, the dilemma was clear: They were always long on heart but short on cash. And in the new era of the NFL, this wasn't enough. You needed deep pockets to make your mark, deeper than in the days when they were going up against the Barron Hiltons of the world, and it eventually became too much for Sullivan and his family.

"It was his ego that kept them going, that kept them in Boston," Montville said of Sullivan. "They went through that whole nomadic stretch there, where they went from BC to Harvard to BU. . . . they played all these different places, and he kept it afloat. And, he figured out a stadium thing. I mean, they built that housing project of a stadium for low money out in Foxborough, but they did it without state money and . . . it was all out of his head that it all came about. I think he was running around a lot with creditors chasing him, and working in the margins, but he kept it together. He's the reason they're still here."

It was believed that Kiam, who had achieved a large measure of success as a businessman running Remington products, would be able to provide the franchise with all the things that the well-meaning Sullivans could not afford. He was well-to-do and well liked. In fact, in the eyes of the public, Kiam was adored, known more as a TV pitchman than a businessman, appearing in his own commercials and telling people, "I liked the shaver so much, I bought the company." Surely, he could do for the Patriots what he did for Remington, and his Steinbrenneresque bravado made it clear that change was in the air.

"I'm looking forward to winning," said Kiam, who made his first appearance at Foxboro Stadium the following week to watch the Patriots upset the Bears, 30–7.

But over the course of the next two seasons, things went back into the dumper. Many of the standout draft picks of the mid-1970s were either on the backside of their career and were on their way out of the game, or had already left. They were unable to re-stock, as the drafts of the late 1980s yielded little talent. Berry re-signed after the team went 5–11 in 1989, giving way to defensive coordinator Rod Rust. A year later, the Patriots completed their fall from grace. In 1990, they went 1–15—including a fourteen-game losing skid to end the season. Many afternoons, it was a strange scene down at Foxboro Stadium; with a capacity of 60,292, it was rare that they were able to draw more than 45,000 on any given Sunday. For the fans who did show up, it was a sur-real experience.

"A friend of mine and I we had season tickets—purchased in 1990—and we used to walk through the front door of the adminis-trative office, walk through Victor Kiam's office and out to the sta-dium," recalled Dan Pires, who would later go on to cover the team for the New Bedford *Standard-Times*. "It was incredible."

As bad as they were, the 1990 Patriots wouldn't be remembered for their on-field incompetence, but their off-field actions. *Boston Herald* reporter Lisa Olson, working on a practice-day story, was verbally assaulted and sexually taunted by several players. The league's investigation, which resulted in a 108-page report, said tight end Zeke Mowatt was seen fondling himself at an arm's length from Olson and asking her: "Is this what you want?" Others gyrated their hips behind the reporter, echoing Mowatt's com-ments. In the league report, Olson recounted how the players "po-sitioned themselves inches away from my face and dared me to touch their private parts." She depicted the incident as "mind rape."

The franchise had had two such incidents in the past. In 1986, a female sports writer was harassed by a player who wanted her to leave the locker room. And a female television reporter was harassed by two players in 1988. But there was never anything of this magnitude. The team fined Mowatt $2,000 over the incident, but that wasn't the end of it. Kiam added fuel to the fire, publicly labeling Olson "a classic bitch," and later telling the *Herald*, "I'm sure [the incident] looms large in Lisa's life but I can't get excited about it. It's a flyspeck in the ocean. It isn't [a factor affecting] winning and losing. That's what we're interested in. Anything that takes [the player's] eye off the ball should be dismissed out of hand.

"The players are doing their jobs, and that includes taking a shower. They should be able to walk around naked. Why can't she conduct her interviews out on the field?" he added. "I feel we're caught up in the tempest of the times. Freedom of speech is fine, but letting women into a locker room goes beyond that. Players should be able to retain the dignity of the individual. [The *Herald* is] at fault here."

Patriots fans piled on. Olson later reported that she received a hundred obscene phone calls and 250 pieces of hate mail regarding the incident, and added that she had her tires slashed, and the perpetrator left a message that threatened, "The next time it will be your neck." When her apartment was burglarized, a note ordered her to "leave Boston or die."

Kiam later apologized—after a boycott of Remington was threatened. "I am deeply concerned that the remarks I made, some of which were taken out of context, appear to condone the actions of a very small group of players, harassing Lisa Olson of the *Boston Herald*," he said. "I did not and do not condone these actions in any way, shape or form. In addition, I reiterate the policy of the Patriots to allow access to our locker room for all accredited members of the media."

In the end, Tagliabue assessed $72,500 in fines on the Patriots for the Olson incident. Mowatt was fined $14,500. Robert Perryman and Michael Timpson were fined $5,000 each, while the Patriot organization was fined $48,000.

As Rust's one-year career as a head coach came to an unceremonious close, the team had found itself in the midst of what one writer would later refer to as a "perfect storm of negativity." Kiam was painted as an unfeeling, uncaring owner who wouldn't spend the money needed in order to bring a winner to town. Rust was career coordinator who was in over his head as a head coach. And the Lisa Olson incident was not only reprehensible, but a public relations nightmare of the highest order. The team was on the verge of moving from New England, and no one cared. It would take a massive effort to pull it back from the brink.

CHAPTER TWO

# "WE'RE GETTING THE BAND
# BACK TOGETHER"

This may have been the best day in Patriot history. For once, everything had been done right. The Patriots had gone out and signed the
best coach to be had. The Patriots were not scrimping, dishing out
millions for [Bill] Parcells and saying they would spend more to go
after free agents. And the Patriots, lest we forget, also have the top
draft choice in the country. . . . Gosh, it's wonderful being a Patriot
fan. I found myself saying this as I began to float off my chair in ecstasy. I found myself saying this one month after watching the worst
pro football ever played, and just two weeks after watching the Patriot organization disintegrate totally on one wacky weekend. So I
had to pinch myself.

— *MICHAEL MADDEN*, THE BOSTON GLOBE, JANUARY 22, 1993

If they want you to cook the dinner, at least they ought to let you
shop for some of the groceries.

— *BILL PARCELLS*, JANUARY 31, 1997

In the history of each successful professional sports franchise,
you can always pinpoint a single event that's served as the cata-
lyst for the turnaround. There's always a moment when the switch
is flipped and the team goes from also-ran to contender, from

mediocre to championship-driven. For the New England Patriots, that moment came on January 21, 1993, when they announced they had hired Bill Parcells as their head coach. Parcells arrived in New England with a peerless resume. A former Patriots assistant, he had led the Giants from the dregs of the league to a pair of Super Bowl victories, and had established himself as a modern-day Vince Lombardi—a tough-talking, no-nonsense sort who knew what it took to win football games. He was wooed to the Patriots with the promise of complete and total authority over the franchise on all personnel matters. The franchise that had managed to write its own chapter of NFL infamy with characters like Clive Rush, Bob Gladieux, Victor Kiam, and Zeke Mowatt had finally gained the sort of credibility it had been seeking for decades. And that wasn't all—they had the No. 1 pick in the upcoming draft. And they had a new owner in James Busch Orthwein who had absolutely no interest in meddling with football affairs. All was right with the world. Parcells received a five-year contract worth roughly $6 million, and was welcomed back to Massachusetts by Governor William Weld, one of several celebs who dropped by the press conference to wish Parcells well—and push for a new stadium to keep the team in New England.

"It's my responsibility to make sure we get a first-class facility and that the team remains in New England," said the governor. "This move is going to increase the value of the franchise a lot. I think Bill Parcells is the No. 1 name in football."

"I want to improve the Patriots to the point where we can compete for a championship," Parcells said during his introductory press conference. "I pledge to the fans and the players that I won't rest until we approach that goal. . . . I feel good about it. I missed football. I missed the competition. I just look forward to it and try to build a new team. And I missed the camaraderie with the players."

For his part, the coach said this would be his last go-round. "This is my last deal, no doubt about that. After that, I'm John Wayne," he said. "But you are what you are. Bill Parcells is a football coach.

I'm not anything else. My goal is to get back to that championship game. I'm comfortable here. I've lived here. I have good memories of the time I was here. And Tom Coughlin the Boston College coach and former Parcells assistant said he needed a neighbor to talk to."

The hiring of Parcells was the first step in bringing the Patriots to a level of relevance at or near the level of the Red Sox. Baseball had always been the first love of the Boston sports public, but the arrival of Parcells suddenly turned Boston into a football town. After struggling to break the 50,000 barrier in home attendance for most of the early 1990s, football was suddenly a hot ticket: In Parcells's first season in New England, the Patriots dipped below the 50,000 mark just three times in their eight home games.

Parcells immediately set about reuniting several of the coaches who were with him in New York. Longtime disciples Romeo Crennel, Al Groh, and Charlie Weis were brought in, as well as former Giants strength and conditioning coach Johnny Parker. His offensive coordinator was Ray Perkins, Parcells's first boss with the Giants. The only member of his usual cadre of assistants that was missing was Bill Belichick. A Parcells lieutenant for eight seasons, Belichick left the Giants after Super Bowl XXV for a head coaching job with the Browns. (In his place, Groh would serve as defensive coordinator.) For the coaches that did follow him, the job they faced was a large one, even for a staff that managed to pull New York from the brink of football despair to a pair of Super Bowl titles in a relatively short time. The Patriots had gone an abysmal 9–39 over the previous three seasons. The Foxboro Stadium facilities were still in sorry shape, and the roster was chock-full of ineffective veterans who had little or no trade value. Small wonder that shortly after he took the job, Parcells described the conditions surrounding the team as "the most down-and-out, despondent, negative atmosphere you could imagine."

"The stadium was a dump. The locker rooms were small. You never knew if you were going to have hot water or not," recalled former Patriots assistant coach Charlie Weis in his autobiography

*No Excuses.* "You never knew if a pipe was going to break, and if one did, you didn't know who was going to fix it. Just trying to keep the place serviceable was a struggle. It was a significant step down from what [we] had been around with the Giants."

To try and remedy the on-field issues, Parcells followed the same blueprint he used when it came to assembling his coaching staff: He found as many ex-Giants as he could get his hands on. "Remember in *The Blues Brothers* when they said 'We're getting the band back together' and they went around getting all the old bandmates back together? That's what it was like," recalled Dan Pires, of the New Bedford *Standard-Times.* "He brought the Adrian Whites in, he brought the Bobby Abrahams, the Myron Guytons. He started bringing those guys in, and they tried to cultivate what they had in New York.

"He brought in his group. He brought in his people," Pires added. "These were veteran guys who had won championships. They had won the Super Bowl. But the guys he brought in had a few more ticks on the clock."

Off the field, problems continued to dog the franchise. Orthwein was a Midwesterner, and had reached a point where he either wanted to move the team to St. Louis to fill the void left by the departure of the Cardinals for Arizona—or simply sell the team altogether. A variety of bidders were interested in the franchise, including author Tom Clancy and area businessman Jeffrey Lurie. But that's where Robert Kraft entered the picture. Born in Brookline, Kraft was a smart and savvy graduate of Harvard Business School. He married into the Rand-Whitney Paper Company, acquiring half the company in a leveraged buyout in 1968 and the rest a few years after that. Soon, he started International Forest Products to control the transportation, marketing, sales, and manufacturing of the paper his business used, and quickly became one of the wealthier men in New England. He was also a colossal Patriots fan. He bought six season tickets in 1971, and spent many Sunday afternoons with his sons in section 217, row 23, seats one through six, wondering what things would be like if he owned the team.

Those daydreams started to become a reality in 1985. After floating trial balloons about purchasing the Celtics and Red Sox, he took aim at the Patriots. He started by securing the purchase rights to three hundred acres around Foxboro Stadium, buying a ten-year option on the area. Essentially, he paid a group of Boston businessmen $1 million a year for rights to eventually buy the land—which he would exercise in 1995—for $18 million. He took the next step by buying the stadium for $25 million from a financially strapped Sullivan family in 1988, going fifty-fifty with then-Patriots owner Victor Kiam and eventually buying Kiam out in 1993.

With Kraft owning the stadium operating agreement, all prospective buyers had to go through him if they were interested in buying the team, giving him a clear edge. As a result, after some thought, he decided this would be his best opportunity for ownership. With the operating covenant in his back pocket (which clearly handicapped other potential buyers, much to the chagrin of Orthwein) his advisors told him that he should go as high as $115 million for the team, a price that would seem more than fair for a franchise that had suffered more than its share of losing over the previous ten seasons—and despite the presence of Parcells, wouldn't be likely to enjoy any real level of success for at least the next few years.

So instead of settling for $115 million, he bought the team from Orthwein for $172 million, the highest price ever paid for a sports franchise. "In pursuing the team, I probably broke every one of my personal financial issues," he told reporters after the deal was completed. But at that time, he was seen as a local hero, someone who saved professional football in Massachusetts. The Patriots were seen as a team with one foot out the door, only to be lured back home by Kraft.

"I just think there would have been a great depression and funk if this team left, and people wouldn't have realized it until they weren't here," Kraft told reporters. "Most people's lives aren't easy financially. . . . They are going from paycheck to paycheck, and they look for distractions and entertainment that are fulfilling. And with the sports teams of New England, they can have a piece of them."

What exactly did he save for New England? A franchise that had the worst won-loss record in the league in the four years before Kraft purchased them. A franchise that had finished last in the league in revenue. And a franchise that played in a dingy, rundown stadium with no club seats and just thirty-eight suites, one of the lowest totals in the league. But everyone has to start somewhere. Just as the franchise got an on-field dose of legitimacy when Parcells arrived, Kraft was able to infuse fans with a belief that the team—thought to be close to pulling up stakes and heading out of town under Orthwein—had made a long-term commitment to staying in Foxborough. The fans responded in kind: The day after the transfer of power from Orthwein to Kraft, they purchased 5,958 season tickets in the middle of a snowstorm, a single-day record for the franchise.

The culture had suddenly started to change in Foxborough. There were new uniforms. The old Pat Patriot was shown the gate in favor of a new mascot that featured the streamlined head of a minuteman. The uniforms changed. (The new mascot was still called "Pat Patriot," but most believed the aerodynamic look made him look more like a stylish Elvis Presley in a tricornered hat, and was soon referred to as a "Flying Elvis.") In late 1994, the franchise negotiated a three-year deal to move their games from stuffy old AM radio to legendary rock station WBCN-FM, the new flagship station of the Patriots Rock Radio network. The move expanded their radio audience, improved the quality of the broadcasts and made them appear to be a cutting-edge franchise interested in drawing young listeners into the NFL experience.

On a much larger scale, these moves were all part of an overall seismic shift in the relationship between New England sports fans and their local teams. Since 1967, the Red Sox were a religion, a local mania, a part of New England folklore. They were clearly at the head of the pack, leading both the Bruins and Celtics. The Patriots? They were the fourth choice in a four-team town. They were an amusing little diversion that was good for an occasional side story, but not much else. But in the early 1990s, the ranking started to change. The Red Sox were going through a sustained down period, with three straight losing seasons (1992, 1993, 1994), the first time that had happened since the mid-1960s. Off the field, it was clear they had started to take the market for granted, and, as a result, attendance dipped considerably for the first time in the post-1967 era. The ballpark was old, they played a boring sport, and ticket prices were way too high. Traditionally, the Red Sox management had always spent relatively little on marketing, preferring to let the charm of Fenway Park serve as a drawing card. But that did little to revive interest in the franchise, as the team sank closer and closer to the bottom of the American League East, finally bottoming out in 1992 when they finished dead last in their division, twenty-three games out of first place.

The Patriots moved into the void. If they couldn't market a winning team, they could market the fact that they had one of the greatest coaches in the history of the game, the No. 1 pick in that year's draft and a long-term commitment to the region with local ownership. They also had new uniforms, a new logo, and their games were broadcast on one of America's top rock stations. It was cool to be a Patriots fan again. "They became a fun team to watch," said longtime fan Ian Logue. "They were one of the teams that more or less surprised a lot of people."

The first major move in the rebuilding of the on-field product came in the 1993 draft. With the No. 1 pick, New England had several holes to fill, most notably at quarterback. A variety of punching bags had taken their licks behind a woefully thin offensive line over the last few years, a group that included Hugh Millen, Tommy

Hodson, and Marc Wilson. A new quarterback would provide the franchise with a cornerstone, as well as a new face to sell to prospective season ticket holders.

For the Patriots and their fans, the decision ultimately came down to two quarterbacks: Washington State's Drew Bledsoe or Notre Dame's Rick Mirer. Bledsoe had started just twenty-eight games at Washington State, but had the classic quarterback look. At six feet five and 220 pounds, he had a strong right arm and a pocket presence that made him appear to be the real deal. His numbers didn't hurt, either: Bledsoe left Washington State ranked second on the school's all-time passing list with 7,373 yards. He was named All-Pac-10 and was ninth in the nation in total offense as a junior in 1992, averaging 247 yards per game. And he capped his collegiate career with arguably his best performance as a Cougar, going 30-for-46 for 476 yards as WSU toppled Utah in the Copper Bowl. Even though Mirer's numbers weren't nearly as impressive, his backers pointed to his pedigree. A Notre Dame product, he played quarterback for the Fighting Irish from 1989 through 1992 and held the school record for career total offense at 6,691 yards.

The Patriots settled on Bledsoe, flipping the keys to the franchise to the laconic Washington native. (In retrospect, the move turned out to be one of the best in the history of the franchise. Drafted by the Seahawks at No. 2, Mirer would go on to win the AFC Rookie of the Year Award in his first season. But he ended up as an NFL journeyman, never again reaching the 2,833 passing yards he notched in his first season in the NFL. He played for seven teams in his first twelve years in the league, never completing more than 56 percent of his passes in a single season and spending most of his career as a backup.) In the second round, the franchise grabbed linebacker Chris Slade, as well as wide receiver Vincent Brisby. They also added kicker Scott Sisson in the fifth round, and took a flier in the eighth round on an undersized wide receiver out of Marshall named Troy Brown. By the time the season

opened, there were some thirty new players wearing Patriots uniforms. Many of them were old friends from the Giants days, including former New York special teams ace Reyna Thompson,
who helped Parcells and the Giants win Super Bowl XXV. (The
following year, more ex-Giants followed him to Foxboro, including linebacker Steve DeOssie, offensive lineman Bob Kratch, and
safety Myron Guyton.) For the rookies, it was a crash course in
Parcells 101. Top-pick Bledsoe, as well as Slade and Brisby, were
immediately indoctrinated into the Parcells Way. "He's very easy to
play for from the standpoint that you know exactly what he ex-
pects," Bledsoe told reporters early on. "He's very up-front about
it, and then you can either do it or you don't do it. If you do it, he's
happy with you and you can play. If you don't do it, then you're out
of here."

After a sluggish start to the 1993 season, the Patriots closed
quickly, winning their final four games. And the following year, the
Patriots were able to deliver a massive blow to the Red Sox when
baseball went out on strike. ("They were the only game in town
that fall," Pires said. "That was huge.") The franchise took advantage, sinking extra money into a marketing campaign that made
sure they didn't play before a home crowd of fewer than 57,656 the
entire season. The fans got the chance to witness one of the most
exciting young football teams in the league, a team that closed out
the season with a seven-game win streak and a berth in the playoffs for the first time in eight years.

During that 1994 season, no one player had a bigger role in making the Patriots a relevant NFL franchise than Bledsoe. The transition to New England (and Parcells) was difficult for the young
quarterback, who had lived his entire life on the West Coast, but by
the fall of 1994, he had settled into the starting role nicely, and
forced Parcells to change his overall approach to offense. Like most
old-school coaches, Parcells was a power football type of guy, traditionally using running backs as the cornerstone of his offensive
game plans. While his defense spoke volumes, he was able to ride

the backs of relatively unheralded runners like Joe Morris and Ottis Anderson to a pair of Super Bowls with the Giants. But with the emergence of Bledsoe—and the departure via free agency of Leonard Russell, who had rushed for 1,088 yards the year before, and the subsequent ineffective play of replacement Marion Butts— it was clear the direction the Patriots were headed in. With Bledsoe at the controls, they were going to go as far as their young, strong-armed quarterback could take them. They opened the 1994 season by dropping a pair of shootouts against Miami and Buffalo, rolling up a combined 70 points in the two losses. Bledsoe was clearly the centerpiece, attempting 93 passes in the first two games and coming away with 801 yards passing and seven touchdowns through the first two games. The team won its next three games, with Bledsoe throwing at least 50 passes in two of them.

Turns out, that was simply prelude to what would become Bledsoe's first signature game as an NFL quarterback. While the first start of his professional career came on September 5, 1993, against the Bills, the history will show that the Bledsoe era began in earnest on a chilly Foxboro afternoon on November 13, 1994, against the Vikings, when he went 45-for-70 for 426 yards and three touchdowns in a dramatic overtime win. It was an other-worldly effort for Bledsoe, whose performance sparked a seven-game win streak, a spot in the playoffs, and solidified his status as an elite NFL quarterback. In the locker room after the game, Parcells teared up. "You've given me hope," he said. "That was valiant." That game became a jumping-off point for the Patriots, who were propelled into their first playoff appearance since 1986, against the Browns in Cleveland.

But in the biggest game of his young career, Bledsoe had one of the worst games of the season, going 21-for-50 with three interceptions. The Patriots still had a shot to cut the lead to three late in the second half, but Bledsoe overthrew a wide-open Ray Crittenden in the end zone, and the Patriots had to settle for a field goal. They had another shot late, but Bledsoe threw four straight incomplete passes to end the game—and the season—with a 20–13 loss. "I don't see this as a great accomplishment," Parcells said afterward. "I see it as progress, but we don't get to go on. We tried everything we had today, but we just made a couple of mistakes, and that's what this game is about at this time of year. . . . We got into a stale period there for most of the third quarter and then we didn't get too much done and we were pressing a little bit at the end. When you press a little, this is what happens."

Even though they fell short, the season was deemed a success by the local media. "This was a team that pulled us from the depths of despair," wrote columnist Dan Shaughnessy in *The Boston Globe*. "We had a baseball strike, a hockey lockout and a dreadful Celtics team. There was little reason to get charged up about sports. And then along came Parcells and Drew Bledsoe and Ben Coates and Maurice Hurst and the rest."

But behind the scenes, the bad blood between Parcells and Kraft had started to boil. When Parcells had been wooed by Orthwein, the former owner had made several promises in hopes of getting the head coach to come to New England. That included total control over all player personnel decisions. Parcells was old-school, and the idea of total control over his franchise seemed like a no-brainer. *Vince Lombardi had total control with the Packers. Chuck Noll had total control with the Steelers. Look how things turned out for them.* And even though he was able to coexist with George Young when the two were together in New York—and the results spoke for themselves in the form of a pair of Super Bowl titles—he still wanted complete autonomy on all personnel moves. So when Kraft named Bobby Grier as the director of player personnel a month after the playoff loss, it was the first step in the eventual dissolution of the relationship.

Grier had been an assistant coach with the Patriots, in charge of the offensive backfield in 1981, as well as from 1985 to 1992. Because Grier was new to the personnel position, Parcells still made most of the calls for the 1995 draft, which was ultimately one of the finest in franchise history. The top pick was cornerback Ty Law. Linebacker Ted Johnson was taken in the second round and running back Curtis Martin in the third. Both Law and Martin would go on to become perennial Pro Bowlers, while Johnson quickly became one of the anchors of the defense at inside line-backer. In addition, they were able to land another Parcells favorite when they signed kick returner and running back Dave Meggett.

With a cadre of young stars, it appeared New England was ready to challenge for supremacy in the AFC. The fans were certainly behind them: For the first time in franchise history, every home game was sold out before the season began. In a region that had been dominated by the Red Sox, the Patriots were able to carve out their own niche, a remarkable feat considering how far they had come in the five years of the Lisa Olson–Victor Kiam fiasco. "I've never seen anything like it," longtime Hub radio host Eddie Andelman told *The Boston Globe* that summer. "The Patriots were the team everybody was talking about all summer, even though the Red Sox were in first place." The frenzy reached a fever pitch for the opener against the Browns. Facing the team that had knocked them out of the playoffs the year before, New England pulled out a dramatic 17–14 win over Cleveland in front of 60,126 ecstatic fans at Foxboro Stadium. The victory was capped with a 14-play, 85-yard drive orchestrated by Bledsoe (who ended up 30-for-47 with 302 yards and no interceptions) and punctuated by Martin's first career touchdown in the final moments of the game. The hype machine went into overdrive, much to the dismay of Parcells. "I told the players in the locker room after the game to be happy and enjoy it," he said in his postgame press conference. "But this is a marathon we're in, not a sprint. It was only one game. We've got a long way to go yet."

Parcells's words would prove prophetic. All the good feeling that had been built up through the end of the previous season and the season opener would go out the window within a couple of months, as the Patriots lost their next four games by a combined score of 115–26. The offense was out of sync and the defense was playing poorly. After a 37–3 home loss to the Broncos that left New England at 1–4, he unloaded on his team and himself in a postgame press conference. "I'm running out of patience. There's lots of players I'm mad at for what's going on down here, but I take responsibility for that, because I'm the one that's allowed this to happen somehow," he said. "When you feel like your team has better ability than what they're showing, then you feel like you're failing as a coach."

And after another loss to Kansas City ended up dropping them to 1–5, the Patriots began their turnaround. The roller-coaster ride that defined much of the Parcells era in New England continued, as the Patriots won five of their next eight to vault right back into the wild-card hunt. Then came a December 16 game against the Steelers at Three Rivers Stadium. New England was hanging with the eventual AFC Champions through the first three quarters, and went into the final two minutes tied at 27. But a late Pittsburgh TD pass and a Ben Coates fumble sealed the Patriots' fate. They lost 41–27, dropping them out of the playoff picture for good. After a 10–7 loss at Indy the following week, the season wrapped with a 6–10 record.

Changes would have to be made. During the off-season, Parcells made a key addition to his coaching staff, hiring Belichick as his secondary coach after he was fired as head coach of the Browns. The reunion was a long time in coming. The two had worked together for eight years with the Giants, and Belichick was considered the yin to Parcells's yang. Considered Parcells's top lieutenant, the man nicknamed "Doom" had gained a rep as a defensive whiz, the sort of coordinator who could give opposing quarterbacks fits. "Bill Belichick is one of the most respected defensive coaches in the game today," Parcells said. "He was an instrumental part of my staff for eight seasons in New York and helped build one of the premier defenses in the league at that time. He is familiar with everyone on my staff and will be a tremendous asset to the team."

Behind the scenes, the power struggle between Parcells and Kraft continued, and it ultimately came to a head on the first day of the 1996 draft, April 20. The Patriots held the seventh pick of the first round, and Parcells was telling people behind closed doors that he wanted to take a defensive lineman. But Parcells later told Bill Gutman in his autobiography, *Parcells: An Autobiography*, he was called into Kraft's office shortly before the pick was to be made, and it wasn't going to be a defensive lineman but a wide receiver out of Ohio State named Terry Glenn. "I didn't know what was happening," Parcells said. "They said that Glenn was going to be the pick. I said we had agreed it was going to be a defensive player and that was it. I was mad as hell. I said, 'OK, if that's the way you want it, you got it.'"

"The next thing you see is Will McDonough chasing Bob Kraft down the stairs, screaming at him and basically calling him a liar," recalled Pires of the odd scene that included the owner, the head coach, and the longtime *Boston Globe* football writer. "'You told me this,' and 'You were going to take this guy.' That was when the Great Wall of Bob Kraft was erected. That's when he put the wall there. That's when it all started going downhill."

(Glenn wasn't the only draftee who was the source of contention between Kraft and Parcells. In the sixth round, New England selected Nebraska defensive tackle Christian Peter, who allegedly had a history of violence against women. Peter's record also included eighteen months on probation after he pleaded no contest to sexually assaulting a former Miss Nebraska; other arrests for trespassing, urinating in public, refusing to comply with the order of a policeman, and threatening to kill a parking attendant; and being accused of rape by two Nebraska students, one of whom ended up filing a federal lawsuit against Peter and the university.

Kraft and the team ended up releasing the player less than two weeks after the draft.)

Immediately after Glenn's selection, Kraft reportedly boasted to several members of the media, "Well, there's a new sheriff in town." Parcells, so put out by the decision—and Kraft's statement—later told Gutman that just over a week after the draft, he made up his mind to quit, but ended up reconsidering because he had made up his mind it would be his final year in Foxboro. "For about twenty-four hours, I made up my mind that I was finished here," he said in his autobiography. "I didn't want any more to do with this guy [Kraft]. But now, here's what I'm going to do. . . . I'm not leaving here 6–10. I'm going to come back here and prove I'm better than that.

"I did a lousy job. I know that. But next year, we've got a chance to be pretty good. I'm just going to have as little to do with [Kraft] as I can and just focus on coaching the team. Then when it's over, I'm out of here. I'm going to retire. This will be my last year coaching." To that end, in May 1996, Kraft issued a statement that said, in a sense: *Fine. If you want to leave, go ahead and leave.* Kraft said he had agreed to Parcells's request to shorten his five-year deal to a four-year contract. "At the same time, we agreed that at the end of this season, if there were a mutual feeling that he should coach the Patriots beyond the 1996 season, he would have that opportunity," said the New England owner in a public statement. "I believe we have one of the best coaches in the NFL. Bill continues to have my full support, professionally and personally."

Despite the bad blood behind the scenes, all was well as the Patriots approached the 1996 season. Glenn looked to be the perfect addition to the receiving corps, but took his share of tongue-in-cheek lumps from Parcells during training camp. (When a reporter asked how Glenn was doing in his attempt to deal with a balky hamstring, Parcells said sarcastically, "She's coming along." The remark drew a stern response from Kraft, who told the Associated Press, "That's not the standard we want to set. That's not the way we do things." Kraft's wife, Myra, also chimed in, saying it was "disgraceful. . . . I hope he's chastised for that. It was the wrong thing for anyone to say.")

The enmity continued to build. Kraft later told McDonough that he had almost fired Parcells immediately after the draft. Sounding very much like Sullivan talking about Fairbanks in the final days of the 1978 season, he made his feelings on Parcells very clear. "I had it up to here with that guy," Kraft said. "It just isn't any fun to go down there. [What happens with Parcells] is my decision. I own the team. He works for me. With me, it's a matter of respect. We give him everything he wants, and still he shows no respect for me."

While the bickering behind the scenes continued, the on-field product started to take off. And just as the franchise had enjoyed a spike in the on-field product in the mid-1970s under Fairbanks and the mid-1980s under Berry, they again started winning under Parcells. With one of the most talented young offenses in the league—featuring a rapidly improving Bledsoe, a running back with the heart of a lion in Martin, and a lighting-quick receiver in Glenn—the Patriots were able to make the playoffs. And after No. 1 seed Denver was upset, New England was able to beat the Steelers, and then defeat the upstart Jacksonville Jaguars in a bitter cold day in Foxborough for the AFC Championship. On a day that felt more than a little like a return to the bad old days—a bank of lights went dark midway through the game, causing a delay—the Patriots beat Jacksonville to advance to the Super Bowl. Carried away at the presentation of the championship trophy after the game, Kraft called Parcells "the greatest coach in the history of the game in modern times."

But the winning didn't make the bad blood disappear. In the days leading up to the Super Bowl, the Parcells–Kraft storyline was all anyone talked about. And at a pregame press conference, Parcells and Kraft shared a podium. They were once again forced to discuss their uneasy truce. "I know there's been a little bit kinda swirlin' around here, so my final statement on this to everyone is the same as it has been," said Parcells. "Bob and I agreed a long time ago that we would go through this year and we would discuss the situation about the future when the season's over, and we're going to do that as expeditiously as possible. And I also can assure you that it's gonna be done in a very civil and a very friendly manner. That was our agreement, and that's what we're going to do as soon as this season's over, OK?"

Kraft made a few perfunctory comments of his own, and then added: "I thank [Coach Parcells] for one thing: With everything that has been stirred up over the last week, [four] years ago and one day—to the day—we bought the team, and here we are in a Super Bowl. There's a pretty special karma going on, and we're excited about it. And I thank you for the opportunity."

As for the game, the Packers were clearly put out by the Parcells "will-he-stay-or-will-he-go?" brouhaha. Feeling it took the spotlight away from them—as well as their All-Pro quarterback Brett Favre—they used it as fuel for their fire. The game started relatively well for the Patriots, who were within striking distance of a far superior Green Bay team late in the third quarter when Desmond Howard returned a kickoff 99 yards to put the exclamation point on a 35–21 Packers win. Again, the Patriots were in a New Orleans Super Bowl. And again, they would go home as losers.

But that was just the beginning of the soap opera. Parcells wouldn't join them on their trip back to New England. The head coach flew home separately from his team, and the speculation began immediately. They didn't have to wait long, as Parcells officially stepped down as head coach of the Patriots on January 31, 1997, almost four years to the week after taking the job. His farewell press conference was something straight out of a Patriots nightmare. In it, he read from the letter of resignation he presented to Kraft, and then touched on a variety of topics.

"I want to express my deepest gratitude to the fans in New England for the tremendous support that they have given me. . . . I want to thank the players. I think all of you guys that followed the team know how much I liked coaching this team this year. They are a great group of kids, they've achieved a lot, and they did a lot of things nobody thought they could do. I take my hat off for them. I do think the future for them is quite bright with what they have.

"I want to thank the coaching staff, which I think operated under very difficult circumstances this year with my being a lame-duck coach going to camp and the pressure of not knowing what was going to happen and that kind of thing. So I'm grateful to them for the efforts that they put forth.

"Now Bob and I, there's been a lot written about this, Bob and I were forced together, OK? He did not hire me here. I was here when he got here. And Bob has been supportive of our program. He's tried to do everything that he can do to help us get to where we are. And in all honesty, we didn't ever have time to sit down and talk about how things should go. . . .

"As I said, he was forced in here. He's coming from another industry into this. I'm already here. I'm kind of set in my ways on some things. We didn't really have time to sit down and iron out how it was going to go. But I want to tell you something. This day is not about a power struggle, OK? I'm gonna tell you, it's not. . . .

"And there were a lot of people that deserve a lot of credit. Bob Kraft is one of them and Bobby Grier's another one. We were all trying to do this thing to get it to where it is. Now, as I said, this isn't about power and who picks who, and who does that. It's not about that. We just have a little philosophical difference, OK?

"And Bob owns the team and he has every right to run a team exactly the way he wants to run it. And I personally have no problem with that, and I wish him well in that regard. And I think that things will go well here because I think things are in place. And as I said, I hope the franchise is better off for me having been here."

He was asked about control over player personnel, and he responded by quoting a friend who once told him: "If they want you to cook the dinner, at least they ought to let you shop for some of the groceries."

It was a line that would go down as one of the most memorable in the history of the franchise. It clearly irked Kraft, who responded by saying: "I think we've been shopping at Bread & Circus. . . . I think [our players are] pretty good. . . . I think they're fresh. . . . I'd like to have groceries like that next year." The owner then spoke, "We owe a tremendous debt of gratitude, and I don't even think thanks is enough or appropriate for Bill Parcells for the contribution he's made to this franchise over the last four years. . . .

"The issue of the relationship of Bill and I has some interesting turns, and I'd just like to speak from my point of view on a personal basis. It's been a very cordial relationship. I can't think of any time on a personal basis when we didn't have a good time. And he's just a fun guy to be around and you folks know, as you call 'Tuna Talk,' his turn of phrases is truly unique.

"On a professional basis, I think we have a different philosophy. You know, he told me right from the beginning he coaches year to year. Which is different than anything I've ever been involved in. I have three other companies that we've built up. We tried to get the very best people, very good people, into those companies and make our decisions long-term looking at a three- and five- and ten-year horizon, and figure out the best things we can do for the long term.

"On a final note, I want to make it clear to everyone in this room that Bill is a person who was responsible more than anyone for getting us to the Super Bowl this year, and the person who four years ago arrived at our destination and brought credibility more than anyone else to this franchise, and he's left us a wonderful foundation to build on. And I promise you that our organization and family are going to do everything we can to build on the credibility he's brought and the legacy that he's left us.

"I guess I'll just take questions but I'm gonna deflect them. I'll only say that I hope and pray by this time next week we'll have another conference like this announcing the new head coach of the New England Patriots."

The media was stunned. "That was unbelievable," said Pires. "It was really just weird. You sat there and thought, 'Wow. Do I believe what I just saw and heard and experienced?' But that was the perfect bookend to the way the season started. It began with the draft and the whole thing with Will McDonough chasing Kraft down the stairs, and ended with that press conference."

"It's beginning to seem like Kraft is just another owner on some personal flight of fancy, some Jerry Jones wannabe who uses his money as a passport to the inner sanctum of American sport," wrote Bill Reynolds in the New Bedford *Standard-Times* the next day. "Is it any wonder that he and Parcells eventually clashed? Call it a New England version of Jones and Jimmy Johnson. Colliding egos in Foxboro. But no more. Now Kraft is the show. For better or worse."

In Parcells's place, Kraft named Pete Carroll as the new head coach. A likable guy who had risen quickly through the ranks to achieve some level of notoriety as a defensive guru, Carroll had been the Jets' defensive coordinator from 1990 through 1993, and was named head coach of New York in 1994, leading the Jets to a 6–10 mark. New York showed him the gate after just one season, but he quickly landed on his feet as defensive coordinator in San Francisco. And after two years with the 49ers, the Patriots came calling.

From the start, it was clear that Carroll was in over his head in New England. "You knew that at the beginning—the veteran guys had no respect for him," Pires said. "Pete was like the substitute teacher. There was no respect for him. Bob Kraft went out, and I don't know what he was thinking. He went for the kinder and gentler guy after Parcells, and it wasn't the way to go. Pete is a very good person, a very good guy with a very good heart. If he was your next-door neighbor, you'd love him, because he'd always offer to cut your grass and paint your house for you."

With Parcells out of town, the players started lining up to take their shots at their deposed coach. While several players spoke their mind freely—including linebacker Chris Slade, who told reporters, "If I was getting $10 million and he was coming back, I wouldn't want to be here"—it was Bledsoe who fired the loudest shot. "He didn't say anything to any of the players," Bledsoe said of Parcells. "You'd like to think that, when you go through some of the things we all went through with the guy, he'd at least say goodbye. But from the get-go, Bill has been about Bill. That's the way it is. That's the way he is.

"It's exciting to come in here to a positive atmosphere, where the coaches are excited about working with you and where you're excited about being here," Bledsoe added. "It's not like before, when you came in every day wondering if you were going to get beat down. You always wondered what he would say. Now, you don't feel like somebody is waiting to cut you down when you came to work."

The troubles began when the team organized a weekly basketball league. While most coaches would have opted out of the process, Carroll became an active participant, suiting up every week alongside his players. He was an excitable guy, given to phrases like "jacked" and "pumped" to describe his state of mind. He was as far from Parcells as you could get. Parcells was an East Coast guy straight out of the Lombardi school of coaching, an old-school disciplinarian who used intimidation to run his team. Carroll was a West Coast guy who believed in the power of positive reinforcement, a coach who would try and win his players over with a combination of feel-good charm and ebullience. At first, it appeared to be a savvy move. "Pete Carroll has turned the team over to the players," defensive back Willie Clay told reporters soon after Carroll took over. "It's different this year. This is the New England Patriots, coached by Pete Carroll. It's our team. Last year, we were just players on Bill's team."

In the long term, trying to be the players' best friend was a bad move. "He was a person who was in a position of authority, and he took himself out of that position and made himself one of the guys. That's never what you want to do, especially in a competitive environment. That was like suicide," said one reporter who covered the team in the 1990s. "You have younger guys making a lot of money, and if you don't have a position of dominance over them, you're going to get swallowed up. That's what happened with Pete."

The trouble continued when it became clear that Carroll had relatively no authority over the players. Bobby Grier had started to consolidate his power as vice president of player personnel, and if a player had a problem with Carroll, he simply went over his head to Grier, who was backed by Kraft. "The infrastructure there wasn't supportive of Pete, because there were the backdoors to Bobby Grier, and that hurt," Pires said. "You had Pete; he was brought in by the Kraft's as a softer, gentler guy. Then, you had Bobby, who was kind of a holdover, and him and Parcells didn't get along, per se, especially with the Terry Glenn thing. You're kind of setting up a bad foundation, and that's what all made it start to crumble."

It wasn't just Carroll who suffered the consequences. All the old Parcells holdovers, including veteran personnel man Charley Armey, were minimized under Grier. Armey would later recall an incident where he was asked to leave a meeting on draft preparation because he was a Parcells guy. "They made a decision to go with Bobby, who was very capable as the director of player personnel. He wanted to come in and do things in his own style and put his stamp on it," Armey said. "That's what happens in this business, when someone comes in and wants to have a chance to do things their way. They really want to do it their way.

"Bobby came in and was given the opportunity to be the director of player personnel and run it the way he wanted to. And, of course, that meant you can't have two guys in the same saddle—there's just not enough room. So that meant I had to get off the saddle."

For his part, Parcells wanted to return to his Jersey roots. While the Giants job wasn't available, the Jets had an opening—they were coming off two seasons under Rich Kotite in which they went 3–13 and 1–15—and Parcells would be more than happy to hop back to New York. But he was still under contract to the Patriots. To circumvent the contract, New York management came up with a wild idea: Parcells would be a "consultant" with the Jets for the duration of the 1997 season. Then, on February 1, 1998, he would become the head coach and chief of football operations. In addition, Belichick would serve under Parcells as the assistant head coach and defensive coordinator, moving into the corner office when Parcells stepped down at the end of his contract.

New York team president Steve Gutman saw nothing wrong with the idea, saying the plan did not violate the rules set down by NFL Commissioner Paul Tagliabue. "Consultants consult," Gutman said. "He does not make decision. He does not run the football team. He does not coach the football team. This is designed to create an element of stability and create an opportunity to put a football program together, and have it last for a very, very, very long time."

Predictably, the ruse sent Kraft over the edge. The Patriots cried foul. "This so-called consulting agreement is a transparent farce, and the latest in a series of actions by the New York Jets and Bill Parcells which further demonstrates it has been their intention all along to have Bill become head coach of the Jets for the '97 season," read a statement issued by the team. "We will immediately ask Commissioner Tagliabue to review this agreement between the Jets and Bill Parcells to determine if there has been a violation of Parcells' agreement with the Patriots and the Commissioner's ruling last week, which prevents him from serving in this de facto coaching position for another NFL team."

The NFL issued a statement saying Parcells could not serve as head coach of the Jets while still under contract to the Patriots: "Commissioner Tagliabue ruled last week that Bill Parcells cannot serve in 1997 as an NFL head coach or in a comparable position without the New England Patriots' permission. Our office has had subsequent discussions with both clubs regarding that decision as recently as yesterday. The Jets were neither denied nor given permission to make a consulting agreement with Parcells for 1997. If asked to review the agreement between the Jets and the Parcells as it may affect the Patriots' contract rights for 1997, the commissioner will review the matter, including holding a hearing if necessary. Any ruling on the consulting agreement would depend on the specifics of the arrangement."

Tagliabue eventually brokered an agreement between the Patriots and the Jets that allowed Parcells to return to the Meadowlands. New England got a third- and a fourth-round draft pick in 1997, as well as a third-round pick the following year. In return, the Jets suddenly became a force to be reckoned with, both on and off the field. Within three years, New York would reach the AFC Championship Game, while Carroll and the Patriots would begin a slide back toward .500. Along the way, Parcells and the Jets took great delight in gleefully tormenting his former employers, swiping several players from the Patriots throughout the late 1990s, including Otis Smith, Ray Lucas, William Roberts, and Tom Tupa. But the biggest catch was Curtis Martin. The dynamic running back rushed for 1,160 yards in 1997, and figured to land a big payday as a restricted free agent. Knowing the Patriots might not be able to match the offer, Parcells got Martin to sign an offer sheet for six years and $36 million. The Patriots, who had the opportunity to match the offer, declined to do so and instead received first- and third-round draft picks from the Jets.

"They made a lot of mistakes in the late 1990s," Pires said. "They made a classic mistake with Curtis Martin. In retrospect, that was a huge mistake. They kind of marginalized the guys' talents. They figured, 'You could always draft a running back.' Ten years later, the guy was just then thinking of retiring."

It all contributed to the downward spiral that was New England sports in the late 1990s. The 1996–97 Celtics posted the worst record in the history of the franchise, going 15–67, but missed out on the No. 1 draft pick when the NBA lottery didn't go their way. That same winter, the Bruins' string of thirty straight playoff appearances ended. The Red Sox had worked their way back from their struggles of the early 1990s, but won just one playoff series over the course of the decade. It created an angry sports populace, and the venom boiled over frequently. The feelings of many athletes and fans were summed up in a now-legendary Rick Pitino rant that came in March 2000 after the Celtics suffered a last-second loss to Toronto that drew boos from the Boston crowd. "The negativity that's in this town sucks," he said in a stunning postgame press conference. "I've been around when Jim Rice was booed. I've been around when [Carl] Yastrzemski was booed. And it stinks. It makes the greatest town, greatest city in the world lousy. The only thing that will turn this around is being upbeat and positive like we are in that locker room . . . and if you think I'm going to succumb to negativity, you're wrong. You've got the wrong guy leading this team."

While New England remained competitive through the late 1990s, Martin's defection to New York changed the tone of the rivalry. And after three seasons that saw the team go from 10–6 to 9–7 and then, 8–8, it was hardly a surprise that less than twenty-four hours after the Patriots beat Baltimore in their 1999 season finale, the Patriots fired Carroll. It was quick and painless, a transaction most everyone knew was coming, including Carroll.

Many of the New England veterans admitted to letting themselves get fat and happy once Parcells was out the door. "I think he knew he was coming into a tough situation following a huge personality. I don't think he anticipated what that was going to be," Bledsoe told reporters after the announcement. "Does this team need an intimidator? I don't know. There are some guys on this team that may need somebody to lay down the law. I would like to subscribe to the theory that we're all professionals."

"You work for Parcells, like a lot of these guys did, and he is the leader. Now Pete comes in and he lets you lead yourself," offensive lineman Heath Irwin told the AP after the ax came down on Carroll. "Maybe a lot of these guys are better taking orders than giving orders. . . . I think it was bad timing. You're always going to be compared to him. People are always going to be looking over your shoulder and saying, 'You aren't like him. He didn't do it that way.' I don't know if there's ever been a guy who came in after a great coach and was really successful."

"I'm proud of being 27–21 and making the playoffs the first two years I was here," said Carroll, who won more games in his first three years with the Patriots than had Parcells or his successor, Belichick, in their first three seasons in New England. "I'll forever be disappointed that we didn't win more."

"This is a business of accountability, and two years ago we won the division. Last year we barely made the playoffs and this year we're 8–8," Kraft said in a press conference. "We need a momentum change."

For the Patriots, there were several candidates for the job, some of whom were apparently interested in a job that still held some measure of cachet in NFL circles—even with the Parcells-Kraft divorce still fresh in the minds of many. However, for the most part, those who did interview with the franchise were not the same sort of retreads that dominated the previous search, which ended with Parcells. While that process included Mike Ditka and Buddy Ryan, this time the franchise focused mostly on newer faces, younger coordinators who were looking to move up. They included Baltimore defensive coordinator Marvin Lewis, Oakland defensive coordinator Willie Shaw, Chicago offensive coordinator Gary Crowton, and Steve Sidwell, who had served as defensive coordinator under Carroll. The change in interviewees was perhaps the first sign that the Patriots were serious about changing the direction of the franchise. The second sign came when the Patriots immediately faxed the Jets about speaking with Belichick about their head coaching position. It was hardly a surprise. By all accounts, Belichick and Kraft had developed a close personal relationship when Belichick served as an assistant coach in New England under Parcells. It was a relationship that continued even though Belichick left Foxboro after the 1997 season to follow Parcells to New York.

But the Jets trumped the Patriots. Later that day, Parcells made a dramatic announcement: He was done with coaching and was stepping aside as the head coach of the Jets. Belichick would take over as head coach. On the surface, it appeared to be a perfect fit, a natural progression for Parcells's top lieutenant. The two had worked together for several years with the Giants, the Patriots, and the Jets. They had helped create legendary defenses; they had taken the Giants to the Super Bowl twice and the Patriots to the Super Bowl once; and they had resurrected the Jets as an AFC power. If there was going to be someone who would continue Parcells's legacy, it would be Belichick, his No. 1 man. In New England, the media took the move as the latest step in what had developed into a burgeoning feud between the Jets and Patriots that many called "the Border War." The division foes—whose battles had never reached the intensity of their baseball brethren—were managing to create a rivalry of their own, thanks in large part to the bitter relationship between Kraft and Parcells.

However, early reports out of New York indicated the transition would not be as smooth as the Jets had hoped. Newspaper reports at the time indicated that Belichick and Parcells had an "animated" discussion on Monday about Belichick possibly taking the job. "His response was, 'If you feel that uncertain about it, maybe you should think about not taking this job,'" Belichick would later say of Parcells. It would later come to light that Belichick did have many reservations about the job. Longtime owner Leon Hess had died the previous May, and the Jets were in the process of being sold. What if a new owner came in and wanted a different head coach? Or what if—and this was even worse—the new owner wanted to bring in a general manager or player personnel man above Belichick who had differing views on how the game should be played?

Belichick was leery of unstable ownership situations. All he had to do was think back a few years to his final year in Cleveland, which had played out like something out of a bad soap opera. There was instability involving the franchise, the ownership, and much of the player roster. He wanted none of that this time around. And so, in the hours before the 2:30 P.M. press conference, he walked the halls at Jets' headquarters, informing members of the staff (including Parcells) he was about to resign. And moments before he walked into the press conference—a gathering most believed was being held in order to officially name him the new head coach of the New York Jets—he told team president Steve Gutman, scrawling on a piece of paper that he had resigned as "HC of the NYJ," joking he hadn't typed out a note because he was computer illiterate. With Parcells reportedly locked in his office, he then spoke uninterrupted for twenty-five minutes rumbling about his abrupt decision to turn his back on the $1.4 million-a-year position because of "various uncertainties surrounding my position as it relates to the team's new ownership."

"I have to make a decision that I understand what's at stake, and I just don't feel that I can lead the Jets in the year 2000," he told reporters. "The uncertainty surrounding the ownership of the team, and a number of other things, had an effect on my decision. I know the commitment that needs to be made, and I don't feel in the current situation I can lead the Jets with 100 percent conviction. The situation is one of great uncertainty, and I just don't feel I can go forward.

"We were supposed to have a new owner by December 15, and now it's January 4," he said. "It's not fair to the organization to drag it out until the middle of February.

"My family has been in a situation where I was the head coach of a team in transition, of a team that went through a lot of changes, and it frankly wasn't a real good experience for me or them," Belichick said. "I'm not saying that would happen here. I don't know what would happen. I have no crystal ball."

Belichick also may have wanted the security of a contract extension. "Was there something in place? Yes, but in my opinion, the circumstances changed so significantly it wouldn't be fair to make a halfhearted commitment with all these questions in the back of my mind," Belichick said.

And then there was the relationship with Parcells. The two had been connected at the hip for much of Belichick's coaching life, but it was clear Belichick had started to chafe under Parcells. "Bill and I have conversed about this for months and even years," Belichick said. "Another thing that has been brought out repeatedly is 'Belichick has known about this transition for a year, he's had plenty of time to get ready for it.' Well, I remember back in 1987 with the Giants, that was a strike year. We were coming off the Super Bowl and we had a terrible team. We couldn't beat anyone. We were not very good. Bill told me in 1987, 'I can't keep doing this. One more year and you can have it.' I heard it at New England, too. I've heard it since 1987 for an extended period of time.

"We all know how Bill is. He sometimes reacts emotionally to a loss or a bad season or a series of bad performances. Every time Bill says that, I take it with a little bit of a grain of salt. Because that's what it's been for the last 12, 13 years, whatever it is.

"Until Monday morning, when he made me aware that this was the final decision and not 80 percent, 90 percent, 83 percent, 77 percent, that this was it, I didn't believe it. It had gone as high as 99, but I've seen it back off and come back up again. Until Monday, when it was, 'This is what I'm going to do,' then that's really when I thought, 'Well, this is what I have to do.' That's how this whole sequence of events has transpired."

Belichick was coy about any sort of long-range plans, saying he was content to simply spend time with his family, and he said he would be perfectly happy to sit out the year, if it came to that. "My wife has been pretty thrifty and clipped some coupons and we've been able to save some money and I think we'll be able to live comfortably for a while," he said. But he did offer up the fact that he had hired a lawyer to contact the league in an apparent attempt to free himself from his contract with the Jets.

After Belichick finished speaking, a surprised Gutman took his whacks at Belichick. The Jets president took to the podium and said: "We should have some feelings of sorrow and regret for him and his family. He obviously has some inner turmoil." As for Belichick's contract, which had three years remaining, Gutman said Belichick has a signed contract "that is clear, unambiguous and specific with respect to the areas of uncertainty that he [Belichick] has raised today so far as they relate to football and the New York Jets."

(Gutman's words would clearly pain Belichick, who wouldn't respond to Gutman immediately, instead waiting a few years before telling the New York Post that, "I can't think of anybody in pro sports and certainly in my thirty years in professional football who has said more and won less than Steve Gutman." Gutman would offer a reply in the weeks prior to Super Bowl XXXIX, when he told Rich Cimini of the New York Daily News his assessment on how things worked out for Belichick: "My only thoughts are that he's a great coach and he's had great success," said Gutman. "I'm very admiring of him. How can you say anything but?")

After the press conference, the NFL said they would bar any other team from contacting Belichick about a head coaching job while they examined his contract, which the Jets still considered binding. If he went to another team, New York would almost certainly be owed compensation. This wasn't what Kraft had envisioned, and he started wondering about a possible fallback plan. According to Michael Holley's book Patriot Reign: Bill Belichick, the Coaches, and the Players Who Built a Champion, Kraft secretly flew to Miami to interview head coach Butch Davis, who had recently taken the Hurricanes to a national title. The interview went so well that Davis came to Boston for another. But it didn't get any farther than that. After NFL commissioner Paul Tagliabue and federal judge John W. Bissell both said the Jets' deal with Belichick was valid, it was left to old enemies Parcells and Kraft to settle things, and the two sides were able to strike a deal. It was an awkward process for both of them, as they hadn't spoken in the three years since Parcells left Foxboro for the Meadowlands.

"Tuesday night, I called Bob Kraft personally and spoke with him and kind of asked him if he was interested in Bill coaching the team," Parcells told the Associated Press. "We spent quite a bit of time talking about the past, mended a lot of fences and kind of explained our feeling to one another. . . . We came to an agreement that regardless of what happened with Bill Belichick, this kind of border war between the Patriots and Jets needed to come to a halt. . . . Quite frankly, I was kind of anxious that we make an attempt to repair the relationship, and he agreed."

An agreement was struck: Belichick would take the reins in New England; in return, the Jets would receive New England's first round pick (No. 16) in the 2000 draft plus its No. 4 and No. 7 picks in 2001. The Jets sent the Patriots a fifth-round pick in 2001 and a seventh-rounder in 2002. It was comparable to the deal the Patriots received when Parcells left Foxboro for the Meadowlands in early 1997. Then, the Patriots received four draft choices: a first-rounder, a second, a third, and a fourth, although not in the same year.

"It resolves a lot of issues lingering a long time and helps Bill get back into coaching, where he wants to be," Parcells told reporters at the time. "I think Bob has the coach he wants, and we were compensated pretty well."

Predictably, the New York tabloids ripped Belichick on his way out of town. The *New York Post* blasted "BELICHICKEN" across the back page, and football fans in New England wondered why Kraft went to the wall for a guy with a career coaching mark of 37–45 and a less-than-hospitable personality when it came to dealing with the media and his players. "Why was Kraft going to hire

[Belichick] to be the caretaker of his organization?" asked Michael Holley in a column in *The Boston Globe* earlier that same month. "The fact that he was even thinking about it shows that he has already gotten off to a bad start with his job search for a new coach/general manager. The first thing Kraft should do this morning is find the list with [Bill] Belichick's name atop it and torch it. I'd hate to see the second name on the list."

In the late 1980s and early 1990s, Belichick had achieved great success as a defensive coordinator with the Giants, but no one was quite sure that he could make the transition between coordinator and head coach. He was certainly an intriguing figure, intriguing enough to have been through multiple interviews in several different locations. He had first interviewed for the Cleveland Browns head coaching position after the 1988 season—and, by all accounts was impressive—but the job went to the defensive coordinator for the Jets, Bud Carson. In 1990, the Phoenix Cardinals had interviewed him for their vacant head coaching position, an interview he appeared reluctant to take. "As I've said many times before, I'm very happy with my job," Belichick said at the time. "The New York Giants are a good organization and a good team. But at the same time, it would be foolish not to investigate a potentially better opportunity for me and my family."

For the Cardinals job, Belichick was one of six finalists, part of a list that included then-49ers offensive coordinator Mike Holmgren, Rams defensive coordinator Fritz Shurmur, Redskins assistant head coach Joe Bugel, Cal State Fresno coach Jim Sweeney, Cincinnati Bengals offensive coordinator Bruce Coslet, and Cardinals interim coach Hank Kuhlmann. Bugel ended up getting the job, but no matter—the Cardinals were not considered one of the better jobs in the NFL. In fact, they were one of the least relevant franchises in the history of the game, and that wasn't going to change, no matter the coach. After moving from St. Louis to Arizona a few years prior, they had little fan base. They didn't even have their own stadium. Until 2005, they played their games at Sun Devil Stadium on the campus of Arizona State University.

In addition to the Cardinals, there were other potential jobs that drew Belichick's interest, including the Tampa Bay Buccaneers. But none had the cachet of the Browns. Belichick was a history buff, and the Cleveland job appealed to him for a variety of reasons, including the fact that no professional football team could boast the impressive lineage the Browns had. The franchise stretched back to the 1940s, back to the days of the All-American Football Conference. It was the team of Paul Brown and Otto Graham, of Lou Groza and Jim Brown, of Marion Motley and Ozzie Newsome. And there was a smart and canny fan base, one that packed Cleveland's Municipal Stadium in good times and bad, and was clearly desperate for a winner. Belichick, who owned almost every book on football strategy ever written, was a student of the game, and could appreciate that being the head coach of the Browns was unlike any other job in the National Football League. It was a chance to be a part of a tradition that included head coaches like Brown and Blanton Collier.

"I think that Paul Brown was, in my mind, the greatest innovator as a coach that I know of," Belichick said. "The professional aspect of the program—the film study, the meetings, the game planning, the precision of the plays—I think he really took it to a different level. . . . I don't think anybody in professional football does anything that dramatically different in terms of the preparation and coaching of the team that wouldn't very closely follow what Paul did."

While Belichick had great respect for the job of head coach of the Cleveland Browns, he was unprepared for the PR chores that went along with it. "I'm driving around one day," Cleveland *Plain Dealer* columnist Bill Livingston once wrote of Belichick during his time with the Browns, "listening to Belichick's radio show. They take a call, and this guy says, 'First of all, Bill, I want to wish you and your family a Merry Christmas.' And there was, like, twenty seconds of dead air. I remember looking at the radio and scream-ing, 'Well, wish him a Merry Christmas back, you little schmuck.'"

Cleveland offensive lineman Mike Baab recalled Belichick's first sitdown with his new team, days after he took the job. In front of a roomful of players, Belichick shouted, "I've worked too long and too hard for this chance to let you guys fuck it up for me." The bar-rage continued through training camp, as Belichick spent most of his time riding his new charges relentlessly, usually in the most vulgar and obscene manner possible. "He was the most profane coach I've ever heard," Baab recalled in *The Boston Globe* a few years later. "I don't think he was interested in becoming your friend in any way, shape, or form. He didn't endear himself to any-one at all. There was nothing to love there, except the hope we would win."

What was even more stunning for Baab and the rest of the vet-eran Browns was that when some of the veteran Giants paid Be-lichick a visit, he embraced them like a father would welcome a long-lost son. "The Giants players were coming over and embrac-ing him and joking with him and talking to him like they were old friends," Baab said. "We couldn't believe it. He never called us any-thing that wasn't twelve letters.

"That first year, he was completely lacking in people skills."

While he was lacking in people skills, his work ethic and drive were never in question. And while there were clashes with the play-ers, Belichick was initially a big hit with the fans because he made the team much more competitive. Cleveland had finished the 1990 season with eight straight losses and ten of their last eleven. But the 1991 Browns were clearly better: Following a season-opening loss to the Cowboys, the Browns won two in a row, including a last-second win over Cincinnati at Cleveland. After the win over the Bengals, Be-lichick ran to the Dawg Pound right after the game and whooped it up with the rest of them, waving his fist over his head and circling it over and over again like Arsenio Hall saluting his Dawg Pound. The honeymoon continued throughout much of the first thirteen games, when the Browns were 6–7 and hanging in the playoff hunt by a thread. Then three straight losses to end the season doomed them.

But those good times soon fizzled. Even though the Browns' turnaround came quickly, it was soon evident he was unprepared for most of the off-field responsibilities. He alienated football-crazed Ohioians by muttering "I don't give a damn what the fans think" into an open microphone. And it didn't stop there. He was excoriated by the Cleveland media for closing the locker room to reporters during the team's first minicamp—instead, players were brought to an interview area. And as the losses piled up in the early going, the media gleefully took their shots at him, mocking his less-than-dynamic speaking style and his wardrobe.

"I think he's as good a coach as there is," said Cleveland owner Art Modell. "His media relations aren't the greatest. But I didn't hire Don Rickles. He's a very, very painfully shy, introverted man. He likes nothing more than his family and coaching."

On the surface, it appeared Belichick and Modell were a good fit. Belichick's father, Steve, had grown up in Ohio, and was immersed in a football culture at an early age, eventually going on to become a player. (Steve would go on to be a college football coach and scout for over half a century, and would author a book, *Football Scouting Methods.*) As a result of his father's passion, Bill Belichick grew up worshipping the game, and had an appreciation for football history, including the importance of a flagship franchise like the Browns. Modell's roots also ran deep in football. He bought the Browns in 1961 for the record sum of $4.1 million, and even though he fired legendary head coach Paul Brown a few years later, he helped foster a close relationship between the Browns and their fans throughout the 1970s and 1980s. Belichick's family had roots in Ohio, and he was completely familiar with the tradition of football in the state.

But when it came to the football, Modell and Belichick were speaking different languages. Modell was about instant results;

Belichick was about slowly crafting a franchise that could enjoy sustained success. Modell was looking to spend; Belichick was thinking more about saving for a rainy day. Compounding the difficulties was the fact that the NFL had entered a new economic world that not everyone was ready to deal with. Free agency and the salary cap had hit the NFL, and many teams were unprepared for what was about to happen. Teams were forced to make some hard decisions. The free agents placed before the teams—such as defensive lineman Reggie White and cornerback Deion Sanders—were some of the most talented players in the league. But they had some hard choices, weighing risk versus reward. They could go and get the big-ticket free agents, but there was the very real danger those signings could end up backfiring, leaving the team hamstrung when it came to trying to operate under the salary cap.

Most of the teams were flabbergasted when confronted with the dilemma. Some teams didn't spend wisely on free agents, shelling out big money to the wrong players and handicapping their franchises as a result. In those early days, there were three free agents who stood out above the rest when it came to beating the system. In 1994, desperately in need of a quarterback, Detroit shelled out a three-year $11 million contract for Miami backup quaterback Scott Mitchell. In 1996, the Jets delivered a five-year, $25 million contract to quarterback Neil O'Donnell. And that same off-season, the Raiders signed cornerback Larry Brown—fresh off an MVP appearance in Super Bowl XXX—to a five-year, $12.5 million contract. All three players were relative failures in their new homes, with Mitchell and Brown in particular becoming the poster children for ill-conceived approaches to free agency.

And if they didn't overspend in free agency, teams wasted money in hopes of retaining their own subpar players, going broke trying to keep their nucleus together. (Instead, they ended up as perennial visitors to the bargain-basement free agent shopping spree, hoping to find a diamond in the rough that had washed out in other locales but would fit perfectly in their system.) Some teams simply forgot about the real importance of the draft; they wasted picks on players who were doomed to spend their careers on the sidelines. And some teams and their owners were just flat-out impatient, going after quick fixes but not sticking with a long-term plan of success. They fell victim by violating the first rule of the new era of professional football: You cannot craft a champion overnight.

The fact was that no one was really sure how to manage the cap. There were, of course, all sorts of ways to beat it. Every one of the teams was forced to learn the process. "There wasn't really much historically to go on," recalled Belichick of those early difficult days of trying to manipulate the salary cap. "There was still a big learning curve for us to take on.

"Nobody really knew exactly how it worked then. There were a lot of changes from year to year, how certain things were treated on the cap."

To find some guidance on the matter, Belichick picked the brain of legendary Lakers general manager Jerry West on the best ways to beat the system. West advised him to focus on player development and not to buy into a one-player-at-any-cost philosophy. West had used this approach to keep Los Angeles at or near the top of the NBA standings for many years. (Belichick also fell back on his collegiate days. The economics major later professed to have employed many of the same lessons he learned while taking economics classes with Professor Dick Miller at Wesleyan. As a result, the son of a teacher, Belichick, was able get the jump on his competition. He later sent Miller a note of thanks.)

Belichick's early personnel moves with the Browns reflect West's idea. Cleveland stocked up on draft picks and moved cautiously when it came to the free agent pool. That didn't mean Belichick eschewed the big players at the right price. It was believed that the Browns were one of the finalists in the race to land the first major free agent, Reggie White, who eventually chose the Packers. In many ways, Belichick's early forays into free agency with the

Browns closely mirrored his approach in New England. He found low-cost, low-risk high-impact guys, and he used some players he was familiar with at his last coaching stop. The latter included ex-Giants linebacker Carl Banks.

"If you look at what he was trying to do in Cleveland, I think he did realize where the league was going before everyone else, and had an idea of how he wanted to go about setting up his team," Perillo said of Belichick. "If he had stayed there, he would have probably built a winner, in time."

While they were able to make some roster tweaks here and there, the Browns were goaded into making some questionable personnel decisions by the ownership. Modell was interested in winning as much as possible as quickly as possible, and he didn't completely accept Belichick's patient, disciplined approach. As a result, the franchise made some significant errors in judgment, the worst of which involved wide receiver Andre Rison. In 1995, Modell became infatuated with Rison, who was coming off three straight years of at least 1,000 receiving yards. An eventual five-time Pro Bowler, Rison was an undeniable talent. But he was also known to be something of a question mark when it came to character. Off the field, he gained a measure of infamy in 1994 when his fiancée, Lisa "Left Eye" Lopes, burned his Atlanta home to the ground in an alcohol-induced rage. None of this mattered to Modell. He saw only the five straight seasons of at least eighty catches and not the potential trouble that Rison and his contract could do to the franchise. Modell put the full-court press on to get Rison signed. "He's the biggest star we've signed. He's the first home run hitter we've had in a long time. He is truly a potential Hall of Famer," panted Modell, even before Rison had signed his deal. Knowing the Browns were so interested, Rison jacked up his request. Eventually he signed a five-year, $17 million deal that forced an already cash-strapped Modell to take out a loan in his wife's name to pay the $5 million signing bonus. (In total that off-season, Modell spent nearly $24 million in bonuses over the $37.1 million salary cap.)

Predictably, the Rison deal backfired. He would spend just one season with the Browns, and that was the worst year of his career. His contract pushed the franchise over the cap, and his behavior—he missed meetings, fought with quarterbacks, and flipped-off fans—left coaches and fans alienated and served as another wedge that helped drive Modell and Belichick apart.

Overall, it was a bad time for the relationship between the head coach and the owner. That same offseason, Belichick had secretly arranged for thirty-eight-year-old Phil Simms to come out of retirement to quarterback the Browns. The two knew each other from their days together in New York, when Simms led the Giants to a victory in Super Bowl XXI with one of the great Super Bowl performances of all time—22-for-25 with 268 yards and three touchdowns. In May, Simms flew out to Cleveland for what he believed was a surreptitious meeting with Modell to discuss details. But when Simms landed, he found that Modell had arranged a press conference to announce the signing of the Super Bowl MVP. Simms turned around and left, telling his agent, "I feel like I just got my pants pulled down." Belichick seethed, and later told Simms, "You are so lucky you didn't come."

While the relationship between Modell and Belichick went south quickly, he lost his support among the fans in 1993 when, leading the AFC Central with a 5–3 mark, he cut loose quarterback Bernie Kosar—a favorite son of Ohio—in favor of Vinny Testaverde. Then Testaverde got hurt and was replaced by Todd Philcox. That started a precipitous slide to a 7–9 finish. At one point in the 1993 season—as the Browns were losing six of their final eight games with the Philcox-Testaverde combo behind center—a crowd of about a thousand stood outside a Belichick press conference following a loss and screamed, "Bill must go!" for several minutes. His critics pounced.

"It is one thing to be bold, to make hard decisions. It is another to embarrass a player the caliber of Bernie Kosar as the Browns did on the day they cut him back in 1993," wrote venerated *Akron*

*Beacon Journal* columnist Terry Pluto. "Actually, they were right. Kosar wasn't the same player he had been in the 1980s. His body had taken a beating, playing behind inferior offensive lines. But Bernie Kosar at 105 years old was better than Todd Philcox in his prime, and Belichick must have thought the fans were idiots when he said otherwise."

But the players who stayed found a coach who was willing to go to the wall for them—even if he didn't always sound like it. "I think a lot of people don't like him because he is not someone who is going to be open with you. He isn't going to kid around," Cleveland running back Leroy Hoard told *The Boston Globe* in the days leading up to the 1994 playoff game with the Patriots. "But that's not his job as a football coach. He is supposed to get us prepared. And the Bernie thing? I think decisions can be made that people don't agree with. But if you were in his same shoes, you have to ask yourself if you would have done the same thing."

And even a year later, as the Browns finished with an 11–5 regular-season record—and a home playoff game—people were still looking for Belichick's head, much to the chagrin of many of his players. "I've never seen anything like this," Browns left tackle Tony Jones told reporters at the end of the 1994 season. "People just can't forget the Bernie thing and they hate the coach. I can see why people are upset, but they need to support their city. We need to focus on football here. . . . I don't even know if winning a Super Bowl will take care of it. Bill made an unpopular decision and some people aren't going to let it go. I thought our record this year would take care of things, but it hasn't."

"[In Cleveland], he was a young coach with no sense of the importance of communications, with either his players or the media," said Livingston. "He was so isolated that his wife had to plead for understanding for him. I remember her talking about how well Belichick connected with small children and animals. It recalled the scene in *The Caine Mutiny* when Humphrey Bogart, as the embattled Captain Queeg, tells his skeptical officers how much his dog loved him."


And so it was no surprise to Robert Kraft when a fellow executive sent him a tape of one of Belichick's media sessions with the message, "Are you sure you want to hire this guy?" But news of the team's interest in Belichick wasn't a shocker to many reporters who had covered the team—for three reasons. First, in his one year as a New England assistant coach, he and Kraft had developed a close relationship. "There was a time in 1996 when they had a fire alarm at the old stadium, and all of a sudden, there goes a Lexus leaving the parking lot with Bob Kraft driving the car and Bill Belichick in the front seat," recalled Dan Pires, who covered the team for the New Bedford *Standard-Times*. "Meanwhile, Bill Parcells is the head coach."

"It certainly seems like Robert had a lot of talk with Bill about where the league was going and the economics of the league, which I'm sure interested Robert from a business perspective, being a businessman," Perillo said. "It would certainly seem that they had formed this bond back in 1996, and it's believed he kind of wanted to hire him when he hired Carroll."

Second, there was Belichick's approach to managing a football team. While Parcells was clearly interested in cooking the dinner and shopping for the groceries, Belichick knew that many cooks didn't necessarily spoil the meal. Belichick would later admit that he learned that lesson with the Browns in the early 1990s, when he looked around the league and realized that great coaches like Chuck Noll, Don Shula, and Bill Walsh were struggling with the intricacies of the new economic setup, which included Plan B free agency as well as the salary cap.

"Really, in every football organization there [have] to be at least two people—one person has to be primarily responsible for the football team, and one person has to be primarily responsible for personnel," Belichick said. "There's no way I can coach a team and go out there and scout players or keep up with pro personnel. There's no way a person in charge of keeping up with personnel, college, pro, and et cetera, is going to be able to coach a team, so you have to have two people doing it.

"The general manager can have all of the authority he wants. He can pick the players and all that, but if it is fourth-and-one out there, he is not going to call the play. And the guy who is coaching the team, there is no way he can go out and scout all of the players," he added. "I see it as two people working together. It may be more than that involved. It could be two, three, four. It could be however it is structured, but it has to be at least two. That is the bare minimum. And then, beyond that, it is however you want to set it up and branch it out at that point."

And third, it was plainly evident to those behind the scenes that he was not the same coach who stood in front of the Browns that day nine years before and delivered an R-rated diatribe to players, many of whom were his age. The personal growth that occurred between his being a head coach in Cleveland and a head coaching candidate in New England could be measured in light-years. "I was only there that one year," Baab later recalled. "I heard from other guys after that that he lightened up. I heard from some guys three or four years later that he let the guys out of camp early, threw them a beer party. I said, 'Belichick?'

"I'm sure Belichick matured as a coach [while in Cleveland]," he added. "Everyone does."

In Cleveland, the most important thing in his football career was not to be needed or loved. It was to win. "I made winning football games the No. 1 priority, and everything else was a distant second," he said of his time in Cleveland. "It took me time to learn that some of the things I could have handled better. I could have granted more access for the media and more freedom for the players. I'm not as tough as I used to be. You could say I've mellowed."

In New England, he would take those lessons he learned and apply them in his new job as head coach of the New England Patriots. On January 27, twenty-three days after he resigned from the Jets, he was introduced at a press conference at Foxboro Stadium. In stark contrast to the pomp and circumstance that surrounded the arrival of Parcells—which included Massachusetts governor Bill Weld—this was a low-key affair.

"Hopefully, this press conference will go a little bit better than the last one I had," Belichick joked. "Hopefully, my tenure here will be a little bit longer."

"For [the price of] a No. 1 draft choice, we can bring in a man that I feel certain can do something, rather than the uncertainty of a draft choice," Kraft said after agreeing to send a No. 1 pick to their division rivals. "And it wasn't even close when I thought about it that way."

And while the media continued to puzzle over the selection of Belichick, many of the players were openly supportive of the move. "Any time you give up a first-round draft pick, that's something you obviously don't want to do," Bledsoe told reporters. "But to get a coach of the caliber of Bill Belichick, it's probably a worthwhile thing to do."

It was a sentiment echoed by many football insiders. "I think that is a small price to pay for the right guy," Dick Vermeil told the Associated Press, who was running the Rams at the time. "I would give up two first-round picks to have Bill Parcells coach my football team. To me, there have been a ton of first-round flops. There has been a ton of first-round picks that everyone is mad at for the next ten years and they hang around the league. . . . You get the right coach, he will change your organization."

The thaw in the Kraft-Parcells relationship also apparently signaled an end to the Border Wars. "I know the competition will be fierce, but I think these things that were alluded to a lot . . . probably will disappear," Parcells said. "I thought it was in the best interest of everyone to make the attempt, and Bob was receptive toward it, I think. It was important to me. I really do believe in the National Football League and the competition is always strong, but compatibility— we are in this together in a lot of ways—is in everyone's best interest, to have relationships you can work with."

Even though nothing was specified at Belichick's press conference, it was soon made clear that Belichick wouldn't be buying his own groceries. He quickly reached out to Scott Pioli for help in running the team, hiring him full time on February 10 as vice president of player personnel. It was a transaction that was buried beneath several inches of major personnel news: In his first move as head coach, Belichick had announced earlier in the week, he had dumped veterans Bruce Armstrong and Ben Coates in salary cap maneuvers, both victims of the salary cap. But like many of the decisions that had been made by the franchise over the years, it would mark a major turning point in the history of the Patriots.

The relationship between Belichick and Pioli went back many years. The two had met in the summer of 1986 when Belichick was a Giants assistant and Pioli was awaiting his senior year at Central Connecticut State. The CCSU defensive tackle made the ninety-minute drive from his home in Washingtonville, New York, several times a week to watch practices. The two were introduced by a mutual friend, and they instantly took to each other—Pioli the student, Belichick the teacher. Belichick got him a field pass and told him he was welcome to sleep on the pullout sofa in the suite Belichick occupied if he didn't want to make the ninety-minute commute every day. Pioli also got access to the team's immense videotape library and free meals and even the opportunity to sit in on team meetings.

After graduating from Central Connecticut State in 1987, Pioli took a two-year graduate assistant job with Syracuse. He then bounced to Murray State, when he spent two years coaching the offensive and defensive lines. Belichick came calling in 1992 with nothing more than a promise. "I don't know what the title is, I don't know what the pay is," Belichick told Pioli. "All I know is that it will be in personnel, maybe some scouting, maybe some coaching, some quality control stuff. I guess that's all you need to know."

It wasn't much of a sales pitch—especially when it was compared to a much firmer job offer 49ers president Dwight Clark had made him—but in Pioli's eyes, it was a no-brainer. He was off to Cleveland. The two spent their first full year together in Cleveland in 1992, and one of Pioli's first tasks was to drive Belichick to the airport in Pioli's rusted brown Cutlass. At the time, he was making $14,000 a year as a scouting assistant, but he found an occasional hundred dollars stashed in the ashtray, courtesy of the head coach. "He would stuff $100 in the ashtray and wouldn't let me refuse it," Pioli would tell *USA Today* in early 2005. "He'd say, 'Shut up. Get yourself some gas, and maybe go out for dinner this weekend.' . . . That's how Bill was. After big wins, he walked around the building and dropped $100 bills on people's desks. Scouts. Secretaries. Assistants. Just to thank them for the job they did."

(It was an ironic way for a Belichick assistant to begin his football career. Belichick was first hired by the Colts in 1975 for the princely sum of two season tickets and room and board at the team's training camp at Goucher College. In addition, head coach Ted Marchibroda and three assistants lived in a Howard Johnson's motel on Dorsey Road, not far from the Baltimore-Washington International Airport, and they got Belichick a room there as well. They carpooled to practice every day, usually with Belichick driving.)

Pioli quickly gained a rep as a jack-of-all-trades. In addition to his chauffeur work, he took players to the hospital for physicals, made photocopies, and quickly learned the intricacies of the NFL's salary cap. In his years in Cleveland, he also became one of the most dependable scouts in the Cleveland organization. As a result, he stuck with the team when they moved from Cleveland to Baltimore, and became the Ravens' director of pro personnel in 1996, working closely to Baltimore general manager Ozzie Newsome throughout the mid-1990s. "Scott is very detailed," Newsome would say later. "He knows how to build a consensus in the room. He's not stubborn. He and Bill make such a good match. But the biggest thing is that unbelievable trust between them."

After a year with the Ravens, Pioli rejoined Belichick with the New York Jets as pro personnel director while Belichick ran the defense. He worked with Belichick—and his father-in-law, head coach Bill Parcells—as the Jets managed to craft an impressive turnaround, going from 1–15 in 1996 to 12–4 in 1998. The twelve wins were the most in franchise history, and gave the Jets their first division title since 1968. He gained a reputation as a guy who had a good eye for finding cheap labor for the Jets, who were constantly strapped because of salary cap limitations. He was able to find journeymen like defensive linemen Anthony Pleasant and Rick Lyle. He specialized in unspectacular but solid veterans, low-risk, high-reward signings who became perfect fits for the system. "Going back to Cleveland and with New York, he's done a real good job of helping define those type of players," Belichick told reporters who asked about Pioli shortly after the Patriots hired him. "The players who are lower profile and maybe have lower salaries and go on to be productive players, in those two organizations and also when he was with Baltimore." His reputation was akin to that of a talented bond trader, someone who knew that buying low and selling high was the key to succeeding in the new NFL economy.

Now, he and Belichick were bringing that approach to the Patriots, a franchise that had never been used to that sort of economic efficiency. It would prove to be a colossal challenge, greater than either of them could imagine.

CHAPTER THREE

# THE SYSTEM

The Patriots' secret is not overpaying for good players who aren't great, but who collectively fit exactly what the coach wants them to do.

— SPORTS ILLUSTRATED *FOOTBALL WRITER PETER KING*

I think they've done an outstanding job. But unless they get the co-operation of the ownership and the ownership understands how things function, you really don't have any chance to succeed.

— *VETERAN NFL PERSONNEL GURU CHARLEY ARMEY*

If Belichick and Pioli were going to try something new with the Patriots, they had three distinct things working in their favor. First, they were under no pressure to win immediately. The franchise had enjoyed three distinct periods of success. In the 1970s, it managed to build a feisty young team that had, in all likelihood, lost out on a shot at the Super Bowl because of a bad call. In the 1980s, the franchise made its first Super Bowl appearance, as well as a handful of trips to the postseason, before slipping back into mediocrity. And in the 1990s, the franchise pulled itself up from the muck and mire of scandal to again reach the verge of Super Bowl glory—only to fall short to Brett Favre and the Packers. In each instance, the Patriots had young, opportunistic teams that appeared poised on the verge of sustained success. But as each one of those teams came close to glory, the franchise would dip again, a year or so later, suffering a major setback with either a major front office defection or a scandal that proved impossible to overcome. In the 1970s and 1990s, the good times were silenced when front office squabbles served to rip the franchise apart. And in the 1980s, the fallout from the drug scandal, combined with woefully inadequate ownership, would continue to harm the team for years to come. In each case, the slide would start slowly, and the franchise would usually bottom out two to three years down the line. It was odd, really: With the traditional team-building techniques employed by the Patriots, there was none of the sustained success or failure—or even mediocrity—that marked most of the rest of the NFL. If you examined the history of the New England franchise through most of its first thirty-five or so years, it would look like the EKG chart of a very ill heart patient—a flatline, accompanied by a major spike, and then by an equally dramatic fall before flatlining again for roughly ten or so years. The franchise had been conducting business as usual for almost forty years, and gotten virtually the same result every time.

And so, in the early days of the twenty-first century, five years removed from the hype and the drama that surrounded Parcells, the trip to Super Bowl XXXI and the subsequent exit of the most successful head coach in the history of the franchise, the team appeared to have flatlined once again. A fan base that had been rendered mostly apathetic by a few years of mediocrity didn't really expect much out of the 2000 Patriots. Despite a brief run of success under Parcells in the mid-1990s, three years of strikingly average on-field performances under Pete Carroll had left the fans shrugging their shoulders. Compounding the relative ennui was the fact that there wasn't the same sustained level of passion surrounding the team that area sports fans had for the Red Sox, who were winning again (they made the 1999 American League Championship Series, and were *Sports Illustrated*'s choice to win the World Series in 2000). The crowd at Boston's Sportsradio 850 WEEI was focused on what was going on with Nomar and Pedro, not Bledsoe and Coates.

But the arrival of Belichick did spark some hope. As a coach, he was mostly a blank slate to New England fans—but he did have that connection to Parcells, which gave some people cause for celebration. "I thought at the time it was a really good hire because it was in the Parcells tree, and it was getting back to that legitimacy," Perillo said. "I had concerns with his track record from Cleveland—obviously, that didn't go well. But in terms of his coaching ability, I felt like he was pretty solid. I'm not going to pretend to have any inkling that I thought he was going to be the kind of coach that he turned out to be, because I didn't. I didn't really even have that kind of hope, to be honest with you.

"But I thought it was a solid choice," he added. "I thought they needed to go back to kind of a disciplined-oriented coach, rather than the player-coach that Carroll was. And I felt it was a good move for the organization, because Robert Kraft obviously felt very strongly about getting him, based on everything he went through to do it. So I felt like if they really want this guy that bad, then it's probably a good thing they got the guy they wanted."

And whenever a New England team can hire away a New York coach, well, that was always a good thing. Patriots fans were still smarting over the loss of Parcells to the Jets and viewed Belichick's move as karmic payback. "There was definitely a feeling that the fan base was basically desperate for anything that resembled Bill Parcells in any way. Pete Carroll was like the anti-Parcells. So Belichick comes to the rescue—and the fact that they stole him from the Jets didn't hurt," said Aaron Schatz, author of the noted football reference guide *Pro Football Prospectus* and founder of Football Outsiders. "Thinking back, many people were saying, 'Hey, we must have done the right thing. If he had to do that to get out of the Jets contract, we must have the right guy.' So I do think people were patient with them."

And so that level of detachment made it possible for the Patriots to operate mostly out of the public eye, giving them carte blanche from their fan base when it came to making radical changes. They could make changes. They could do things differently. Their fan base was going to give them that leeway. *Hey, we don't expect anything out of you this year, or even the next. In fact, we haven't expected all that much out of you for the last forty or so years. If you want to try something new, knock yourselves out.*

Second, they were given more leeway to pursue a unique rebuilding process because, by the end of the twentieth century, it wasn't like the NFL was a hotbed of radical new ideas. In a league where parity reigned, most teams were too nervous to try something progressive, especially if it meant shelling out more cash. There *were* periods of real change in the game, with football radicalism springing up in the form of Tom Landry's flex defense, the West Coast offense, and the 46 defense. But it was clear that few owners had the guts to sign on to revolutionary new ideas. Really, why should they? But by this time, there were billions of dollars in television revenue pouring in, and many owners had gotten fat and happy. It's not like there was a lot of incentive to go out and try to spend money on some revolutionary new idea. *Everyone is rich, so we'll just let conventional wisdom be the law of the land, and let someone else come up with something new.* If the Patriots wanted to try something new, the other thirty-one teams in the league weren't going to stop them.

Third, it was clear the front office and football brain trust would get no resistance from the New England ownership if they wanted to take the franchise in a new direction. After almost a four-year stretch of amazingly poor PR moves, Bob Kraft was content to step out of the spotlight, quite a change for someone who often approached his day-to-day obligations as an owner in the same fashion as someone running for state senate. Shortly after he bought the team, Kraft was almost always in the spotlight. He was energetic and exciting, willing to do almost anything—including ride through the parking lot on game day to high-five tailgaters or walking the outer rim of the playing field before games, slapping five with the fans sitting in the first few rows—if it meant helping change the image of his football team. He initiated a PR blitz that included a grand vision. "My objective in buying the Patriots is to help bring a championship to New England," he said shortly after he purchased full control of the team in 1994. He was seen as someone who pumped life into a dormant franchise, pouring millions into his franchise and helping bring it to the cusp of a Super Bowl.

And it wasn't just on the field. Away from the gridiron, Kraft was lionized in the media as a model owner. It was later made public that he walked away from a lucrative deal to sell the team back to Orthwein. *Finally, a big-shot owner who doesn't care that much about money!* He was the sort of guy who boots malcontents like Christian Peter off his football team. *He cares about the image of his franchise! No thugs around here!* He made the Foxboro Stadium experience safer for families, stepping up security and threatening to confiscate the tickets of those who dared to cause trouble. *A family-friendly environment!* When he was compared against previous Patriots ownership—a veritable rogues gallery of men like Victor Kiam—he was a giant among men.

For his efforts, he was praised in most every area of the sporting press as the man who not only saved football in New England, but someone who had the potential to revolutionize the role of owner in modern American sports. In early 1996, Kraft appeared on ABC's weekly news roundtable *This Week with David Brinkley*, speaking in grand terms about the obligations of a modern owner. "Owning a team like the Patriots, any team, is being caretaker of a public trust," he said. "And I take that very seriously. I walk through our parking lots before games sometimes, and I feel a tremendous sense of responsibility—and accountability—with these fans. This team matters to them, and mattered long before I came along. These Sunday afternoons are an important part of their life. We can't take those Sundays and just move on to the next city and not worry about the people we leave behind."

"Kraft sounds like a cornball, but he is right, he is the caretaker of a trust; these aren't dry-cleaning franchises or fast-food joints or used-car dealerships," wrote columnist Mike Lupica. "He is honest enough to know that no matter how much of his money he put up to get the Patriots, the team still belongs to the fans he visits in the parking lots around the stadium every Sunday, shaking hands, talking to them, listening to them."

But after his very public spat with Parcells, a series of events conspired to change the public perception of the owner. He slowly morphed from the man who saved football in New England to Jerry Jones, version 2.0. In 1997, he got the tag as the man who pushed the local legend out the door because he interfered in the team-building process, a process that had certainly worked for Parcells in the past, and would have almost certainly worked again, if not for Kraft's meddling. *After all, Parcells has two rings. Kraft has none. What's up with that?* And after Parcells's departure, he replaced the man who had been the acknowledged heavyweight champion of the world with a featherweight, a man who appeared to be a swell guy, but wildly overmatched for the job of NFL head coach. As Carroll took the reins, the boot camp environment that prevailed throughout much of the Parcells era went out the window. (Oddly enough, foremost among the off-field troubles involved Bledsoe. The quarterback, who was usually a model citizen in the community, took part in an infamous stagedive at an Everclear show at the Paradise Rock Club with teammate Max Lane in 1997, an event that injured one female concertgoer and forced the club to close for thirty-four days.) There were fights at area clubs and embarrassing acts of lewdness, many of which involved wide receiver Terry Glenn. The wide receiver, whom Kraft had pushed so hard to draft, got into a number of off-field incidents, including a memorable scrape in November 1999. At a Big Brothers charity event at a nightclub in Saugus, he allegedly urinated on a limo outside the nightclub. He was later charged with offensive touching, civil battery, and infliction of emotional distress. (The lawsuit was later settled out of court in 2001, four days before it was scheduled to go to trial.) The day after the 1999 incident, Glenn was nearly three hours late for a team meeting and was fined by Carroll, but not before being stopped for driving to endanger and speeding through the streets of Walpole in an effort to get to practice on time. (To be fair, Glenn wasn't the only Patriots player involved in trouble that night. Teammates Lawyer Milloy and Vincent Brisby engaged in fisticuffs.) The family-friendly image Kraft fought so hard to create for his team was going out the window.

And there were other problems. In 1997, Kraft starting trying to unsuccessfully to get the city of Boston to agree to build him a new stadium along the South Boston waterfront. It was a period of un-questioned growth in the NFL. In all, nine teams would move into new stadiums between 1996 and 2000, out of old and dilapidated venues like RFK in Washington, D.C., and Tampa Stadium in Tampa Bay and into new buildings like FedEx Field and Raymond James Stadium, thanks in large part to governmental financing. Kraft clearly believed the Patriots should enjoy the same bounty. But it was not to be. He ultimately gave up in the face of intense opposition, first from South Boston natives who wanted no part of a stadium in their backyard, and second from politicians who were not interested in providing public funds to help finance such a venue. His primary foil was Massachusetts Speaker of the House Thomas Finneran. Finneran, fed up with Kraft's attempts to get a stadium deal pushed through, would later call the New England owner "a whining multimillionaire" and "a fat-assed millionaire." (Finneran would later say the comments were meant to apply to Baltimore Ravens owner Art Modell, not Kraft.)

Meanwhile, with a dysfunctional front office, Kraft's team was starting a slow slide back to mediocrity. It began a year after Super Bowl XXXI, when they finished 10–6 and beat Miami in a wild-card matchup before losing a divisional playoff game to Pittsburgh.

In 1998, they went 9–7, and suffered a first-round playoff defeat to Jacksonville. And in 1999, there was an 8–8 record and no trip to the postseason. Without a winning football team to fall back on—and no Parcells to take the heat—Kraft's public image started to dissolve. Whether it was on Beacon Hill or the sports pages, Kraft had become an all-purpose punching bag for the entire Commonwealth. "There is no direction because the owner wanted to be the Big Football Guy around here. And so he is. And this is what you get," said *Boston Globe* columnist Dan Shaughnessy midway through the 1997 season with the Patriots standing at 5–5. "The Patriots' season is not over. The decline is not irreversible. But the only hope is that these talented players can take all this embarrassment and turn it into positive energy over the next five weeks. They used to have a coach who could do this for them, but that's no longer the case. They'll have to do it themselves. And the reason for that is Bob Kraft."

Remarkably, things would get worse for Kraft before they got better. Prior to the 1998 draft, he took an ill-fated trip to Syracuse with Carroll and Grier to ostensibly assist with the workout of defensive back Tebucky Jones. This was simply not the sort of thing that an owner does. The story was told and retold so often it became a cautionary tale, the sort of anecdote that gets retold so often it becomes an urban legend. *He pulled up in a limo, hopped out, and held the stopwatch himself,* went one version of the story. *He went and told people that Jones would make a good "press corner,"* said another version. *As if he knows what a "press corner" is.* It left him open to another scalding in the media, who continued to remind him of the incident time and again. "I did not realize that Amos Alonzo Kraft was the true architect of this team," deadpanned columnist Mike Barnicle in *The Boston Globe*.

And then came Hartford.

When Kraft purchased the team in 1994, it was believed by many that Foxboro Stadium was on its last legs. The NFL had started to make noise about moving the Patriots into a new venue in the late 1980s, but by the early 1990s, many in the league office believed the problem had reached a crisis point. "Foxboro is an unacceptable venue for the long-term future of the Patriots franchise," said NFL commissioner Paul Tagliabue in 1993. By this time, the stadium had very few of the amenities of the type that had become commonplace throughout the NFL, such as chairback seating, club seats, luxury suites, and deluxe locker rooms. As premium seating became a major source of revenue for professional sports teams, Foxboro Stadium was becoming functionally obsolete. Tagliabue added, "Time is growing short," when it came to proceeding on a new stadium, intimating that if the team did not a get a new deal done with the state, the ownership would face the distinct possibility of seeing the franchise moved.

Throughout the mid 1990s, several potential deals were explored: One would put a stadium in South Bay, a patch of land just outside the city, and another discussed a megaplex that would be built somewhere in South Boston to house both the Patriots and the Red Sox. But neither of those deals would come to fruition. With the NFL waiting impatiently—and the South Boston stadium deal dead on the table—Kraft made a decision: He entered into an agreement with Connecticut governor John Rowland that would provide the franchise with $350 million to build a new venue. The announcement came down in late November 1998 that would move the team from Foxborough to Hartford in 2001, into a new stadium that would be the cornerstone of the city's downtown redevelopment plan. Just three years after he described himself as more than an owner, the "caretaker of a public trust" who had a "responsibility" to the fans, he was cementing a deal that would ship them out of town.

"Anyone want to buy a house?" quarterback Drew Bledsoe asked the media with a rueful smile the week the move was announced.

But the Connecticut deal was a flawed one. The site where the stadium was to be built was polluted, which added to the cost of the stadium construction. As a result of the pollution, it soon became evident that Connecticut wouldn't be able to deliver the stadium in 2000, 2001, 2002, or even 2003. Despite the fact that the Hartford deal could have been worth as much as $1 billion over a thirty-year period, Kraft and the Patriots soon resumed negotiations with Massachusetts lawmakers. The Massachusetts legislature approved the needed subsidies; the Patriots agreed to build the stadium for $225 million, while Finneran and the state provided $70 million in infrastructure, most of which came in improvements to Route 1. Both sides were able to claim victory. The local politicians held the line on state contributions, while Kraft got to boast that he accepted less money to stay in Massachusetts.

But even with the agreement to keep the team in Massachusetts, things were not well. Between his failed attempts to get a stadium built in South Boston, his brief flirtation with Hartford, and the perception that he had pushed Parcells out the door in a flap over personnel, the image of Kraft as a benevolent owner had been turned on its head. Now he was a meddler who had overstepped his bounds and gotten burned because of it. By the late 1990s, he had even stopped riding through the parking lot on game days to shake hands with the fans because he was afraid of the reaction he would get. A few years after becoming just the second owner in NFL history to have his own interview station at Super Bowl Media Day, Kraft cried uncle. He clearly did not want to be in the spotlight with anyone anymore. He had seen the glare, and would be content to step back into the shadows.

In that context, what he did next was hardly surprising. In May 2000, Bobby Grier, who had been the source of so much tension between Kraft and Parcells, was let go by Belichick, who also fired national scout Dave Uyrus. (It was the latest move in a series of events that showed just how much control Belichick was given by

Kraft. He had fired strength and conditioning coach Johnny Parker shortly after he was named head coach in January.) "This is an unpleasant thing for me to do," Belichick said in a statement. "I recognized that Bobby Grier has made significant contributions to the New England Patriots over many years, in various capacities, as has Dave Uyrus. I enjoyed a good working relationship with Bobby in preparation for the recent draft, as I did in 1996. . . . This decision is unrelated to any specific event, performance or personal relationship. It is more a reflection of my general feeling to proceed in a new direction with regard to the structure and operation of our personnel department."

"At that point, everybody understood that things had bottomed out," said Schatz. "Bobby Grier's drafts were horrific, and it was going to take time to rebuild."

The decision spoke volumes as to the state of the Patriots' front office. There would be none of the relative ambiguity that plagued the franchise in the Carroll-Grier years. Publicly, there was now one voice calling the shots, and that was Belichick's. While Belichick joined the likes of Atlanta's Dan Reeves, Seattle's Mike Holmgren, Denver's Mike Shanahan, and Minnesota's Dennis Green as coaches who had the last word, in truth, it was really a duo that was now at the top of the Patriots' food chain—Belichick and Pioli. And whether it was a lesson learned from his fractious relationship with Parcells or the first signal of a new comfort level he had with Belichick that he never reached with his former coach, it was clear there was a new level of trust between the front office and owner. In Foxborough, football men were now making the decisions. And after the early days of 2000, Kraft would never again be perceived as the meddlesome football owner he was when Parcells was running the show.

"When I bought the team, I was a kid with peach fuzz who hadn't shaved. And I got nicks and scrapes," said Kraft, years after his experience with Parcells. "You have to get knocked around and see for yourself firsthand. It's an intoxicating business, and you can get seduced by it. . . . My involvement in the trenches was something I would change."

"Any time you own something and you're trying to learn the business, you get involved and find out exactly how each part of the business and organization is going to function. To his credit, Kraft found out the best way for it to function was for him to adapt his personality," said veteran NFL personnel man Charley Armey.

In the early days of 2000, with the Patriots roughly $10.5 million over the salary cap, the idea they were going to be a Super Bowl contender in a year was laughable. Coming off an 8–8 season, they not only had to institute a whole new blueprint for success—complete with a new GM, a new head coach, new assistants and support staff—they had to think about potential free agents who were out there, as well as clear out the dead weight while slashing salaries. If constructing a football team was like building a new house, Belichick and Pioli had to tear everything down, haul away the garbage, and start from the ground up.

"I think that when he got here in 2000, everybody recognized that the team wasn't that good," said Paul Perillo. "I don't think that was a great team, but I think it was a pretty good team. I think they deteriorated under Carroll because they had no discipline.

"By the time 2000 rolled around, most people realized the team wasn't great. I think they had gotten it through their minds that they weren't a Super Bowl team, from a fan's perspective. I think it was a good time for Bill to come in. Now, he inherited a terrible cap situation, and everybody knew that—everybody, being the Krafts. They said, 'Do what you need to do to get it back into shape here.'"

Step one was bringing in Charlie Weis as the offensive coordinator. A former assistant under Parcells, he quickly became invaluable to the success of the franchise. A salty, sarcastic Jersey native, Weis wasn't above using R-rated language to verbally assault his players, dropping f-bombs throughout practice. (One veteran would later recall he had never been harangued in such a "colorful" manner when Weis laced into him.) Weis had risen quickly to the job of Giants assistant. Just a year after he was coaching high school football at Franklin Township High, he was named a defensive and special teams assistant for the 1990 Giants. When he was named offensive coordinator by Belichick prior to the start of the 2000 season, it was his second tour with New England, as he had coached the tight ends (1993–94), running backs (1995), and wide receivers (1996) with the Patriots under Parcells. He remembered his first go-round with the Patriots fondly.

"I was fortunate to be handed positions where there were good players. I came here and we were 2–14 and I had those crummy players Marv Cook and Ben Coates. Then they moved me from there to those crummy running backs and we drafted Curtis Martin. Then I messed him up so bad, so they moved me to wide receivers and they drafted Terry Glenn and signed Shawn Jefferson," he said, tongue in cheek. "So a lot of coaching has to do with how good your players are. Don't have any illusions that the coach is the reason why that happened."

Because they were so far over the salary cap, it would be impossible to try and turn the roster over that quickly. It would also be impossible to pursue any of the big-ticket free agents. Pro Bowlers like offensive linemen John Runyan and Ruben Brown, tight end Shannon Sharpe, and defensive ends Robert Porcher, Tony Brackens, and Simeon Rice were all considered the major targets in free agency during the off-season, but they were way out of New England's league. And most of the next level of players who were available via free agency took notice of the situation. The agent for former Jets and Cardinals running back Adrian Murrell—who had never gained more than 301 yards *in a single season*—got wind of the Patriots' new approach, and canceled a trip to New England.

"Until they're serious about what they can offer us, there's no point in Adrian making a trip there," sniffed his agent, Stephen Hayes.

There were 342 unrestricted free agents on the market that off-season. If the big-name free agents were Plan A and the Adrian Murrells of the world were Plan B, the Patriots were forced into Plan C. They would target players who would essentially be stop-gaps, players who could help get the Patriots closer to their goal of a title. These players were not likely to be the centerpiece of a championship team, but they would be able to help keep the franchise competitive over the next year or two. To get started, Belichick followed in the footsteps of Parcells, doing much the same thing Parcells did when he first arrived in Foxborough: He started seeking out many of his former players who were available in free agency, going with guys who knew his system and his coaching methods. That would make the transition easier. Prior to the 2000 season, that included defensive back Otis Smith and lineman Bobby Hamilton. They would be joined midway through the 2000 season by tight end Jermaine Wiggins, a former Jet. (Before the start of the 2001 season, they would add more of Belichick's guys, including linebackers Bryan Cox and Roman Phifer, along with defensive lineman Anthony Pleasant.)

"I think it was important to Bill to be familiar with guys that he knew and trusted," assistant head coach and offensive line coach Dante Scarnecchia said.

"When we started in 2000, it was critical," Pioli said. "Having a veteran presence, particularly with players who understood our system and understood how we do business and how all the football operations run.

"Just because a player has made a Pro Bowl or has a marquee name because of his salary doesn't mean the player is necessarily a good football player," Pioli added. "That's the problem. Sometimes perception and reality are two completely different things."

Ideally, the rest of the new faces would be able to augment the major free-agent acquisitions and impact draftees who would be signed to populate the upper reaches of the roster. As for the veterans who were already on the active roster, the front office decided to proceed with a simple plan: They would assign a dollar amount to the players based on a series of variables, which included but were not limited to the following: overall ability, age, and previous experience on a Belichick-coached team. If they were not veterans of a Belichick-coached team, were they willing to embrace a new system? If the dollar amount the front office settled on outweighed what they believed would be the players' overall impact on the success of the team, they would part ways.

One thing that would not enter into that system of variables was the idea of paying out based solely on past performance. They could not afford to sign players who *had* contributed; they had to acquire players who were *going* to contribute. This became clear when they were faced with the case of tight end Ben Coates. Coates, a fifth-round pick out of tiny Livingston College in 1991, had made his mark on the franchise record books in several categories, including most receptions in a career (second all-time with 490), most receptions in a season (96, a franchise record in 1994), and most receiving touchdowns in a career (second all-time with 50). He was, without a doubt, Bledsoe's favorite receiver. On many teams, salary cap limitations or no, he would have been in line to receive a big bump in salary. But he and the Patriots did not see eye to eye on a contract, and he was cut loose. It was a shocking move, and showed fans and players alike that things were going to be different.

There were similar cases for other high-profile Patriots. According to reporters who covered the team in 2000, when Belichick asked veteran offensive lineman Bruce Armstrong to take a pay cut, it angered the ex-Pro Bowler. Armstrong had been with the franchise through some of the good times (including a trip to Super Bowl XXXI) and bad (he had been part of the 1991 team that finished 1–15), and figured he had earned a lifetime achievement award in the form of a fat contract that would allow him to be set up nicely for retirement. But under the Patriots' new plan, it wasn't going to happen. When he didn't get the payday he believed he deserved—worse yet, he was being asked to take a pay cut—he balked, and was cut by Belichick. What made it worse for Armstrong was that he was unable to hook on with another team, and was forced to return to the Patriots to play for the veterans' minimum. He wasn't happy, recalled Patriots assistant coach Pepper Johnson in his book *Won for All*. "He allowed his personal feelings to take over, and he decided to shut it down," Johnson recalled. "Everything I heard about him before I came over—that he was vocal and inspirational—I didn't see at all. I think it was one of those cases where he felt it was the money that made the man, when, in truth, it's the man who makes the money."

Other players who were considered overvalued under New England's new system were offensive linemen Zefross Moss and Todd Rucci and wide receivers Vincent Brisby and Shawn Jefferson. All of them were soon gone. In place of veterans like Coates, the Patriots went with younger players, like tight end Rod Rutledge. Rutledge may not have had the numbers that Coates had, but he was a considerably better value, and his lower salary allowed the franchise to make additions in other areas. They replaced Rucci at right guard with Sale Isaia before settling on Joe Andruzzi, and they did the same to Moss at right tackle, bringing in Grant Williams and Greg Robinson-Randall to fill the spot. While they could take some chances on fringe players—the way things were set up under the collective bargaining agreement, they wouldn't be on the hook for all that much if someone like running back Raymont Harris, special teams ace and wide receiver Aaron Bailey, cornerback Antonio Langham, or linebacker Chad Cascadden didn't work out—they were not going to be taking big gambles or major risks. With their salary cap situation, they couldn't afford to be wrong.

Some veterans were spared, including Pro Bowler Larry Whigham. But the biggest payday that off-season went to veteran safety Lawyer Milloy, who was given a seven-year, $35 million deal. When Milloy signed, Belichick acknowledged the stresses that the new NFL economy placed on traditional team-building techniques. "The way the system is set up now, there are only so many players you can make this type of commitment to," Belichick said of the safety, one of his acknowledged favorites. "You just can't do it to everybody. That's just the way it's set up."

When the Patriots arrived for training camp prior to the 2000 season, there weren't a lot of new, high-profile faces. There *were* some arrivals that would go on to form the basis of the title teams to come—including Andruzzi and a skinny rookie quarterback out of Michigan named Tom Brady—but most of the roster was filled out with those stopgap free agents. And so, as a team, the 2000 squad was remarkably unremarkable, just passive and restrained enough to pass for mediocre. Things were so laid-back in training camp that there were no fights, a bad sign for a team. "I'm not a big fighter, but because of the heat, the constant contact, a guy trying to cheat a drill, somebody loud-mouthing, everyone fighting for jobs, there's always a fight," Johnson recalled. "Yet we went through the whole training camp without one altercation. It might seem insignificant, but it showed the character of the team. There weren't enough mean streaks; there weren't enough guys hitting other guys in the mouth."

When the coach canceled a July 27 scrimmage with the Giants because he felt he didn't have enough healthy players, it was evident the Patriots weren't going to be much of a football team. And they weren't. As the season started, they were just good enough to stay competitive, going 0–4 out of the gate, but they lost those four games by a combined total of just twenty-one points. They won a pair, but then ended up on another four-game skid. "It was a blah team," recalled one season ticket holder. They had just one running back reach the 500-yard mark—Kevin Faulk. Veteran receivers Troy Brown and Terry Glenn both had 900-plus yards receiving. The defense allowed opponents to convert an astonishing

44 percent of the time on third down. And they were one of only a few teams in the NFL not to have a single Pro Bowl representative.

While the team wasn't in a fighting mood during training camp, they were later in the season. Looking to provide a spark, Belichick reportedly paid practice squad veteran Rob Gatrell to start a fight with Milloy during practice in the week leading to the November 19 game against the Bengals. The fight seemed to inspire the team, albeit to a narrow 16–13 win at home over lowly Cincinnati. Belichick denied paying Gatrell to start the fight, but did concede that a little brawling was good. "Each team has its own chemistry and personality. It changes each year as players come and go. Talking to other coaches and players around the league, there are certain teams that are comprised that way. There are players who control the tempo of the way practices go. [Fighting] can be a very positive thing, and if you don't have it, sometimes you need to create it. You need to change up the routine, and there are a lot of ways to do it."

While they were changing up the routine on the field, it looked like off the field they were the same old Patriots. Harking back to the days of Irving Fryar's scrapes with the law and the brawling between players during the Pete Carroll Era, they suddenly had a new mess on their hands. On December 18, Ty Law was stopped by U.S. Customs agents at the Canadian border at 5:30 A.M. and found to be in possession of ecstasy, for which he paid a fine and was released. Fearful of flying home in a blizzard after the previous day's game, Law, Glenn, and Troy Brown stayed in Buffalo with a promise to Belichick to make the next day's team meeting. They did not, and all three were fined, while Law was suspended for the last game of the season. It was clear the lack of respect for the head coach that had started to fester in the final year of the Pete Carroll era was still evident. "There may have been problems in Foxborough under Carroll," wrote Ron Borges in *The Boston Globe* after the incident. "They may have been pumped and jacked win, lose, or lose some more, but no one was ever known to be in ecstasy. Or on it for that matter. At least not while trying to cross the Canadian border."

Turns out that Law missed one of the strangest games in the history of the franchise. The Patriots were at home on Christmas Eve against Miami in a chilling cold. New England was playing out the string, while the Dolphins were gunning for a division title. But the game was marred by a controversial finish. First, Drew Bledsoe's forward pass with three seconds left was ruled an illegal forward pass, and so the game ended. Patriots lose, 27–24. Then, fifteen minutes later (as players were getting showered and dressed), referee Johnny Grier reversed his call, saying the pass was an incompletion, meaning three seconds remained. Players slowly returned to the field . . . only to be told by Grier that he'd changed his mind again and that the final seconds would not be played "for safety reasons." *Then* word came down from the NFL office that the full sixty minutes must be played, so teams *had* to return to the field. With one Dolphin player standing on the sideline wearing just a towel wrapped around his waist and roughly a hundred fans remaining, backup quarterback Michael Bishop heaved a Hail Mary that landed about thirty yards short of the end zone. It was "a fitting end to a sad and silly season," wrote Borges.

As the game ended . . . *finally* . . . the Patriots who remained were on the receiving end of a scalding speech from Milloy. As the Dolphins whooped and hollered on the other side of the wall, celebrating a division title, Milloy seethed. "I want everyone to take a moment and remember something, get it into your heads," said Milloy, according to those who were there. "Remember what you are feeling now, the taste that you have in your mouths. Remember it, because I'm pissed. Five and eleven. We're losers. Losers. I hope every last one of you feels the same way. Don't forget it for a minute, because I don't give a damn what we have to do until the opening kickoff next year. We're not going to feel this way again after next season. No way. We're all going to look back on this and laugh."

Despite the odd end to the 2000 season, there *was* real change in the air. The final record wasn't much to look at, and the team was lacking depth in many key areas. And they still had several questions when it came to the salary cap. However, thirteen of the sixteen games had been decided by eight points or less, and many close to the team believed the blueprint that Belichick and Pioli were constructing was a lot closer to becoming reality than many had originally believed. "They were able to play defense against good offensive teams, without having great defensive players, and still stay in ball games and have a chance to win at the end," broadcaster Gil Santos said of the 2000 Patriots. "That's what I saw developing in the 2000 team—'[Belichick's] defense will keep us in games into the fourth quarter as the next few years go along, which will then give us a chance to win games and get to the playoffs.'"

Between the 2000 and 2001 season, the goal was to continue to try and close that gap. Based on Belichick's previous experiences, he knew closing that gap could be established one of two ways—by adding offensive firepower or reducing the opponents' scoring output. That off-season, Belichick and the Patriots opted to focus on the latter. Early in his coaching career, Belichick discovered that the quickest way to change a team, at least on the defensive side of the football, was with smart, fast, and flexible linebackers. That's not to suggest he did not coach some of the finest defensive linemen or defensive backs in the history of the game. Richard Seymour, Ty Law, Everson Walls, and others. It's just that through the years with Belichick, most of the success or failure of his teams can be traced directly to the play of the linebacking corps. (It's no surprise that many of the players who have played linebacker for Belichick have done so in multiple places: Roman Phifer, Carl Banks, Pepper Johnson, and Bryan Cox among them.) Belichick knows that not many linebackers can do what he asks them to do. He asks them to do a lot of things: show an ability to rush the quarterback or drop into pass coverage, or to show blitz and then drop into coverage . . . or vice versa. In short, linebacker remains the most demanding position on the field, and the linebackers who played for Belichick were quite often the smartest, swiftest, and strongest guys on the field.

"They funnel everything to the linebackers," Santos said of a Belichick-coached defense. "You've got to have the [Tedy] Bruschis and the [Mike] Vrabels. People who can make those plays when the plays are funneled to them. That, to me, is the key to his defense, period. . . . To play linebacker in his system, you've not only got to be good physically, you've got to be very, very smart."

Belichick began to try and create the same scheme in Foxborough using the linebackers (veterans Bruschi, Willie McGinest, and Ted Johnson) already in place with the Patriots. It was a group that had several things in common with many of the other linebackers who played for Belichick with the Giants, Jets, and Browns: They were a mostly veteran bunch of savvy veterans, a talented group who had all made several trips to the postseason. In addition, they had seen the intricacies of a Belichick-coached defense up close the last few years. They had been with New England when Belichick was a defensive assistant under Parcells in 1996, and when Belichick was an assistant with the Jets the three years after that, they had a chance to see his defenses twice a year when the AFC East rivals met.

But many of them had something in their game that set them apart, that allowed the Patriots and Belichick to take the game plan to the next level: an unmatched versatility. Both Bruschi and McGinest had played defensive end while in college, and both had an unquestioned knack for getting to the quarterback. (Bruschi set the Division I record for sacks as an undersized defensive lineman at Arizona.) In the pros, McGinest was moved to outside linebacker, while Bruschi moved inside. Bruschi, in particular, was able to flourish in the 3–4 zone blitz schemes of Parcells and Belichick.

Their play was a revelation, and it led New England to a startling conclusion: If the Patriots could find collegiate defensive linemen—preferably defensive ends—who were talented pass rushers but didn't have the size or strength to play the defensive line in the pros, they could revolutionize the defensive game.

"That 3–4 scheme, Pittsburgh had already done it. It's not the same system, obviously, but I think there was something to that," Perillo said. "McGinest—I think that was a key factor because I think he is a much better standup outside linebacker than he is a defensive end, which is how he was used by Carroll. And he became a better player when Bill took over."

The Patriots began to draw up defensive game plans that would involve a complicated zone blitz scheme around linebackers rather than defensive linemen, a revolutionary concept in today's NFL. "Belichick just took that concept of 'Let's have that rush linebacker on the outside,' [and said] 'Let's just do that for all the linebackers *and* all the defensive line,'" said ESPN's K. C. Joyner. "'Let's just do it across the front. We've got these big linebackers who are playing defensive end, and let's just drop them into coverage, or let's bring this guy who's an inside linebacker.'

"[Belichick] said, 'We move all these people around. Since we're doing that, why limit ourselves to just rushing an outside linebacker? Why not just do that all the way up and down the line?'"

In order to try and take it to that level, the Patriots went out and started signing versatile linebackers who fit the profile. In March 2001, they signed Mike Vrabel, and in August of that same year, they inked Roman Phifer. Like the firing of Bobby Grier, on the surface, the signings were minor transactions; a pair of well-traveled veterans were being added to a 5–11 team. But the addition of these veteran linebackers would go a long way toward establishing New England as a force to be reckoned with in 2001. In particular, the Vrabel signing would change the face of professional football.

To this point in his career, most NFL people had thought of Mike Vrabel as a JAG—a pro football acronym for Just Another Guy. No one was sure where the phrase originated as it pertained to the NFL, but it was known that Bill Parcells had made it popular. The phrase itself wasn't a putdown. There were thousands of talented college players who would have given everything they owned for the chance to be a JAG in the NFL. In truth, it served as a simple description for someone who isn't necessarily a star, but just another player filling out a roster spot. Most of the time, JAGs are offensive or defensive linemen or linebackers who are shut out of a starting job because of a numbers game.

But in the new financial world of the NFL, JAGs had become tremendously important. They were seen as a way to add depth at multiple positions—as well as at special teams—at a relatively reduced rate. Most of them were veterans, low-rent free agents who could sign relatively cheap, incentive-laden contracts.

Vrabel had been consigned to JAG status through no fault of his own. As a collegian, he was cut from the same cloth as Bruschi—a fast, smart, talented defensive lineman at Ohio State. An undersized defensive end with the Buckeyes who managed 36 sacks over the course of his collegiate career, he was drafted in the third round by the Steelers in 1997. Initially, the Steelers tried to make the 260-pound Vrabel bigger. He put on fifteen pounds before his rookie season, bulking up to 275. They saw him as another Kevin Henry, a defensive end who, like Vrabel, was undersized. Henry put on thirty-five pounds, going from 260 to 295 and enjoying moderate success for the Steelers in the 1990s as a defensive end. They had the same plans for Vrabel, especially after they lost defensive ends Brentson Buckner and Ray Seals in the off-season. "He's tough enough and he wants to play," said then-Steelers' defensive coordinator Jim Haslett of Vrabel. "It's hard to keep guys like that off the field. He's really active and emotional. I think someday down the road he'll turn into a 290-pound defensive end."

But he never found a spot in Pittsburgh. As a rookie, he played down. As a second-year player, he played up. In 1999, they put him inside at tackle in their dime defense. The following year, they put him back at right outside linebacker behind Gildon and used him to spell Gildon at end in their dime defense. It was a frustrating time for Vrabel, who couldn't find a spot. He was too small to play defensive end for an extended stretch, and at linebacker, he was stuck on the depth chart behind four excellent linebackers in Gildon, Levon Kirkland, Greg Lloyd, and Joey Porter. He did have a supporter in Pittsburgh head coach Bill Cowher, who said time and again that he loved Vrabel's approach to the game, adding that his work ethic and attitude were among the best on the team. "He's a real active guy; he's a lot of fun to be around," Cowher said. "He loves the game of football." Patriots fans were in no position to argue. In New England, he gained a sizable measure of infamy when he ended the Patriots' 1997 postseason: His sack of Bledsoe and fumble recovery gave the Steelers a narrow 7–6 playoff win over New England.

But with a coterie of talented defenders already at his disposal, Cowher simply could not find a place for him in Pittsburgh. Vrabel languished on the bench, getting occasional reps on special teams, but little else. When the 2000 season came to an end, he was at a crossroads. Maybe it was time to get out of football and give law school a try. Life as a JAG had become too much.

That's when Bill Belichick came calling. The New England head coached viewed Vrabel as more than just your average JAG. He had been keeping an eye on Vrabel as a possible linebacker who could flourish in the New England defense. Belichick saw him as having the same sort of versatility as Bruschi, a linebacker agile enough to rush or drop into coverage, but also smart enough to handle the intricacies of a Belichick-coached scheme. When the two met, the head coach told Vrabel the Patriots had been closely monitoring his play. A skeptical Vrabel confessed he didn't get a lot of time with the Steelers, and was unsure how he'd fit into the New England defensive scheme. Vrabel would later recall the moment for *The Boston Globe*. "Well," Belichick said, "if you play like you did in that second series against Miami in the preseason, you'll be fine."

Vrabel was stunned. It was enough to convince him to sign with the Patriots.

As the years continued and their relationship evolved, Vrabel became Belichick's doppelgänger. No one consistently did a better Belichick impression than the linebacker. And no one became more emblematic of the new Patriots' Way than Mike Vrabel. "When he moved onto this team . . . he's a smart player, in addition to being extremely gifted. He's extremely smart, and able to implement Belichick's very intricate defenses," Santos said. "To me, he was the key free agent signing because he has become so good. He's the one that just jumps off the page at me."

In Michael Lewis's *Moneyball*, Scott Hatteberg is held up as the shining example of the triumph of the Oakland A's team-building approach to the game. The backup catcher, who had already been cast aside by one organization, "was a deeply satisfying scientific discovery," wrote Lewis. "The things he did so peculiarly well at the plate were the things only science—or, at any rate, closer to normal scrutiny—could turn up." Belichick and Pioli would soon find out they had their own Scott Hatteberg in Vrabel. "The guy who I think is the equivalent of Scott Hatteberg, the guy who represents how the Patriots do things differently from other teams and why they win, is Mike Vrabel," said Aaron Schatz of *Pro Football Prospectus* and *Football Outsiders*. "Vrabel—you talk about a guy who was a backup in Pittsburgh, didn't fit their system. And he comes to New England, and he fits in in very specific ways. Multiple ways. And plays awesome."

As for Phifer, he was a step up from JAG status, but not much. He had been in the league for ten years, playing with the Rams in Los Angeles and St. Louis, as well as two years with the Jets. Nicknamed "Jinx" by teammate and fellow linebacker Bryan Cox, he had played eight years with the Rams, but left the year before they won Super Bowl XXXIV. He then showed up with the Jets the year after they advanced to the AFC Championship Game, and proceeded to sit through two years when New York combined to finish one game over .500. Despite his bad timing, Phifer appealed to Belichick on a number of levels. One, they were together when Belichick was the defensive coordinator with the Jets, so Phifer was familiar with what would be asked of him in New England. On the field, Phifer was known as being tenacious in pass coverage. As a result, when he signed as a veteran free agent on August 3, 2001, it was thought he would serve as the inside linebacker on pass downs, while Ted Johnson would play that role on running downs. (It turns out that Phifer ended up being much more than just a pass-coverage specialist. "We'll kind of teach you everything, and then we'll define your role," Belichick told Phifer. But after he left the Patriots at the end of the 2004 season, by Belichick's estimate, Phifer saw 98 percent playtime two years in a row. "Turns out, his role was to play *every* play," Belichick would later say with a smile.)

Two, Phifer was also one of the nicest, unfailingly polite players in the NFL. He was rarely in the locker room. During the 2001 season, the immensely likable veteran had asked for and been granted permission by Belichick to leave after every Sunday game and fly to the West Coast to see his young son. He was allowed to return Wednesdays for meetings. So when he did appear, it was a treat for reporters, many of whom looked forward to his thoughtful and eloquent breakdown of the previous game, as well as what could be in store for the New England defense that week. So when a media member cornered him in the locker room to ask one question about a minor point about the defense, the interview inevitably became a scrum. Too polite to refuse a request from a reporter at even the smallest of papers, he would provide a well-reasoned and intelligent response. Inevitably, another reporter would see this and join in the questioning. And, just as inevitably, twenty minutes later, Phifer would be surrounded by cameras and microphones, unable to break away from what had become a sizable pack of reporters huddled around his locker clamoring for his attention. (One reporter would liken asking the quick question that started the frenzy around Phifer to starting a car fire—all you had to do was toss a match, and the bonfire would provide enough heat for the rest of the reporters for the duration of media availability.)

The Patriots made their biggest splash that off-season on the offensive side of the football with a move that seemed, on the surface, to run counter to the team-building approach that Belichick and Pioli had initiated. On March 7, they announced that they had signed Bledsoe to the largest contract in NFL history, a ten-year, $103 million deal. By this time, the quarterback, the No. 1 pick in the 1993 NFL draft, had become the face of the franchise. His strong right arm had delivered the Patriots several wins in his short time in New England and given a weak franchise a level of credibility. He was also a favorite of Kraft. Other than his infamous stagedive with teammate Max Lane, Bledsoe was every bit the quarterback straight out of central casting—tall, handsome, and plenty brave. Bledsoe was very aware of his image in the community. He was a family man who came from an all-American background in the Northwest, and he brought that image with him to New England. With his wife, Maura, he helped found the Drew Bledsoe Foundation, a group that focused on a program he ran with his father, Mac, called Parenting with Dignity. He wrote a children's book. And he was the international chairman for the Children's Miracle Network, which raised hundreds of millions of dollars for children's hospitals worldwide. For the organization that had lived with the specter of the Lisa Olson incident, Kraft was well aware of the image that Bledsoe portrayed, and was more than happy to have him on his side, financial circumstances be damned. "I remember feeling sad when Bobby Orr left," Kraft said when the announcement was made official, referring to the NHL Hall of Famer who left the Bruins for Chicago near the end of his career. "I saw this as an opportunity to sign one of the great Patriots for the rest of his career."

But all-American quarterback or no, Bledsoe's cap numbers—$8.66 million for the 2000 season and $9.3 million for 2001—were certainly not in line with Belichick's team-building approach. The front office was preaching economic efficiency, and it certainly wasn't economically efficient to have one player taking up that much room under the cap, even someone like Bledsoe. To his credit, Bledsoe recognized that he had to work with the team on a new deal that would give them more room to operate under the cap. "My cap number is high and it would help the team if there were a renegotiation. I'm not going to hold the team hostage for the very last dollar," Bledsoe told *The Boston Globe*. "The Patriots have been very good to me and I know they will continue to be. At some point, there needs to be something done so we can remain competitive in the free agent market and re-sign our guys."

Bledsoe would get his dollars, but the cost cutting continued in other areas of the locker room. Whigham left in free agency to join the Bears, where he quickly returned to the Pro Bowl. Slade, another ex-Pro Bowler, left for the Panthers. And popular defensive tackle Henry Thomas chose to call it a career. But no player came to symbolize the Patriots' cost-cutting ways like nose tackle Chad Eaton. Eaton was a fan favorite while playing in New England from 1996 until 2000. The six-foot-six, 300-pound Eaton had a career-best six sacks in 1998, and the Washington State product was seen by many as an anchor along the defensive line, the sort of guy a young team like the Patriots could build around. However, when Eaton's agent and New England sat down at the bargaining table, it quickly became apparent the two sides were far apart. Eaton was informed the Patriots would love to have him back in

Foxboro, but at a sizably lower rate than what Eaton and his agent were asking. As a result, Eaton quickly signed a deal with the Seahawks, a contract that included a $3.5 million signing bonus—$800,000 more than all the signing bonus money New England doled out throughout that off-season.

And while the Patriots were doing their level best to cut corners here and there, they received a unique compliment prior to the 2001 season when free agent defensive lineman Tracy Scroggins decided to use the team to try to jack up his price on the open market. After the 2000 season, the thirty-one-year-old Scroggins was a talented defensive end who registered twenty-nine sacks in the previous four seasons. On the surface, he appeared to be a good fit with New England. He was an underrated pass rusher who looked like he could come relatively cheaply. Plus, the Patriots appeared to have an in: he had played with New England assistant coach Pepper Johnson, and the Patriots believed the ebullient Johnson would serve as the perfect recruiter for Scroggins. The only problem was Scroggins had zero interest in joining New England. He had spent the last nine seasons in Detroit, and, as it turns out, was simply using the Patriots to draw interest from the Lions in hopes of signing a new deal. The plan worked, as Scroggins returned to Detroit for the 2001 season with a big new contract. The Lions ended up going 1–15 that season, while New England won the Super Bowl. "If he had known his team would be 1–15 and he wouldn't play that much, he might have looked at it differently," said Johnson, who later added that other players tried the same thing with the Patriots that off-season, only to return to their own teams or go elsewhere.

Without Scroggins, and with their own payroll noticeably slimmer than the previous off-season—one local media outlet snarkily reported their cost cutting was "Walmart-esque"—they started casting about for veteran free agents who could make an impact. Even though they appeared to have more money to work with and more financial freedom, their overall approach again prevented them from going after some of the more expensive players. But that didn't really seem to fit their style. Belichick and Pioli were not looking for quick fixes à la Andre Rison in Cleveland. It didn't appear that there were going to be any home run hitters in this class of free agents anyway.

And years later, when Patriot fans would wax nostalgic about the early days of the rebuilding process, they would usually only remember the free agents who succeeded. But there were plenty of other low-cost veteran acquisitions in 2000 and 2001 who never made an impact, a motley crew that included tight end Eric Bjornson and defensive end Jon Harris. Most of these players shared some common traits: They all had moderately successful college careers, but all kicked around the league for roughly four or five years, unable to achieve any real level of success at the professional level. They joined wide receiver David Patten and running back Antowain Smith as players who had never been able to find a home in the NFL. Some washed out quickly. But some flourished with the Patriots, and were immediately signed to incentive-laden deals. It was a great deal for New England, which was getting a bonus on two levels. First, Belichick was able to obtain smart players who could quickly pick up on the intricate schemes he had put into place. Second, they came relatively cheaply, at least by NFL standards. Many of them agreed to easy contracts that weren't going to gum up the New England payroll: If they performed, they would be paid handsomely for their efforts. If not, they could be cut loose for a minimum.

A perfect example of the Patriots' maneuverings in the new NFL economy was Smith, a running back who was cut by the Bills in a salary dump. In the NFL, there were few men like Smith: The polite Alabama native didn't play football until his senior year of high school, but became an All-Conference running back, and he quickly drew the eye of college scouts. However, Smith put off college for two years while he worked to support his ailing grandparents, toiling in a dye factory near his hometown of Millbrook. After his grandmother died, he played a year of football at East Mississippi, and then went on to play two years at the University of Houston. But after four years with the Bills—including a 1998 season that saw him rush for 1,124 yards—he was pushed overboard. New England picked him up easily, signing him to a one-year deal worth $477,000, as well as a $25,000 signing bonus. (In the end, Smith was able to earn roughly $1 million his first year with the Patriots because of performance incentives. He ran for 1,157 yards and 12 touchdowns.)

After the 2000 season, there were soon several men of faith on the New England roster who had stories like Smith's. Patten was a deeply spiritual man who wasn't drafted out of college, but he had spent time working several part-time jobs, including as an electrician, a landscaper, and a laborer who hauled seventy-five-pound cases of coffee beans, before finding a job with the Albany Firebirds of the Arena Football League. He later said he signed with New England because of the spiritual element offered by the franchise. Pleasant was another religious man (his nickname in the locker room was "Moses") who aspired to work as a minister after his playing days were over. And running back Robert Edwards was an immensely likable young man who, after rushing for 1,115 yards as a rookie in 1998, was trying to work his way back from a freak knee injury he suffered while playing beach football the weekend of the Pro Bowl in Hawaii.

"When I hired Bill," Kraft recalled years later of those days in 2000, "I said, 'Just don't bring thugs or hoodlums to New England.'"

"I know what kind of player Bill wants in his system. The word we use is 'makeup,'" said Pioli, remembering the most important words of their rebuilding plan prior to the 2000 and 2001 seasons. "We're very concerned about a player's makeup. My job is to find players who are compatible with their head coach."

They would add more of those in the 2001 draft, in particular, first-round selection Richard Seymour. Many expected the Patriots to chase a wide receiver with the sixth pick, Michigan's David Terrell. He was a six-foot-three burner who provided a big target for any quarterback. As a senior, he was considered one of the top pass catchers in the country, notching 1,130 receiving yards and 14 touchdown catches. Over the course of his three-year collegiate career, he caught 152 passes for 2,317 yards and 23 touchdowns. Seventeenth in the league in passing in 2000, conventional wisdom said that New England's drafting of Terrell would allow the offense to really take off.

Instead, the Patriots went with Seymour, a defensive lineman out of Georgia. On the surface, it was a puzzling decision. It didn't appear that the Patriots were in need of a defensive lineman, and as a collegian, he didn't have the sort of numbers that would make him a priority. But a positive meeting for both sides before the draft showed Belichick and Pioli that Seymour appeared to be just the sort of player they were searching for. The young lineman had a maturity that was far beyond his years, with deep ties to a large and spiritual Southern family. He was versatile; he would go on to be able to play end in either the 3–4 or 4–3, as well as defensive tackle in the 4–3 or nose in the 3–4. And it was clear he yearned to improve. He became a constant companion of Pleasant, who started mentoring the youngster. Within weeks, it was clear that Seymour was the prime example of the Patriots' new approach to drafting, which valued intangibles almost as much as it favored talent.

"They put a great emphasis on the word 'fit,'" said Charley Armey of Belichick and his approach to team building. "They have players who fit their philosophy. They don't try to pound a square peg into a round hole. They find a guy that fits their philosophy and what they're trying to achieve, and they go out and get them, and that's been the key. Players have to fit. They have to fit a certain philosophy."

And just in case any of them weren't sure they fit into New England's new philosophy, Belichick used a very simple technique to teach players during training camp in 2001 that while they may thirst for individual recognition, the results of *team football* are key to *individual recognition*. He started by reading a list of names.

It was an odd list, one that didn't appear to have much rhyme or reason behind it other than the fact that the players were all in alphabetical order by last name.

"Donnie Abraham. Sam Adams. Trace Armstrong. Matt Birk. Daunte Culpepper. Hugh Douglas. Mark Fields. La'Roi Glover. Martin Gramatica. Brian Griese. Robert Griffith. Torry Holt. Brad Hopkins. Joe Horn. Tim Ruddy. Larry Izzo. Lincoln Kennedy. Chad Lewis. Brock Marion. Derrick Mason. Donovan McNabb. Steve McNair. Keith Mitchell. Samari Rolle. Rod Smith. Ron Stone. Matt Stover. Korey Stringer. Jason Taylor. Jeremiah Trotter.

"What do these thirty players have in common?" he asked in a conversation recalled in "Patriots United." "All thirty made their first trip to the Pro Bowl in 2000, and all were on playoff teams in 2000. They didn't make it because every single scheme and game plan revolved around these individuals, but because their teams embraced a program, chemistry gained momentum, and they won. Almost seven of every ten Pro Bowlers came off playoff rosters." The lesson was clear: *Your* chances of making a Pro Bowl roster are better if the *team* is a success. And no one had to remind the 5–11 Patriots that they were one of a precious few teams that didn't have a single Pro Bowl player on their rosters in 2000.

Throughout the early days of training camp in 2001, the message seemed to resonate with the players. There were no Gatrell-Milloy steel cage matches, but there was plenty of pushing and shoving, much to the delight of Johnson. That dream house was a lot closer to completion than anybody thought. "The players were a little more relaxed on the outside, yet I saw that the competition was up, saw guys motivating each other, and there were a couple of fights as well as a lot of pushing," Johnson said of the difference between training camp in 2000 and the following year. "I said, 'Yeah, that's a training camp.'"

Using a carefully crafted series of core beliefs in the fifteen months since they'd taken control of the franchise—valuing team above individual, putting a premium on economic efficiency, and using nontraditional methods of evaluating talent—they had radically overhauled the personnel. Sixty-five of the eighty-eight players who were on the roster in the summer of 2001 were brought in by Belichick and Pioli, an astounding amount of turnover in such a short time. On the defensive side of the football, there were wholesale changes at the key position on a Belichick-coached defense: linebacker, with Vrabel, Phifer, and Cox joining Bruschi, McGinest, and Ted Johnson. On the offensive side of the football, Belichick was working with a veteran quarterback whose sizable salary appeared to run counter to his team-building approach, but who was still a three-time Pro Bowler, and was now surrounded by a considerably sturdier offensive line and two running backs, Robert Edwards and Antowain Smith, who had both topped the thousand-yard mark within the past three seasons.

From the outside, the Patriots were a different organization than when Belichick and Pioli first arrived in Foxborough. They had restored order to a previously dysfunctional front office and created a viable system, one with a solid sense of direction and vision where none had stood before.

Belichick and Pioli appeared to have the complete and total backing of ownership. In addition, they brought a consistent sense of economic efficiency when it came to acquiring personnel, opting to consider the big picture every time. "We'll do what we think is best for the football team" was the response Belichick almost always gave when he was questioned about a personnel move. It was a philosophy that left some players and their agents shaking their heads, but also left others within the organization realizing that for the first time in several years, there was a genuine meritocracy. Veterans could not skate by on reputation anymore. They had to work for their money. And if they didn't work, they wouldn't be playing for the Patriots.

As a result, that summer, the local image of the Patriots was considerably sunnier than when Belichick and Pioli first took control of the franchise. On the surface, things appeared shaky—they were coming off a season where they finished 5-11—but there was suddenly a feeling of consistency, a feeling that the Patriots had a strong hand at the wheel. That impression was due in large part to the fact that Belichick forbade all his assistants to speak to the media. Pioli rarely, if ever, addressed reporters, and Belichick expected scouts, personnel men, and trainers to do the same. If there was going to be news, it was going to be Belichick who would deliver it. Where there were questions among fans and players before as to who was calling the shots in the Carroll-Grier era, now everyone knew there was absolutely no question publicly as to where the organization stood on any personnel matters.

Now, they just needed to see if the system worked.

# CHAPTER FOUR

# "TONIGHT, THE DYNASTY IS BORN"

> Drew Bledsoe collected the richest contract in history, $103 million (I have trouble even writing a number like that), for the privilege of getting hammered behind a line that is mostly prayer. The Pats have signed a ton of free agents, mostly backup types and none as good as one guy they lost, DT [Chad] Eaton.
>
> —*PAUL ZIMMERMAN, SI.COM, JULY 15, 2001*

As camp broke in 2001, many media outlets didn't share Pepper Johnson's optimism. Almost universally, the Patriots were panned as having no hope. "The Pats signed a bunch of free agents from the NFL's five-and-dime store," wrote Street & Smith's *Pro Football Preview*. "Belichick better hope that Robert Kraft is a very patient owner who can still see the big picture if the team is 4–10 and playing in front of 30,000 empty seats this December," said *Pro Football Talk*. And that sort of pessimism was well founded, as New England stumbled to a road loss against the Bengals to open the season.

Two weeks later, things started to change. Sunday, September 23, marked the first series of games for the NFL since the attacks on New York and Washington on September 11, and the tragedy hit the franchise indirectly, as New England offensive lineman Joe

Andruzzi had three brothers who were New York City firemen, one of whom worked in the station closest to the World Trade Center and was among the first firemen on the scene that morning. (Jim Andruzzi had climbed as high as the twenty-third floor of the North Tower—on his way to the eightieth floor—but on his way up, he was rerouted to help another firefighter who was having chest pains. That radio message likely saved Andruzzi's life, as he ended up helping the other firefighter out of the building just as the North Tower came down.) Joe Andruzzi memorably recapped what his family went through in an emotional press conference a few days later. The three brothers and their father, a retired New York City police officer, were made honorary captains for the Jets game and received a huge ovation before taking part in the opening coin toss. It was an emotional moment, one many teams could have drawn strength from.

Despite all that, the Patriots were down to the Jets 10–3 with 4:48 remaining when Bledsoe rolled right, escaping the pocket while trying to scramble away from New York defensive lineman John Abraham for a first-down and stop the clock. A step from the sideline and roughly a yard shy of the first-down marker, everyone started to pull up slightly, including Abraham, who appeared to be playfully gunning for his old pal Bryan Cox, who was standing along the sidelines. "Seeing that Drew was almost out of bounds, Abraham started running at Bryan Cox, who was standing about three feet from me," Johnson recalled in *Won for All: The Inside Story of the New England Patriots' Improbable Run to a Super Bowl*. "He was doing as a joke with a former teammate, and he stopped before reaching him." But not Lewis, who, as Johnson recalls, hit Bledsoe with a "real hard shot, jarring the ball loose and sending Drew sprawling over the sideline."

For all the team building and preparation, all the drafting and scouting that goes into making a successful professional football team, there are moments that no one can account for, moments that no one can see coming. These are moments that can not only change the course of a player's career, but also alter the course of football history. This was one of those moments, a seminal event in the history of the Patriots that would alter not only the careers of two quarterbacks, but the very fortunes of everyone connected with the franchise.

From the stands and on television, it appeared as though there was nothing wrong with Bledsoe, nothing that a few extra moments on the sidelines couldn't remedy anyway. He lay on the ground a bit before being helped to his feet. On the sidelines, everything appeared to check out: He passed concussion tests, and was sent back into the game for another series by Belichick before being yanked in favor of backup Tom Brady. But as Brady continued to try and lead the Patriots back, it became clear that Bledsoe was hurt much worse than anyone had realized. The hit had caused Bledsoe to suffer a sheared blood vessel, and he had lost a lot of blood. "It's some type of internal injury, which isn't what it appeared at the time of the play," Belichick said the day after the game. "Initially, it seemed that he had been knocked out for a second. Then, after the game, it became apparent this wasn't an issue." Shortly after the game—which ended as a 10–3 defeat for New England, sending them to 0–2 on the young season—Bledsoe was taken to Massachusetts General Hospital, where he had blood drained from his chest.

That game would be Bledsoe's last start for the Patriots.

For the moment, Belichick's legacy as a head coach rested squarely on the shoulders of Brady, an untested second-year quarterback out of Michigan who had just turned twenty-four the month before. A youngster who didn't get off the bench as a rookie—he threw just one pass in his first season with the Patriots, a six-yard connection to running back J. R. Redmond in the final moments of a blowout loss at Detroit—he had worked his way up from No. 4 quarterback to the backup role by the start of his second season, bypassing a series of older veterans like John Friesz, who were looking for the No. 2 spot behind Bledsoe.

While not much was known about Brady publicly, he was already popular with many of his teammates. He had managed to win many of them over during his rookie season where he displayed his willingness to work, time and again, on the smallest of issues, the tiniest of points. Like a politician, Brady had spent much of his short career in a Patriots uniform building a consensus, winning the hearts and minds of those in the locker room by dint of sheer effort. He did that in a variety of ways. Between the end of the 2000 season and the start of the 2001 season, the team held sixty off-season workouts. Brady made every one of them, and received one of the highest honors the coaching staff can bestow on a player—the best parking space in the players lot.

In truth, Brady's year on the bench was part of a bigger program, one the Patriots were just starting to take advantage of. Every NFL team had begun using the five-man practice squad, which had been established in 1989 as a way of supplementing an NFL roster with players who weren't quite ready to start. But over the years, few teams would manipulate the practice squad like the Patriots. Under their new team-building approach, New England had, in effect, begun redshirting players in much the same way college programs did. The process would work like this: The Patriots would select a player who appeared to have the mental and emotional capabilities to succeed in the NFL, but didn't quite have an NFL-ready physique. So they would find a spot for them somewhere, whether on the practice squad or another spot on the roster. (Over the next several years, their redshirts would include wide receiver David Givens, offensive linemen Stephen Neal and Russ Hochstein, and defensive lineman Jarvis Green, all of whom would go on to become major contributors.) All of them would spend much of their rookie season either on the bench or on the practice squad as they became NFL ready.

During *his* redshirt season, Brady spent portions of his time as the scout team quarterback. The job involved running the opposing offense, trying to give New England's starting defense a taste of the strengths and weaknesses of the opposing quarterback. So if the 2000 Patriots were facing the Detroit Lions, chances are he might spend the week running around trying to look like Charlie Batch or Stoney Case. It was a thankless job, really, one many veteran quarterbacks considered beneath them. (There are, at this moment, likely ten teams where a veteran backup has ceded the scout team duties to a younger No. 3 quarterback out of sheer embarrassment.) But the scout team role was one Brady took to with zeal, using it as his opportunity to show Belichick he had bought into the system. And after running the scout team, Brady would continue to practice, staying on the field and working with the other scout teamers.

With Bledsoe out for the foreseeable future, Brady also took over the job of public face of the franchise. There are certain responsibilities that go with being a starting quarterback, and one of them is to hold a weekly press conference. Each week, you become the go-to guy for TV cameras and reporters alike. The comments of the starting quarterback get replayed over and over again throughout the week by television stations all over New England, and they're dissected by football fans everywhere who are hoping to glean a few bits of insight into this week's game plan. And over the years, the Boston sports media had gotten used to Bledsoe as that very public face. He had been a starter in the league for many years, and had his press conference routine *down*. He was polished and professional in front of a large group of media, speaking in a deep monotone and offering up just enough to let people believe they had some small insight into that week's game plan—but not so much that the Patriots would tip their hand as to what they were planning for the week.

When Brady met the media for the first time, it was quite a change. When he arrived for his first weekly press conference as a starter the morning of September 26, 2001, he had a backpack slung over his shoulder and a baseball cap pointed backward, looking for all the world like a college student on his way to class.

But it was clear there was a new day in Foxborough. He didn't have the same occasionally glazed look of a weary Bledsoe, who appeared many times like he had heard every question you could conjure up about quarterbacking the New England Patriots. For Brady, this was all brand-new, and he appeared to embrace the moment. This was now *his* team. He was at the controls. "Who wants to shoot?" he asked with a smile after walking in, dropping his bag, and grabbing both sides of the podium.

The rest of his introductory press conference had the same genial, slightly goofy tone, alternating between humility and a confidence that bordered on cockiness. *Are you going to be nervous?* "Not a bit, man. Not a bit," he said, reminding people that he had played in front of 112,000 people at Michigan. "I prepare as hard as I can every week. I was ready to start last night if they had told me to start last night. I'll be just as ready this week."

As Brady readied for his first start, the game marked a crossroads for the franchise, and for Belichick in particular. As the Patriots began preparing for the Colts, Belichick's career coaching mark in New England was a not-so-robust 5–13. For the short term, his job certainly appeared safe. There was no drumbeat among the talk shows or newspaper columnists about his future in Foxboro, even after an 0–2 start. But with his franchise quarterback sidelined for the foreseeable future and a collection of relatively anonymous players on both sides of the football, one had to wonder what sort of long-term effect the Bledsoe injury might have on Belichick's grand plan for football in Foxborough, or even his coaching career overall. It wouldn't matter that he lost the starting quarterback in Week 2 to a freak injury, just as it didn't matter that the situation in Cleveland had spiraled beyond his control. At that stage of his coaching career, the only thing that mattered were the wins and losses. When you're dealing with a billion-dollar industry like the NFL, there is no room for nuance or gray areas—there are only wins and losses, a final, unforgiving register that measures the success or failure of a head coach. And with the losses starting to pile up faster than the wins (his career mark as a head coach was 42–58 entering that Sunday against Indianapolis) it appeared Belichick's second go-round as a head coach had the potential to end in much the same fashion as his time in Cleveland. Then, almost certainly, his NFL legacy would be written for all to see. He would be tagged as a guy who made a strong assistant, but wasn't able to handle the responsibilities that went along with a head coaching job.

But the old guys weren't going to let that happen.

While Brady was now the Man upstairs in Super Box A, it was a far different story downstairs in the locker room. That's where the old guys had really started the process of "regulating" the locker room, policing the team and making sure everyone did what he was supposed to do. No one was really sure whether it was simply a pleasant coincidence or part of an overall bigger plan, but Belichick and the Patriots had assembled the oldest team in the NFL, with some of the hardiest veterans. They included Bryan Cox, Anthony Pleasant, Otis Smith, Ty Law, Lawyer Milloy, Tedy Bruschi, and Willie McGinest, guys who had already spent several years in the NFL and were considered at or near the top of the pecking order. These were the guys who made sure that rookies were seen and not heard—and provided the occasional snack for teammates. (Rookie left tackle Matt Light was forced to bring his linemates Subway sandwiches on more than one occasion.) These were the guys who spent much of their time bringing all corners of the locker room together through dominos. (Smith brought the first domino set into the locker room early on, and a table was soon set up. It quickly became a favorite gathering spot among players for several reasons, not the least of which was that an unwritten rule quickly arose: Media were not to disturb anyone sitting at the dominos table.) And these were the guys who were charged with

protecting Brady from the media on the eve of his first professional start.

As he did throughout much of the season, it was Cox who took
the lead. Once considered a locker room risk because he had
racked up hundreds of thousands of dollars in fines for various
run-ins with the league, he had matured into a leader. He told reporters during training camp in the summer of 2001 that a light
had gone on, telling him it was time to shape up. As a result, he
quickly became a favorite among teammates and reporters alike.
And in his short tenure with the Patriots, the irreverent linebacker
had done everything in his power to shake things up, beginning
with his choice of uniform number. "We went [7–9 and 4–12] in the
two years I didn't wear number 51," said Cox, who wore number 52
in his two years with the Chicago Bears. "I need to get 51 back."
Only problem was, Mike Vrabel had number 51. Cox instead wore
number 0 throughout training camp before swinging a deal with
Vrabel for the number. Cox was quickly voted a defensive captain,
and did his part to shield Brady from the spotlight in the week leading up to the game. In a move designed to take some heat off the
youngster, Cox did what Bryan Cox had done throughout his
career: He made an outrageous comment. "They can be beat," Cox
said of the powerful Indianapolis offense. "They put their pants on
just like we put our pants on. We can compete. We can play. We can
win. I'm looking to knock Peyton [Manning's] head off. That's
point-blank football. You can make them out to be Supermen. You
can give them some credit—they've put up a lot of points this season. But I'm not built like that." His off-the-record comments were
even more pointed. "I'm not the kind of man to suck another man's
dick," Cox said privately when asked about the Colts' quarterback.

It was the first of several occasions where the veterans deflected
the attention from Brady in hopes of shielding the youngster. "I
think that was intentional," Perillo said of the veterans' exerting
their influence. "I think they said, 'We have a kid here who has
never played. We have to take the focus off him and put it on us.'"

It was a savvy move: A ravenous Boston media flocked to Cox's incendiary quotes. While Brady's statistics tell the story of a remarkably average outing—at least statistically—Brady was downright pedestrian in his first NFL start, going 13-for-23 with 168 yards against the Colts with no touchdowns and no interceptions. But the players around him all took their games to a higher level, including the New England defense. Under first-year defensive coordinator Romeo Crennel, a longtime assistant with the Giants with Parcells and Belichick, the unit made its first real statement of the season in the first quarter when Indianapolis wide receiver Jerome Pathon boldly came over the middle on a crossing pattern, only to be blasted by Cox. It was a tackle that set the tone for the season, and showed people that this Patriots team was not to be messed with. "That established a new era of toughness on this team that probably had been lacking prior to that hit," Weis would say later.

Manning was intercepted three times, with two of them being returned for scores (one for 78 yards, another for 23 yards) on the way to a 44–13 win over previously unbeaten Indianapolis. After the game, Brady was quick to credit Bledsoe: "The one thing he told me was, 'Tom, the most important thing for you today is to go out there and smile and have fun. You're as prepared as you could be. I have a ton of confidence in you and just go out there and have fun. Let everything else take care of itself.' That's kind of the way it worked out." If his numbers against the Colts were pedestrian, his statistics the following week seemed to indicate he had taken a step backward in his development. A 26–13 loss to the Dolphins in Miami that remains one of the worst of Brady's career (12-for-24, 86 yards, zero touchdown passes and four sacks) left New England with a 1–3 record.

In retrospect, those first two starts were essentially window dressing, an overture to a career that really commenced on the afternoon on October 14, 2001, against the Chargers. It was a game that was bursting with intriguing storylines. It marked the return of local hero Doug Flutie as San Diego's quarterback. The former

Boston College star had led the surprising Chargers—who finished 1–15 a season before—to a 3–1 start. Along the way, Flutie was looking to improve his personal career record in Foxboro to 13–1 at the expense of his hometown team, who he was still steamed at for cutting him loose years earlier. In addition, there was the continued drama surrounding the New England quarterbacking situation. Could Brady take charge of the team and turn the season around? Or had the season already been lost with the injury to Bledsoe?

Looming over it all was the return of wide receiver Terry Glenn, who had just finished a four-game suspension for violating the NFL's substance abuse rules. Throughout the start of the 2001 season, Glenn had been a major distraction. He believed that the franchise wasn't completely supportive of him when the league came down with the penalty over the summer, so he missed five training camp sessions. Glenn then left training camp altogether on August 3. Belichick, who made the decision to suspend him for the season, said Glenn had "ample opportunity" to return, but didn't. Twelve days later, the team suspended him for the 2001 season, and the team requested he return the roughly $11 million in bonus money he received. However, Glenn publicly fought the ban, and had it overturned by an arbitrator, setting the stage for a big return that Sunday against San Diego.

On a wet and cloudy afternoon in Foxboro, Glenn received a warm ovation from the fans, and caught the first touchdown pass of Brady's professional career. (He flung the ball into the stands in celebration.) He ended the day with seven catches for 110 yards, and helped spark the Patriots to a 16–13 lead midway through the third quarter. But San Diego answered with a quick flurry, and Derrick Harris's fumble recovery and touchdown run gave the Chargers a 26–16 lead with 8:48 left in regulation. With four minutes left, little remained of the Patriots' hopes. They had lost three of their first four games, had a rookie quarterback at the helm, and were down by ten with ten minutes left. While the season wouldn't be lost if they fell to 1–4, it would certainly put a major dent in their postseason plans.

But behind Brady (who ended up going 33-for-54 for 364 yards and two touchdown passes), New England scored on each of its last three possessions—including an eight-play, sixty-yard drive that tied the score with thirty-six seconds left—to stun the Chargers 29–26 in overtime. Down the stretch, Brady was magnificent, going 13-for-18 for 130 yards and a touchdown over the final 8:48 to pull out the first come-from-behind win of his career, showing his trademark cool the whole way. "Never a doubt, huh?" he said with a small smile afterward. It was the first time in his professional career that New England fans had a chance to witness a Brady comeback drive, and it started a streak of three wins in the next four games to improve their record to 5–4 and vault them into the thick of the AFC playoff picture, with a key contest against St. Louis looming on Sunday, November 18.

At the start of the season, the reason ESPN decided to make the Rams-Patriots game part of their *Sunday Night* package wasn't because of New England, but it was looked at as a chance to get as many St. Louis games on national television as possible. With offensive stars like Marshall Faulk, Kurt Warner, Isaac Bruce, and Torry Holt, the Rams were one of the league's marquee teams, boasting an offense that would ultimately go on to be considered one of the best in the history of the league. With Brady's emergence, New England had started to develop into an interesting team, but hardly one that was worthy of a national television audience.

The Patriots whipped up a series of exotic defensive fronts, including one series in which they had seven defensive backs on the field, all trying to slow down the Rams' offense. Despite a constant series of blitzes, Warner passed for 401 yards (the most passing yardage New England would allow all season) and three touchdowns. The Patriots did themselves no favors. Late in the first half, Antowain Smith fumbled the football deep in St. Louis territory as

New England was driving for a score that would have given them a
17–7 lead. Instead, St. Louis took possession and drove 97 yards at
the end of the first half to take a 14–10 lead. The Rams wouldn't
trail the rest of the night, taking a 24–17 decision that was only
that close because the Patriots scored a late touchdown to draw to
within seven. A year before, this was the sort of loss that would
have been chalked up as a moral victory. After all, not many teams
were able to hang with St. Louis. But in 2001, there was no sense
of victory, just a maddening defeat for a team that had highly
touted St. Louis on the ropes before it committed the backbreak-
ing turnover. "I thought we just missed too many opportunities tonight," Belichick said. "Both sides made some plays, but in the end
we just couldn't quite make enough of them. And obviously, that's
real disappointing."

But St. Louis certainly took note of the Patriots. A day later,
Martz predicted that the Patriots would be the team representing
the AFC in the Super Bowl.

While Brady had led them back into the race, Bledsoe worked out
on his own, hoping to return to his old job sooner rather than later.
After the Chargers game, he was cleared for light jogging, and for
the first time since the injury, he was listed as "doubtful" instead of
"out" on the weekly injury report. But as the team rallied around
Brady—and more and more media members started to become
drawn to the younger and more charismatic quarterback—Bledsoe
became a sad, almost solitary figure, going through workouts in
Foxboro Stadium all alone. He would run the stairs of the old
place by himself, going up and down the aisles while thinking
about his return to the field. Less than nine months after he had
signed the largest contract in the history of the National Football
League, Bledsoe was a man without a country, a football player
facing an uncertain future. He had never been a backup before,

and he confessed privately to reporters that it was an odd feeling sitting and watching another quarterback guide *his* team.

Things couldn't have been sunnier between Bledsoe and owner Bob Kraft. At the press conference announcing his nine-figure contract extension earlier that year, Kraft and Bledsoe took turns praising each other, which sparked comparisons to the classic Boston owner-player relationships of the past like Tom Yawkey and Carl Yastrzemski. Bledsoe said Kraft was a "mentor. . . . He supplies me with some guidance that my parents wouldn't be familiar with as schoolteachers. It's still an owner-player relationship, but we're both going to be here for the long haul. The success that we ultimately have will benefit us and when we don't have success, it cuts *us* to the core. We feel it together."

That feeling didn't exist between Belichick and Bledsoe. The two never appeared to mesh. They were pleasant enough to each other publicly, but the sense of veterans' entitlement that permeated the New England locker room under the Grier-Carroll administration was gone, and with it any real chance that Bledsoe had at winning back his job.

There were several sticking points between Bledsoe and Belichick. Bledsoe's salary cap number was certainly not in line with Belichick's approach to team building. The quarterback was seen as inflexible, not able to adapt to the new approach laid out by Belichick and Weis. And then, perhaps the most damning of all, there was Bledsoe's approach to the off-season. Bledsoe was infamous for his quick getaways at the end of the year. (Before the final game of the 2000 season, he rented a helicopter, the quicker to get him to a nearby airport to take a private plane back to the West Coast, where he could start his off-season. He had it warming up throughout the second half.) Even though he was also a West Coast guy—Bledsoe had deep roots in Washington and Montana, while Brady spent the majority of his life growing up in the Bay Area—Brady stuck around. He recognized the importance of team building, of the bonding that slowly becomes the fabric that holds a locker room together. "I think it's important being around the guys you're going to play with. You're out there running and sweating together, and everyone is going, 'This sucks,' or you're cussing out your strength coach," he would say years later. "That's what it's all about."

As a result, Bledsoe was in danger of becoming a footnote, the Wally Pipp of the New England football world. There was clearly a showdown looming between the veteran quarterback and the new coach, and it all came to a head on November 19, the day after a narrow Sunday night loss to St. Louis. Bledsoe had finally received medical clearance to play, and Brady had now thrown seven interceptions in his last thirteen quarters. The quarterback debate was gaining steam. Belichick was going to be faced with a situation similar to one that ultimately doomed him in Cleveland: Which quarterback should he choose? That Monday, he made his decision. Belichick told the veteran during the weekly quarterbacks meeting he would be going with Brady as his starter the rest of the season. From that point, the relationship between Belichick and Bledsoe was forever altered. One account said there was a "very heated" argument between the two, and another said Bledsoe was "extremely pissed off." Later, Belichick told WWZN Radio's Sean McDonough that Brady would be the starting quarterback for the "foreseeable future."

"As we go forward, I don't anticipate that changing unless something unforeseen happens," Belichick said, later adding that "something unforeseen" would be an injury to Brady.

Admitting the decision was "talk show material for everybody" the next day, the coach delivered strong, straightforward answers. "It is what it is. Nobody scripted it this way. It just worked out that way. My job—I have been here two years—my job is to make the decisions for the football team, and that is what I am going to do. I am going to make the best decisions I can for the football team. That is what Mr. Kraft is paying me to do and that's what I am going to do. I am going to make the decisions that I feel are best for the football team, T-E-A-M, as in team. I can't make them for an individual or a group, I have to do what is best for the entire team.

"This is not about Drew losing a job," Belichick added. "This is strictly about the team. It's about getting the team ready. I don't think you can get two quarterbacks ready. I feel that for us to get our starting quarterback ready, we need to give that player the majority of the reps. When Drew was the quarterback, it was the same way."

Bledsoe was stunned. In a memorable locker room press conference later that morning, he was asked about his feelings on the matter. "Next question," he replied shakily in a tone quite unfamiliar to the legions of fans who were used to his usually sure and steady voice he delivered each Wednesday. He would later explain: "I looked forward to the chance to compete for my job, and I'll leave it at that." Later in the week, after cooling off, Bledsoe expanded: "My intention is to do the same thing I've done for nine years—and ever since I was drafted by this team—and that is to do whatever I can to help this team. In this particular case, that means continuing as I have to help Tom on the field, and help him during the week. One thing that falls into that category is to conduct myself in a manner that allows the players on this team to support both Tom and I. I feel like I've done that to this point, and I don't need to change."

With no quarterback coach on staff after the death of Dick Rehbein before the start of the season, Bledsoe became the de facto quarterbacks coach, helping guide Brady. Publicly, Brady clearly relished the idea of working with the nine-year veteran. "I tell you, he's great," Brady said of Bledsoe a few weeks before Belichick made his decision. "He just cuts through everything. He's there with me all the time. I know as a quarterback you really put your trust in certain people. . . . He's one guy that I have a lot of trust in because I know that he'd never let me down. He's fighting for plays to get called, because he knows if he was out there what kind of plays he'd want to be calling."

Quarterback debates can rip a locker room apart. Almost every team, at one time or another, has gone through the process. But this one looked like it could be different. On the surface, the New England locker room appeared to be a tranquil place. When they were asked to make a choice between Brady or Bledsoe, almost everyone in the locker room parroted the company line: whatever it takes for us to win games. "We all know we have to go out there and play regardless of what happens," said Troy Brown. "It's not something that's going to split the team up or cause any hard feelings. I'm sure Drew is disappointed. But we have got to be ready to carry on every Sunday no matter what happens and no matter who is out there. This is the National Football League, and you have to make tough decisions sometimes and this was a tough one coach Belichick had to make." Mike Compton said the same thing. "We've got three good quarterbacks and we have confidence in any of the three," he said. "Whoever is out there is going to do the job fine. And if he couldn't do the job, he wouldn't be here."

Off the record, it was a far different story. While reports circulated that Bledsoe had gone to Kraft to lobby for his job, there were players in many corners of the locker room who believed he should be the starter again. Quietly, the locker room had split into three factions. In the first group were the mostly younger players who favored Brady. After all, he had managed to get the team back on track, and had the offense playing with a renewed vigor. There was a genuine meritocracy in place: Brady was playing well, so why not let him keep the job? It was a distinct change from the Bobby Grier–Pete Carroll era, when veterans felt entitled and received the bulk of the playing time, whether they were past their prime or not. *It's about time they decided to shake things up around here.* In the second group, most of the veterans cast their lot with Bledsoe. This was a collection of players who saw the demotion of their fellow veteran—a longtime member of the franchise who had, after all, helped deliver an AFC championship just five years before—as a cautionary tale. A player's time in the National Football League is a relatively short one. Coaches should understand that and do whatever they can to make accommodations to help out a player who has paid his dues. *If Belichick did it to the $100 million man, there's no reason he can't do the same to me.* What kept much of the Bledsoe-Brady debate from reaching a crisis inside the locker room was the third group, a smaller faction that had a growing voice as the season continued. There were many veterans in the Patriots locker room that fall who had been signed the previous off-season who knew they were approaching the end of their playing careers and realized that if they could hitch their wagon to Brady's star, they might have a real shot at football glory. As a result, many of those veterans truly believed it when they delivered the company line. *Whichever quarterback will help us win more games, I'm all for it.* That group included Cox. And as he did so many times throughout the 2001 season, he tried to defuse controversy by serving as a lightning rod. This time, instead of protecting Brady from the media prior to his first start against the Colts, he engaged in a spirited defense of Belichick's decision. "This is real foolish. You guys are trying to undercut Bill. He's trying to make a decision that's best for the team. [The media doesn't] know the situation," he said. "Some of the media up here are not capable of making the choice of who should be the quarterback. They don't know. They don't see the tape."

For all the success the team had enjoyed, the 2001 Patriots had clearly reached a tipping point, a tenuous situation that could have ultimately affected the long-term history of the franchise. Brady or Bledsoe? In truth, it was a decision that was fraught with peril, and the whole thing could have collapsed on any number of levels if the parties involved hadn't conducted themselves professionally while in the public eye. Bledsoe could have lobbied for his job, going to the media every day and complaining about his situation. The drama would have played out publicly and polarized the locker room, and fans would have rolled their eyes at the situation. *Same old Patriots*. Kraft could have leaned on the coaching staff to reinstate a player he had grown close to; after all, the quarterback had compared him to a parent when he signed his record-setting deal that spring. (Some wondered if the owner would have had the good sense to stay out of such a personnel matter five years earlier, especially one involving his favorite player—and especially involving Parcells.) And Belichick, recalling the Kosar-Philcox-Testaverde debate from his days in Cleveland and the hideous fallout that ensued, could have easily bowed to any pressure that Kraft might have brought to bear on the situation and gone back to the veteran.

But none of that happened. For the first time in Belichick's career as a head coach, a controversial decision had received the full endorsement of the ownership. When things are going well—and none of your favorite players are threatened—it's one thing for the owner to say he will not interfere with personnel moves. It's a whole different thing when he sticks to his word. With his decision made (and supported by the owner), the head coach was truly free to put his final major imprint on the system. Brady would be the starter. The triumph was impressive, and appeared to coincide with a major breakthrough in Belichick's public persona. In a late-season win over the Jets, a normally reserved Belichick was ebullient at the end of the game, slapping five with his players and celebrating a narrow victory over a division rival. "I've never seen him that excited," said Phifer afterward, shaking his head in disbelief. "That was the first time I've ever seen him hug anyone. I was surprised." And after the Patriots beat the Browns in Foxborough on December 9 and the fans had cleared out, the Cleveland writers—the same ones who dogged him for being an out-of-touch automaton—looked down at the Foxboro Stadium field in amazement to see Belichick happily playing touch football with his kids.

But the real coup de grace came after the final regular-season game against Miami, when Belichick took a victory lap around Foxboro Stadium with the team, a big smile on his face. According to many of the players who followed him from Cleveland to New

York to New England, he *had* changed. He was no longer the young coach who cursed out his charges with the Browns less than ten years before. Now, he was a different man, a changed man, and he was thoroughly enjoying himself. Pleasant had played for Belichick in Cleveland, as well as the Jets. He signed with New England prior to the 2000 season. "He's still consistent as far as being strict about things and wanting guys to do things right," Pleasant said late that season. "But he's not as dogmatic as he was in Cleveland. He's more willing to give now than he was back then. In Cleveland, it was more like 'This is my way—this is the way we're going to do it.' He wasn't willing to make changes."

"Everybody has emotion," said cornerback Otis Smith, who played for Belichick in New York and followed him to New England before the 2000 season. "He's not as totally cold as people would say. He's a human being, and his emotion changes from situation to situation. Sometimes, it comes out and the camera catches it. I'm almost sure he doesn't want it to happen that way. But that's the way he is. . . . It's not like he's trying to impress anyone by doing that. He's just being Bill Belichick."

And it was quite clear that Belichick was learning from the same lessons that helped doom him when he was with the Browns. "When you're the head man, you have to listen to other people," Smith said. "I think he's done a great job of that, of listening to his coaching staff and believing in what they present to him. Not only his coaching staff, but some players that have been around the league and know and have an idea of what they're talking about. He takes time out to listen to what they have to say."

Late in the season, Belichick admitted he finally learned to let go of the little things and trust the people around him. It was a process that was a long time in coming. "I agree that being able to delegate and have confidence that other people are going to handle things and get it done is a really big step [in learning how to be a successful head coach]," he said. "It's a big step for me to take, because I kind of like to be involved in the details and all that. But as

I've found out, I think that there are a lot of people—when I delegate—who do a better job of doing it than I would have anyway. And that certainly as come through to me many times."

While it was a transitional year for Belichick, it was also a transitional year for the franchise, which would be spending its final year in Foxboro Stadium. As the winning streak continued, the new stadium, CMGI Field, started rising in the background. It eventually loomed large over the far corner, peeking over the rim of the old stadium, a symbol of the luxury that was to come. For an optimist, the metaphor was clear: There were better days on the horizon. No matter how the 2001 season ended, the franchise would finally be shaking off the ghosts of Foxboro Stadium, a venue inextricably linked with the (mostly) sour fortunes of the franchise through most of the stadium's thirty-year existence. In its place, there would be a state-of-the-art facility to provide support for a franchise that had suddenly become one of the AFC elite.

And as the stadium neared completion and wins continued to mount and the Brady legend started to take hold throughout New England, it was clear the legendary stories about the ineptitude of the franchise were starting to fade into memory. There were no more stories of head coaches nearly getting electrocuted by microphones; no more stories of star receivers leaving the stadium at halftime and getting into a car crash on the way home; and no more stories about pulling players out of the stands moments before kickoff. Recklessness has been replaced by responsibility, chaos by efficiency. And unnecessary drama had been replaced by a sense of stability.

On the final home game of the regular season, many of the great old Patriots showed up to pay tribute to the old stadium, including Steve Grogan, Steve Nelson, and Mike Haynes. And, for one day, the old jokes about the cold showers, faulty plumbing and dinky locker rooms were put to rest, replaced by nostalgia for an era of Patriots football that was about to come to an end.

"I've been to a lot of stadiums in my fourteen years in the National Football League. I played on a team in San Francisco that won five Super Bowls. And Schaefer Stadium, to me, was always that grand, beautiful home," said tight end Russ Francis. "You can go back to the home you grew up in as a child, in the old neighborhood, and say 'This is not quite as nice as I remember it.' You can look at that 1973 Dodge Charger and think, 'This is not quite as cool as the new Dodge Magnum.' But it will always have a very special place in your heart."

Before the stadium closed its doors for the last time, there was one final game, a divisional playoff contest against the Raiders that was played in a driving snowstorm. CBS announcers Greg Gumbel and Phil Simms were under attack for much of the game by snowballs, with one barely missing Simms's face in the fourth quarter. Oakland held a narrow 13–10 lead with just under two minutes remaining, but the Patriots were driving with a first and ten from the Oakland 42. In his first playoff game, Brady had shown remarkable poise, running for his first career touchdown and keeping his head against a veteran defense, all in the middle of the first snowstorm of the season. And when he dropped back to pass, it looked like the story of this game would be similar to the comeback wins over San Diego, Buffalo, and the New York Jets that Brady was able to engineer earlier in the season.

But the New England quarterback was hit from behind by Oakland defensive back—and former college teammate—Charles Woodson, who came in untouched on a corner blitz from the defensive left side and knocked the ball from Brady's grip. The ball squirted free, falling to the ground. Linebacker Greg Biekert was right behind Woodson, and had the football in his sights. Brady tried to prevent Biekert from recovering the fumble, sticking his leg out quickly, but Biekert collapsed on the football. With time dwindling down, it appeared this is where the 2001 season would end for the New England Patriots.

However, officials in the press box requested a replay. It appeared that Brady might have tucked the ball away before trying to throw, which would have made it an incomplete pass, not a fumble. The tuck rule had been on the books for several years: "When a Team A player is holding the ball to pass it forward, any intentional forward movement of [the passer's] arm starts a forward pass, even if the player loses possession of the ball as he is attempting to tuck it back toward his body," reads Rule 3, Section 21, Article 2, Note 2 in the NFL rule book. In the loss to the Rams in November, there was a controversial tuck rule call involving Kurt Warner. While Coleman continued to watch the play on the field, up in the press box, Oakland officials fumed. Raiders executive Amy Trask stood over veteran official Art McNally and uttered: "You better call 911, because I'm going to have a fucking heart attack if you overturn this call."

Coleman then returned to the field and delivered his verdict: "After reviewing the play, the quarterbacks arm was going forward—" The crowd drowned out the rest. "Obviously, what I saw on the field, I thought the ball came out before his arm was going forward," Coleman later told a pool reporter. "Then, when I got to the replay monitor and looked at it, it was obvious his arm was coming forward. He touched the ball. And they just hooked it out of his hand. His arm was coming forward, which makes it an incomplete pass."

"Yeah," Brady said with a broad smile, practically winking at the media when he was asked about the call after the game. "I was throwing the football. I was going to throw it and he hit me as I was going to throw it. How do you like that?"

As the Raiders fumed, Brady and the Patriots continued their drive, getting to the Oakland 29 with twenty-seven seconds left. That set the stage for Adam Vinatieri. To this point in his career, the kicker was known among most Patriots fans as the Man Who

Ran Down Herschel Walker. An undrafted free agent out of South Dakota State, Vinatieri began his career with the Amsterdam Admirals of the World League, but quickly hooked on with the Patriots after sending tapes around the league in hopes of finding work as a kicker. Bill Parcells thought so much of Adam Vinatieri that he cut veteran Matt Bahr in favor of Vinatieri. And as a rookie in 1996, he was able to catch Walker from behind on a kick return, making a touchdown-saving tackle after the former track star had sprinted seventy yards down the sideline. The Patriots ended up losing the game, but the move earned him the respect of his teammates as more than just another kicker. And at six feet, 200 pounds, he was certainly more than just another kicker: He was a well-known workout warrior, spending as much time in the gym as the rest of his teammates.

He had a rough start as a rookie, making just three of his seven field goal attempts to open the season, and many in the media were wondering when Bahr was going to return. But Vinatieri remained unflappable. Like many of the Patriots who would come of age professionally in the 2001 season, the early slights contributed to a thicker skin. He never backed down from doubters, even after missing three field goals in a 17–10 loss to Buffalo. "You've got to be able to put it behind you," he said afterward. "You're not going to have perfect games every time. If you dwell on something in the past, it's going to carry on into the future. You can't do that. You just watch the films, correct your mistakes, and go on to the next day, and hopefully, the next week, you can redeem yourself. Then, if you go 4-for-4, then maybe they'll forget about the last game." Two weeks later, all talk of Bahr went out the window when Vinatieri booted five field goals—including the game winner in overtime—to help carry New England past Jacksonville. "Every week, every game, you're kicking for your job," Vinatieri shrugged after making the first game-winning kick of his career. "If you get some mixed emotions, that's going to carry over into your next game, your next kick."

He started to settle in nicely, and developed a reputation as a fairly reliable kicker. He enjoyed a small level of success in pressure situations, booting eight game winners in his first five seasons with the Patriots. In 2001, he took it all to a new level, kicking three regular-season game winners that year alone, bringing his career total of game-winning field goals to eleven. But of those kicks, only two of them came in two do-or-die situations, one on September 12, 1999, to help New England beat the Jets, 30–28, and the other one on December 2, 2001, to again beat New York, 17–16. The others came with the game tied. If he had missed any one of those nine kicks, the worst that would have happened was that the game would have remained tied.

But against the Raiders, it went beyond a do-or-die situation. It was a forty-five-yarder, directly into a harsh snowfall. Pregame attempts from beyond forty yards had been difficult, and that was before the snow really started to fall. "We were pushing the envelope a little bit," Vinatieri would recall later. "As the game went along, the range ended up dwindling down a little bit just because we knew footing and the snow was going to be a problem. Going out there for that last one, that was about our range. But the guys up front did a great job, my snapper [Lonie Paxton] and my holder [Ken Walter] did great. I knew it was straight enough, but I had to wait a while to see if it was going to be long enough." Vinatieri boomed a low line drive that had everyone in Foxboro Stadium holding their breath. People watching on television weren't completely sure it made it through the uprights, while those in the stadium were just as uncertain . . . until the roar went up from those sitting behind the goal posts. The kick had just barely made it over the crossbar. The game was tied at thirteen.

"It was a situation where I felt like I made pretty decent contact and I kind of line-drived it a little bit more. I obviously would have liked to get a little bit more elevation on it, but once I knew it cleared the line and I looked up," he said. "I kind of waited and held my breath for a couple of seconds until it went over the bar, and then it was time to celebrate."

After celebrating the fact that their kicker had forced overtime, Brady and the Patriots never let their foot off the gas pedal. New England won the coin toss, and the Raiders, perhaps rattled by the call, were clearly on their heels. As snow continued to fall late into the New England night, Brady orchestrated a fifteen-play, 61-yard drive that brought the Patriots to the Oakland eight-yard line, making it a 23-yard field goal attempt. Compared to the 45-yarder that tied the game at the end of regulation, this one was a relative chip shot. He easily connected. Patriots win, 16–13. And as Lonie Paxton celebrated in the end zone with snow angels, the real old-timers reacted with glee, recalling the playoff loss to the Raiders twenty-five years before, a game that had turned on Ben Dreith's controversial roughing-the-passer call. "What goes around comes around," said Gil Santos, who broadcast both games. "Revenge is a dish best served cold. If you don't like it, that's just too bad. Been there, had to suffer through it. Now, it's your turn."

For Patriots fans, who were used to years of bad coaching, bad bounces, bad calls, and just plain bad football, it was like something out of a dream. "We've been trained to expect the breaks to go against us," Dan Shaughnessy wrote in *The Boston Globe* later that week. "These Patriots are different. They get all the breaks. And now they are one game from a trip to the Super Bowl. They are underdogs but we have learned not to bet against them. Something always happens. They've got the good karma and cosmic rays. The larger forces are with them."

"I was interviewed by someone on some talk show a day or two days after that particular game, and the guy asked me, 'Where does it rank?'" Santos said of the playoff win over the Raiders. "And I said, 'That was the best Patriots win I've ever had the good fortune to broadcast. And the only thing that would ever top that game is if we win the Super Bowl on the final play.'"

Two weeks later, Santos would get his chance.

During their postseason run that year, Tom Brady gradually came to be identified as the face of the Patriots. But Troy Brown was the heart of the franchise. An eighth-round draft pick out of Marshall in 1993, Brown was a chatty young man as a rookie. And on a Bill Parcells–run team, it was better to be seen and not heard. "He used to talk a lot," recalled sportswriter Dan Pires of Brown, "and what Bruce Armstrong and Ben Coates did was put him in a barrel and roll him down the ramps at Foxboro Stadium." Brown spent most of his first few years operating on the fringes of the league. After a thoroughly unspectacular rookie year, he was released on August 28, 1994, only to re-sign midway in the season as a return man. A promising career was again derailed briefly when the Patriots signed veteran returner Dave Meggett. (Meggett was a Parcells favorite from way back, having played with the Giants from 1989 through 1994.) But Brown was re-signed several times before working his way into the rotation as a receiver midway through the 1996 season.

Even though he had continued to get more and more snaps at wide receiver, he still worked extensively on special teams (but after 1996, it was almost entirely on punt returns) and became a clear favorite of Belichick when the new coach arrived. In his first year under Belichick, Brown's receiving numbers doubled. But it was more than that. This was the sort of player Belichick could use: a versatile player who wouldn't blink, no matter what situation he was dropped into. "Troy Brown," the coach said on more than one occasion, "is a football-playing dude." And in 2001, Brown emerged as Brady's No. 1 target, catching 101 passes in the regular season and shattering the single-season mark on his way to a spot in the Pro Bowl. But it was special teams where he had initially made his mark. "Special teams got me on this team," Brown said. "They got me this opportunity. I'll always play them."

Entering the AFC Championship Game against the Steelers, it was clear the Patriots were going to be at a disadvantage against the typically ferocious Pittsburgh defense. In addition, even though Steelers quarterback Kordell Stewart was erratic at best, running back Jerome Bettis was poised to return, and it was believed their emotional leader would give them the spark necessary to get over the top and into the Super Bowl.

The one place where New England held a clear edge was on special teams. Belichick had gotten his start as a special teams coach with Denver, Detroit, and the New York Giants, and he knew that in a tight game special teams could serve as a tipping point. Early in his tenure with the Patriots, Belichick's approach was made clear when he told special teams coach Brad Seely that no player was off-limits when it came to choosing special teams. On most teams, the special teams—other than a return man or a punter or kicker—were mostly backups, scrubs who were simply looking to play their way into a starting role. In New England, starting safety Tebucky Jones served as a gunner on punt coverage. In addition, starters like Brown, Roman Phifer, Richard Seymour, Brandon Mitchell, Tedy Bruschi, and Mike Vrabel all routinely joined Jones on special teams.

In stark contrast, the Steelers' special teams were spotty. Kicker Kris Brown was shaky, having missed a league-high fourteen field goals in the regular season. And the Patriots held a wild card in Troy Brown, who had broken two punt returns for touchdowns earlier in the season. On those two punt returns, Pittsburgh noticed, he had taken them directly into the teeth of the opposing special teams unit. On both attempts (one against the Browns and another against the Panthers), he had barely moved five to ten yards left or right, preferring instead to find a seam and— *whoosh*—take off. The Steelers told reporters during the week that if they could force Brown outside on returns, they would have an excellent chance at negating his breaking a long one.

So much for special teams homework. In the first quarter, a

sixty-four-yard punt by Josh Miller was negated when Troy Edwards intentionally stepped out of bounds while running downfield in kick coverage. On the next attempt, Brown gathered in the punt at the New England 45, and—*whoosh*—took it straight into the heart of the Pittsburgh special teams unit. He squeezed past linebacker John Fiala and got a little hop step over downed cornerback Jason Simmons before cruising into the end zone—alongside wide receiver Freddie "Boom Boom" Coleman—to make it 7–0.

That was just act 1 of a three-act play. After the Patriots got the ball back, Brady quickly moved New England into Pittsburgh territory. But after finding Brown (who finished with eight catches for 121 yards) on a crossing pattern that brought the Patriots to the Pittsburgh 40, he was hit from behind by Steelers safety Lee Flowers. Flowers landed on the back of Brady's legs, and the quarterback's right leg appeared to fold awkwardly beneath him. He was quickly yanked from the game in favor of Drew Bledsoe, sidelined with a balky left ankle.

It had been a strange few weeks for Bledsoe, who had stood on the sidelines in the snow and watched the greatest playoff win in the history of the franchise the week before. But now, with his father in the Heinz Field stands watching—even though it was wildly unlikely he would play—he was back at the controls, starting the beginning of act 2 of the AFC Championship Game. "Guess who's back?" he asked with a smile when he entered the huddle for the first time since September 23, 2001. And on his first play from scrimmage, he found David Patten on a fifteen-yard pass, a vintage Bledsoe bullet that got New England to the Pittsburgh 25. On his second, he rolled out toward the sideline, scampering for some daylight inside the Steelers' 25. A step from the sidelines, he was knocked sideways by Pittsburgh safety Chad Scott, a hit that had eerie parallels to the Mo Lewis tackle earlier in the season. With Brady on his way to the locker room and Bledsoe on the ground, there was a moment where everyone wondered if, once again, this was where the ride would end.

But Bledsoe popped up quickly, shouting encouragement to his teammates. And with just over a minute to play in the first half, he hit Patten in the far corner of the end zone, giving the Patriots a 14–3 halftime lead. He was 3-for-3 for 36 yards and a touchdown pass—the only touchdown the New England offense would get all day.

Act 3 came in the third quarter when Pittsburgh lined up for a thirty-four-yard field goal attempt. True to form, Kris Brown's kick was a low line drive. Brandon Mitchell got up high enough to block it, and Troy Brown scooped up the football. He was brought down from behind by the kicker, but not before he lateraled the football to Antwan Harris, who scooted into the end zone for the score that would seal it.

For a coach who, like Belichick, got his start on special teams (Cowher was special teams coach for the Browns in 1985 and 1986), the game provided a galling reminder of how poor play by special teams can affect a season. The two touchdowns allowed in the New England playoff loss were among four touchdowns allowed by Steelers special teams in their final four games—two on punt returns and two on failed field goal attempts. Of the four touchdowns Pittsburgh allowed in the postseason, three were on special teams. As a result, two days after the loss, Cowher fired special teams coach Jay Hayes, and Flowers ripped their special teams play, saying they didn't approach that aspect of their game "seriously enough."

The Steelers would draw to within 21–17, but couldn't get any closer, with a Vinatieri field goal ending matters, giving New England an unlikely trip to the Super Bowl. It was a galling loss for Pittsburgh and head coach Bill Cowher, who came down with a nasty case of foot-in-mouth disease in the week leading up to the game. The lantern-jawed coach told reporters that he set aside Monday and Tuesday before the AFC Championship Game against the Patriots so the team could take care of their travel plans for Super Bowl XXXVI. (It was a move that was common practice around the league. Not that it mattered to Belichick, who used the perceived slight to the Patriots' advantage, telling his players the Steelers were disrespecting them.) "All week, all they wanted to talk about was their defense, their receivers, and their place in history," Bruschi said. "Well, guess what? Their place in history is losing to the Patriots in the AFC Championship Game and going home." Linebacker Willie McGinest gleefully joined in, mocking the fans with taunts, "Cancel those reservations." It also didn't help Pittsburgh matters that, prior to the game, the Patriots had discovered a room next to their locker room with several boxes of "AFC Champions" T-shirts. Belichick took one of them and gave it to safety Lawyer Milloy, who left it on the blackboard during pregame preparations. After the game, assistant coach Pepper Johnson ripped it from the wall tossed it to the floor and stomped on it. Player after player—and coach after coach—did the same thing as they returned to the locker room, including Belichick.

For Bledsoe, the win was an overwhelming, surreal moment. As the game ended, his eyes filled with tears, and he collapsed to the turf in an emotional embrace with Bruschi. "The team has done great all year, but for me personally it's been a very long year," he said. "It started all the way back in training camp with the loss of my quarterback coach [Dick Rehbein] who passed away. Then we started out 0–2 and I got injured. Then I wasn't able to get back on the field.

"I have to say honestly that I had envisioned the scenario being the case because that's what you have to prepare for during the week. But to actually have it happen and then to be kneeling on the ball at the end of the game and going to the Super Bowl . . . it's just a little overwhelming."

It was also more than a little overwhelming for hordes of Patriots fans who, when Belichick took over the team twenty-five months before, had inherited a team that was 8–8 and taking on water. But between January 2000 and February 2002, New England had changed thirty-eight of the fifty-three players on the roster. Twenty-one of the thirty-eight newcomers were free agents, including seventeen veteran free agents signed in 2001. Those seventeen included ten unrestricted free agents and seven veterans let go by other teams. Of that group, seven started this season, five played as top-of-the-line substitutes, three were key performers on special teams and two were backups. The New England model appeared to shatter the myth that salary cap constricts a general manager in his efforts to overhaul a team.

One of the things that helped speed the process was the fact that much of the roster was stocked with ex-Jets and ex-Browns who were known to Belichick from his days in Cleveland and New York. In the days leading up to the Super Bowl, Belichick said he didn't go out and target those players, but that level of familiarity helped to speed the turnaround.

"It's a little bit overstated in thinking that an objective when you take a job is to hurry up and bring as many players as you can from the place that you left," Belichick said. "What I would say is that when you get into a new situation and you have a need on your team and you're considering two or three guys for that need, because of the familiarity and because the player knows your system, you have a tendency to go with the guy you know and who knows you. I think it happens more that way than 'Gee, I want to try to get six guys from that team.' That's not really the thought process.

"I think a good example of that for us this year was Fred Coleman. We had some problems at receiver. A couple of guys got hurt and then Terry [Glenn]'s situation and we brought in three or four receivers. I can't sit here and tell you that Fred Coleman was better than all the other guys. But what we did know about Fred was that he was tough and dependable. Charlie [Weis], Scott Pioli, and myself had seen him in practice for over a year and we had seen him in training camp and we knew what he could do, he knew our system, it was in the middle of the season and we felt like he could come in and probably contribute quicker than some of the other people we had.

"That's not to say that the other guys aren't going to be good football players or that they couldn't contribute some where else. But at that point in time, Fred was probably just a little bit better fit for us. It wasn't so much that he was an ex-Jet as it was that we were familiar with him."

But maybe the most impressive thing about the group was the fact that the Patriots had the third lowest payroll in the league, and had doled out just $2.123 million in signing bonuses—roughly $1.5 million less than the bonus Seattle gave prized defensive lineman Chad Eaton when he left New England earlier that spring for Seattle via free agency—to gain all seventeen. (The largest signing bonus—$625,000—went to Mike Compton.)

Of course, all that was great. But few gave the Patriots any real shot at actually *winning* Super Bowl XXXVI. The Rams were considered heavy favorites; among bookies, they were getting 14 points, the second-highest line in Super Bowl history, and a Super Bowl victory was going to be their crowning achievement. "I think the team was confident," St. Louis GM Charley Armey said years later. "We had a very good football team at that time. We were very, very confident that if we would go in there and play well, we would have an opportunity to win the ball game." That feeling was well founded: They had won Super Bowl XXXIV two years previously, and they were set to move into some rarefied air. Rams officials talked of creating a special Super Bowl ring for the achievement, connecting their Super Bowl XXXIV jewelry with the rings they would presumably receive for winning Super Bowl XXXVI to create a Super ring, so those who won both titles would be able to walk around, in effect, with a pair of diamond-encrusted knuckle-dusters on their middle and ring fingers. The cockiness would ultimately doom the Rams. "With that high-flying offense and not really knowing a lot about them, we really felt confident going into the game," said former St. Louis linebacker Don Davis, who would join the Patriots two years later. That idea was confirmed weeks later when NFL Films released the official Super Bowl XXXVI DVD. Prior to the game, St. Louis wide receiver Ricky Proehl is seen smiling and waving at a cameraman. "Tonight, the dynasty is born," says Proehl with a grin.

There was none of that coming from the Patriots, either on or off the record. The only real pregame drama involved whether or not New England would go with Brady or Bledsoe at quarterback. (Even U2 got into the act the Wednesday before the game, deflecting the burgeoning controversy with mock-serious tones at a press conference to discuss their halftime performance. "We're not going to be fielding any questions on that issue," said guitarist the Edge when asked about the Brady-Bledsoe debate. "It does have to be said that Bledsoe has a superior long pass and that Brady's ankle has been a problem . . ." Lead singer Bono quickly interjected, saying the choice between the two was a "very sore subject" within the band, before adding, "We're here to bring peace," he said. "We want to bring peace to Bledsoe and Brady.") But with the former fully healed from the injury he suffered against the Steelers, Belichick officially named Brady the starter Wednesday afternoon. And in his final press conference before the game, the usually tight-lipped Belichick let slip a key piece of information: Many things would be different this time around. "I think the most important thing in this game for us is that our team needs to understand how we have to play," Belichick said the Friday before the game. "We can't play St. Louis the way we played them the first time, or we're going to have the same result."

For even the most casual of fans, it was an easy-to-follow contrast in styles. The Rams were all about offense. Mike Martz had led St. Louis to a 500-plus point season for the third consecutive year, the first time a team had ever done that. Meanwhile, the Patriots were the Little Engine That Could, a collection of players led by a quarterback who was looking more and more like Joe Hardy and a defensive mastermind of a coach who had never met an offense he couldn't stop. That contrast extended to the team introductions. After an extended pregame show that included Mariah Carey, Paul McCartney, the Boston Pops, and former New York City mayor Rudolph Giuliani, the introductions began. (The length of the pregame show—three and a half hours—was galling to many of the players. "I hope you enjoyed the pregame show," Brady told reporters afterward. He took a nap in the locker room while the spectacle unfolded on the Superdome floor. "We all hated it.") The Rams offense was introduced first, and, as was the custom in these circumstances, they were done so individually. Wide receiver Torry Holt came out without his helmet, maximizing his close-up on football's biggest stage. New Orleans native Marshall Faulk got the loudest ovation.

The Patriots, meanwhile, had decided to eschew the traditional introductions, instead coming out as a group. In the press box, reporters from around the world gasped at the show of unity, and many of them seized on the theme. *What a great idea to show community and togetherness! This is truly America's team!* But New England's idea was not rooted in any sort of post-September 11 good feeling designed especially for maximum exposure at the Super Bowl. It actually started at the season opener in Cincinnati, when Bengals public address announcer Tom Kinder started announcing the New England defensive unit while they were still in the locker room. The perceived lack of respect riled many of the Patriots, and it was safety Lawyer Milloy who said, "To hell with it. Let's run out there as a team." It was a practice they continued throughout the season, occasionally alternating the defense or the offense.

As the game began, Belichick's pregame proclamation rang true. The Patriots were again whipping up a nasty series of fronts for Warner and the Rams, with Belichick using his defensive backs to present a whole new series of looks. But instead of running a series of constant blitzes, as they did in their first game against St. Louis in November, there were only a few. The receivers were jammed off the line by a swarm of defensive backs who threw off the precise timing patterns that were such a big part of the success of the St. Louis offense. They focused not on Warner, but on his receivers. On the night, Belichick used four defensive backs on nine plays, five defensive backs on ten plays, six defensive backs on thirteen plays and seven defensive backs on one play. Warner and the Rams' passing game were out of rhythm all night, their flow disrupted by the physical play of the New England secondary.

The secondary received plenty of support because of the linebackers. Those fast, smart overachievers that Belichick and Pioli had targeted over the previous twenty-five months because of their smarts and versatility—the Phifers and Vrabels—along with the veterans like Bruschi, Johnson, and McGinest, were asked to do a lot against the Rams. They not only had to provide occasional help in coverage, but there was almost always a spy on Faulk, who spent much of the game being knocked off his very precise timing routes by linebackers, especially outside linebackers McGinest and Vrabel, when he lined up in the slot. (NFL Films has a memorable series of clips from the game that show Faulk getting chipped time and again by New England's outside linebackers.) And with fewer down linemen in the game, they also provided support in the pass rush. While there weren't many blitzes, when they did come, they came from the linebacker spot, and they made a sizable difference. New England blitzed just once in the first half, but it was a doozy. On first and ten from the St. Louis 39-yard line, Vrabel came hard from Warner's right side. When Rams right tackle Rod Jones erroneously blocked down instead of out (he confessed to being confused by the coverage), Vrabel had an open lane to Warner. Vrabel didn't get the sack, but he crushed the St. Louis quarterback, who rushed his throw. It was consequently off the mark to Bruce in the right flat. Ty Law intercepted it easily and took off down the sideline for a 47-yard return. The touchdown gave New England a 7–3 lead with 8:49 left in the second quarter.

By midway through the second quarter, the Patriots' defensive approach looked familiar to old New York Giants fans. When New York met Buffalo in Super Bowl XXV, the Giants—and defensive coordinator Bill Belichick—decided to try and rob Buffalo of its passing game. The Giants allowed All-Pro running back Thurman Thomas to do what he wished and sought to punish the fleet Buffalo receivers with a series of exotic looks in the secondary. The stratagem worked. The Giants edged the Bills, 20–19, and Belichick's game plan is now on display at the Pro Football Hall of Fame. In that game, Buffalo made in-game adjustments. Realizing that New York was giving up on stopping the run, Thomas ran wild in the second half, finishing with 135 rushing yards and nearly leading Buffalo to victory.

Eleven years later, the Rams decided to try and stick to their original plan of pass, pass, pass. They ended up with twice as many passing attempts as rushing attempts on the night. In retrospect, with all the defensive backs and so few linemen or linebackers, the Rams almost certainly could have run the ball with ease against the Patriots. (Faulk did get 76 yards on 17 carries, one of his lowest rushing totals of the season.) But Mike Martz and St. Louis were content to keep passing the football. It remains an age-old debate among football fans throughout the Midwest. "You have Marshall Faulk as an MVP tailback in his prime—in his hometown. What makes more sense? Give him the football," Armey said. "He's in his prime, an MVP." As a result, New England—not the Rams—was able to control the tempo. And after a Proehl fumble shortly before the end of the first half, the Patriots added another touchdown when Brady hit Patten with an eight-yard strike in the corner of the end zone. It was their only offensive touchdown of the night, and marked the third consecutive postseason game in which the Patriots got just one touchdown out of their offense, and it made the score 14–3.

The Brady-to-Patten connection spoke to the real difference between the two teams. During the season, that pass play was in the Patriots' playbook as a simple down-and-out, part of their red-zone package. Patten, lined up to the right of the quarterback, would simply take off for the end zone and then make a ninety-degree turn toward the pylon. But two days before, New England decided to tweak the play. They had noticed that when guarding a wide receiver in similar situations, St. Louis cornerback Dexter McCleon had developed a tendency to jump the route and make a lunge for the football. So Belichick and Weis told Brady and Patten to alter the route slightly. Instead of making a beeline for the pylon and turning to look for the pass, Patten was to break for the pylon, but then break again toward the corner of the end zone. Once the situation presented itself in the game, Patten made the adjustment—after McCleon bit—and made the catch in the end zone that gave New England the lead.

It was more of the same in the third quarter, as Otis Smith picked off a Warner pass to set up a thirty-seven-yard field goal from Vinatieri with 1:18 left, making it 17–3. Remarkably, the Patriots appeared to have pushed their lead to 24–3 when Phifer forced a Warner fumble on New England's two-yard line and Tebucky Jones took it all the way back for a touchdown. But a holding call on McGinest—the original regulator appeared to mug Faulk in hopes of keeping him from busting loose out of the backfield—negated the return, and the Rams made the Patriots pay on the next play when Warner scored on a keeper to make it 17–10. McGinest made up for it shortly afterward with a sack on the Rams' next possession, but there was a growing sense that the Patriots' defense suddenly had a tiger by the tail. That belief seemed well founded when St. Louis tied the score with 1:30 remaining. Warner lofted one to Proehl, who put a little deke on Jones and walked into the end zone to make it 17-all.

In the broadcast booth, Madden was saying the Patriots should pack it in and play for overtime. After all, there was 1:21 left on the clock, and New England was out of time-outs. On the New England sidelines, it was a different story. Offensive coordinator Charlie Weis would later recall the sideline conversation in his book *No Excuses*.

"Bill turned to me and asked, 'What do you think?'"

"I think they've got all the momentum," I said. "I think we should go down and try and score."

"OK, call something safe. If we get a first down here, we'll go ahead and be more aggressive. Let's make sure we don't start off with a sack."

Both coaches told Brady that if they got into a fix, they could always drop the plan and play for overtime. *Play smart. Play conservative. Play the game that got you here.* But before Brady walked out to join his teammates, Bledsoe called him back for one more quick word. "Sling it," he told Brady. "Go out there and win the game."

The drive began with 1:21 left on the clock at the New England 17-yard line. Brady avoided a blitzing Leonard Little with a simple five-yard dump pass to little-used running back J. R. Redmond. Brady added another eight-yard pass to Redmond for a first down at the New England 30-yard line before spiking the ball, stopping the clock with forty-one seconds left. The offense had fulfilled Belichick's first two wishes, avoiding a sack on the first play and getting a first down. They now started to dial it up a notch. On the fourth play of the drive, Brady again found Redmond, this time on another short pass. Redmond found a small measure of daylight and just barely made the sidelines, stopping the clock with thirty-three seconds left at the Patriots' 41-yard line.

With first and ten at their own 41, Brady barely avoided a blitz, evading St. Louis safety Adam Archuleta at the last second and flinging the ball toward the Rams' sideline for an incompletion. On second down, the Patriots called "64 Max All-In," a play designed to have all the receivers run in-cuts at a variety of depths downfield. Brady found Troy Brown over the middle for a massive twenty-three-yard gain, taking the ball down to the St. Louis 36 with twenty-three seconds left.

In the booth, Madden was stunned, quickly backtracking on the words he had uttered no more than three minutes beforehand. "At some point, when you're in the Super Bowl, you have to let it all hang out," he said as the face of the New England offensive coordinator flashed onscreen. "And I'll say this: Charlie Weis and this Patriot team, they are letting it all hang out."

The Patriots were now in field goal range for Vinatieri—it would have been a 53-yarder, clearly makeable by a guy who had never missed a field goal indoors over the course of his career—but New England was going to try and edge a little closer. With a first and ten situation at the 36, St. Louis brought a blitz, their final one of the night. But Brady hit tight end Jermaine Wiggins on another short pass, this one a quick six-yard down and out that got the Patriots to the St. Louis 30. Brady walked gradually up to the line of scrimmage and, with seven seconds left, spiked the football, holding it gently in the air after it popped back up off the turf. The sight of Brady standing and holding the football gently aloft with his left hand was an oddly calming image. "He held it as if he were posing for a picture," wrote Michael Holley in *Patriot Reign* of those final few moments of Super Bowl XXXVI. "Bringing style to the mundane, the sixth-round pick suddenly looked cool."

Madden was more to the point. "What Tom Brady just did," he said, "gives me goose bumps."

Brady jogged off the field, and Vinatieri and the rest of the field goal unit walked on. The kicker had started growing a playoff beard shortly before the divisional playoff game against the Raiders, and it had grown long and shaggy over the course of the month. "When he walked on the field today, I saw a bunch of security guards move over to check him out," special teams ace Larry Izzo told reporters when asked about Vinatieri's look during warmups. "I told him he looked like John Walker, like he was ready to go fight for the Taliban."

Gil Santos had been with the team through most of the bad times. He went all the way back to Fenway Park. He'd witnessed the fire in the grandstand at Boston College, the nuttiness of Clive Rush and the Black Power Defense, and the Great Flush at Foxboro Stadium. He was there for Billy Sullivan, the Monday Night Massacre, Victor Kiam's ineptitude, and the battles between Bob Kraft and Bill Parcells. Now, he was preparing to call the biggest moment in the history of the franchise. He had a million thoughts racing through his mind, but went back to Broadcasting 101. *This was a big moment. Don't screw it up.*

"Let them know where the ball is, how long the field goal will be, what hash mark it's at, who's snapping, who's holding, how much time is left," Santos said of the blueprint for those final few moments. "Just describe the play, and that's the way I do any play of any game. Describe the play. Then, after the play is concluded and what happens has happened, that's when you just let the emotion of the moment and your own brain try to put words together to describe what's going on.

"You just react to it. It's just reaction. You have to look at it, describe it, and tell them what's happening. Then you just react."

The reaction was a positive one. Vinatieri's kick went straight and true—it would have been good from sixty yards—and a hail of red, white, and blue confetti rained down on the field. The Patriots had won, 20–17, and were Super Bowl champions. "Hey, New England. You have the best football team in the world," Santos said with a disbelieving laugh in the booth, crying and hugging his wife and son and broadcast partner Gino Cappelletti.

Vinatieri galloped off the field, his face frozen in a big grin beneath his bushy beard. Brady, goggle-eyed in amazement, slapped one of Bledsoe's shoulder pads and shouting excitedly, "We won!" Smith jumped on the shoulders of Law and mugged happily for the cameras. Long snapper Lonie Paxton recreated his snow angel routine from the divisional playoff win over the Raiders, dashing madly for the end zone before falling backward to the turf and waving his hands and arms in celebration. And massive offensive lineman Mike Compton fell to the ground, sobbing in disbelief.

But the lasting image many have of that game is not the Vinatieri kick or Brady's last-second drive, but a shot of the quarterback afterward on the podium. It's an image that's familiar to anyone who followed the team, a small piece of video that was captured by NFL Films that's been replayed over and over. He's standing next to Belichick's father, Steve, and wearing a Super Bowl Champions T-shirt. There's a backward baseball cap on his head, and he's pointing both index fingers at his sisters, who are sitting in the stands. As confetti falls gently around him like snowflakes, he grabs his head and shakes it from side to side with a goofy, disbelieving grin on his face. It was the same goofy, disbelieving grin that Patriots fans everywhere had that night. For all the world, no one ever thought it could happen. *The Patriots had won the Super Bowl.*

In the wake of September 11, the NFL dressed up the victory as a triumph for all Americans, a win for Patriots everywhere, that made even the most cynical fan weak in the knees. ("Tonight, we are all Patriots!" Kraft hollered during the postgame ceremony.) While it would speak volumes about all the things the NFL likes to hold dear—the triumph of teamwork, an underdog's struggle against the odds in an all-for-one effort that everyone could identify with—the win was more about the triumph of a new system. Belichick and Pioli had created a new philosophy in team building, one completely unique to the NFL. They did not have the best players at each position. (In fact, they had just three players selected to the Pro Bowl—Brady, Troy Brown, and Lawyer Milloy. For a Super Bowl champion, it was an amazingly low number.) But collectively, the whole of the team was greater than the sum of its parts. And that whole was driven by a core of players who bought into the system, totally and completely.

Suddenly, the idea of giving up a first-round pick for Belichick didn't seem so odd.

"The message—listen up, you goobers—is that the game is won in the head, not the body," wrote former *Boston Globe* columnist Leigh Montville in the days following the victory. "Thinking counts. . . . Do your homework. Figure out how to cover your weaknesses, maximize your strengths, do what you're supposed to do and 'bingo,' as Mr. Troy Brown might say. Preparation is everything. Anybody can do this! Everybody, helping each other, can do this! It all works."

CHAPTER FIVE

# "THE NEW PRINCE OF THE NFL"

The value board at that point really just clearly put him as the top value. [Tom] Brady is a guy who has obviously played at a high level of competition in front of a lot of people. He's been in a lot of pressure situations. We felt that this year his decision-making was improved from his junior year after he took over for [Brian] Griese and cut his interceptions down. [He's] a good, tough, competitive, smart quarterback that is a good value and how he does and what he'll be able to . . . we'll just put him out there with everybody else and let him compete and see what happens.

—BILL BELICHICK AFTER DAY 2 OF THE 2000 NFL DRAFT

Very tall with a thin build. Needs to upgrade his overall strength. Pocket passer with average quickness. Can slide from pressure, but is not very elusive. Doesn't look to run. Holds the ball a bit low, but has a fairly quick release. Lacks a strong arm. Doesn't rifle the long outs, but he's an accurate passer with a good feel for touch. Sails some throws and hangs some deep balls. Leader. Eyeballs his primary target at times, but shows the ability to come off and find alternates. Generally makes good decisions. Had a good Orange Bowl.

—SPORTS ILLUSTRATED'S SCOUTING REPORT ON
TOM BRADY PRIOR TO THE 2000 DRAFT

Quarterback Rohan Davey was five feet from absolute madness.

A throng of roughly thirty-five reporters had gathered in a narrow area around the locker of quarterback Tom Brady—no more than five feet by five feet, really—jockeying for the best spots before the New England quarterback arrived to address the media. By 2002, if you were a local reporter, these once-a-week sessions were the only way you were going to ask Brady a question. He had stopped going to the podium for press conferences—he said he didn't want to draw too much attention to himself—and answered questions at his locker. The one-on-ones had strictly become the domain of national outlets like ESPN and *Sports Illustrated*.

Despite the fact the Patriots' media relations staff would always transcribe most of the press conference for print media (and the fact that they would provide stepstools to make it easier for TV cameras to get a clear shot of the quarterback), it was still a nasty scrum that often carried over into the lockers next to Brady. Those players who had the unfortunate distinction of being lockered next to the starting quarterback would either be forced to dress before Brady's press conference or wait until the media had left the locker room to finish getting ready.

It was a place where smaller reporters could get hurt if they weren't careful. Media members were always getting squeezed against each other, pushing their tape recorders or microphones forward in hopes of getting some usable audio. Cameras were maneuvering for position, and many reporters would get bopped in the head. You had to push and shove, maneuvering for just the right angle so you could get some face time with the Super Bowl MVP. If you weren't lucky enough to get to the first few rows of questions, maybe you could shout one question above the din in hopes of getting it through to Brady before the media availability session was completed.

Usually, most locker room sessions with Brady were given to the electronic media first, most of whom were simply looking for a quick sound bite that would reference this week's opponent or a feature on another member of the team. *Tom, would you say the Bills are the toughest defense you've faced all year? Tom, has your confidence in Ben Watson grown over the years?* Then, after five or ten minutes, the cameras and tape recorders would edge their way out of the scrum, giving way to a second wave of media, usually the print reporters. At this point, the questions usually became a little more in-depth. For example, it wasn't uncommon for Brady to really break down the intricacies of the game in front of reporters. He once spent ten minutes talking about the differences in the grips between the screen pass and the deep ball.

Throughout most all of the sessions, Brady remained pleasant and attentive to almost every question. (Despite the efforts of his offensive linemen, who occasionally sneak a noise machine into Brady's locker beforehand, one that would either make fart noises or rattle off some sort of profane putdown, usually at the worst moment possible. There was also the occasional threat of silly string.) Even in the spotlight, with multiple camera lights in his face and a sizable crowd of reporters around him, he stood calmly and politely. By the start of the 2002 season, reporters noticed he had developed the amazing ability to smile and talk at the same time, and appear completely and totally sincere while doing so. It was an astounding characteristic, one perfected by politicians and television anchormen alike. He rarely appeared rattled by the spotlight. It was smiling and talking, smiling and talking, smiling and talking. It was disarming to questioners. *Nothing* shocked him. No matter how inane the question might be, Brady always had a camera-ready sound bite. It was a relatively small part of the job of being a National Football League quarterback. But for his teammates, Brady's job as lightning rod for the Boston sports media was welcome. Let the TV cameras and tape recorders surround Brady. They would be happy to rest in the shadows, out of the spotlight.

In the late summer of 2002, Rohan Davey—then, the Patriots rookie third-string quarterback out of Louisiana State—watched the scene with a small smile. He had been drafted the previous spring, and was sitting behind Brady and Damon Huard on the depth chart. To the public, his duties that season consisted of little more than holding a clipboard and working with the scout team in practice, trying to give the starters a good look at what to expect that week. It was a difficult job for Davey, especially when you consider he was the starting quarterback for LSU the season before, helping lead the Tigers to an SEC title and a win in the Sugar Bowl. In Baton Rouge, Davey was king. On the campus of Louisiana State, *he* was Tom Brady. Reporters questioned. Fans swooned. And games were won. Here in New England, he was a glorified valet.

But there was hope. A third-string quarterback has to find his inspiration where he can get it. And Davey had it, standing less than five feet from Brady. There, surrounded by a pack of reporters, stood a guy who was in Davey's position the year before. He was a living, breathing example of the fact that the journey from anonymous third-string quarterback to Super Bowl hero was a shorter trip than anyone could ever know.

At the start of the 2001 preseason, Brady was a third-string quarterback, sitting behind a Pro Bowler in Bledsoe and a veteran backup in Huard. More important, he was on a team that was going nowhere. In 2002, he had become a bona fide pop icon. After winning Super Bowl MVP honors, he was selected as a judge for the Miss USA Pageant, named one of *People* magazine's "50 Most Beautiful People," and had a brief appearance at the Oscars. He caused a near riot when he went to Disney World. He was romantically linked to a variety of high-profile actresses, including infamous party girl Tara Reid. And he found himself on the cover of *Sports Illustrated*—without a shirt—for a cover story that dubbed him "the new prince of the NFL."

Brady's celebrity was a colossal change for a region and a franchise that was used to vanilla-bland, less-than-glamorous athletes. A generation ago, New England had preferred its sports heroes to be the strong and silent type, stoic men who performed on the field and then disappeared into a relatively anonymous private life away from the games. The other cities could boast crossover stars like Joe Namath, Reggie Jackson, O. J. Simpson or Magic Johnson, charismatic figures who transcended sports. In Boston, it was a far different story. The job of Patriots quarterback didn't have the cachet of, say, a quarterback for the Dallas Cowboys or the New York Jets. It was not a glamorous position. Until Drew Bledsoe arrived in the early 1990s, the best-known quarterback in the history of the franchise was likely Steve Grogan, a well-meaning and relatively quiet Midwesterner, one of the most durable, toughest players in team history. However, he was by no means a charismatic figure off the field, which was pretty much in line with the other New England sports figures of the past. Carl Yastrzemski never hosted *Saturday Night Live*. Larry Bird never appeared in *People* magazine. And Ted Williams never showed up on the cover of *Sport Magazine* with his shirt off. And that was the way it was.

Brady was New England's first legitimate sports hero of the twenty-first century. His good looks, charisma, and charm vaulted him into a new realm of sports celebrity, one where sports and pop culture intersected. Teenage girls—and area football fans—swooned over his every move. It was rarefied air. He would go on to play himself in *The Simpsons* and *Family Guy*, and serve as a host of *Saturday Night Live*. He was sought after by national chains as a pitchman. And he was an unabashed bachelor, living a life that he only dreamed of when he was a relatively anonymous backup quarterback. "In case you missed it, one night last week, Brady made his first real visit to Tabloid America when he was seen dancing with pop diva Mariah Carey in a Back Bay nightspot," wrote *Boston Herald* columnist Gerry Callahan in April 2002. "Well, not dancing, exactly. Bumping and grinding, according to *New York* magazine, which first reported the story. Say good night, Tom. It's over. You have officially left the ranks of run-of-the-mill sports celebrities and ascended to an exclusive place where only the most beautiful and successful athletes are welcome, where the E! Channel and ESPN collide, where Jason Sehorn and Angie Harmon rule as First Couple, and Joe Namath is considered a deity."

The spotlight got a little warmer for Brady when, on April 21, the Patriots decided to cut ties with Bledsoe. In Belichick's team-building approach, having two quarterbacks of the caliber of Brady and Bledsoe was an inefficient use of the salary cap (the team didn't need a backup eating up that much of their salary cap), so Bledsoe was shipped to Buffalo for a first-round pick. It was clearly the end of the road for him in New England; he didn't come back to Boston for the post–Super Bowl parade, choosing instead to return home to Montana. And publicly, he assiduously avoided all contact with Belichick when the Patriots visited the White House that spring. On his way out of town, Bledsoe held his head high. He could have easily taken public swipes at Belichick or the rest of the franchise; instead, he took out a full-page ad in two Boston daily papers. Beneath a photo of Bledsoe holding the game ball at the conclusion of the 2001 AFC Championship Game, it was an open letter to New England football fans. He began by thanking all those "who fostered [my] growth as a person and a player. I could not be more humbled by or more thankful for your support." It closed with a final look back at a forgettable season for the once-proud franchise quarterback who had been reduced to holding a clipboard. "The letters I received while in the hospital after my little collision along the sidelines last September were many and wonderful," it read. "You demonstrated to me that to you I was more than just a number on the field. I was a person you cared about. As I raise my three little boys, I will share with them stories of your warmth and kindness. Quite simply, you helped me to learn how people should treat other people, and I thank you for that. Please know that you have made a profound difference in my life and the way I will live it. And while I am excited about my future in Buffalo, I will miss you. Thank you for all you mean to me, and I wish you the very best."

"It was a tough situation, and I think Drew did handle it well," Belichick would later recall. "I've never been in a situation quite like that.

"I think all the parties: Damon [Huard], Tom [Brady], Drew and all the other people on our team did a lot last year to—whatever the situations were, and we had plenty of them—did a good job to focus on the target, focus on the goals, the game and the team concept and achieved results as a team, which is what we did. I think that is something that the players, the coaches and the organization should all be proud of."

Almost a year after signing Bledsoe to an extension he had hoped would make him a Patriot for life, Kraft did not bother to take questions after the deal went down, instead issuing a statement that wished Bledsoe well. "Let me speak as a Patriots fan," said Kraft in a statement. "Drew Bledsoe is a special player. I have great respect for all he's done for this franchise, not only for his contributions on the field but also his contributions off the field. He gave our fans some of the greatest memories in the franchise's history, and there will always be a special place reserved for him in the hearts of Patriots fans.

"For many reasons, and at many levels, this was a difficult trade to make."

Back in New England, with Bledsoe now completely out of the picture, Brady's ascension was fully complete. The amiably goofy twenty-four-year-old who had shown up for his first Wednesday press conference with a backpack slung over his shoulder was no more. In less than a year, he had morphed from anonymous backup to Tom Brady, NFL superstar. That spring, he didn't have to wait in line to get into a club. He didn't have to call ahead for a reservation at a restaurant. Everyone wanted to buy him a drink. Women wanted him, and men wanted to be him. Area businesses were knocking on his door, bypassing other New England sports stars in hope the Patriots' newest star could sprinkle a little magic dust on whatever it was they were selling. He had moved to the top of the Boston sports food chain, quickly bypassing other high-profile Boston athletes like Nomar Garciaparra, Pedro Martinez, Ray Bourque, and Paul Pierce—all of whom had already played in the city for a number of years—in less than one wild calendar year. It was a sudden and surprising journey for Brady, who now couldn't go anywhere in the city without causing a major stir.

"You can age real quick in one year, believe me," Brady said at minicamp that spring shortly after the Bledsoe deal went down. "It was quite a change. A lot of the things I used to do are a lot tougher to do now."

As for Belichick, the Super Bowl victory had moved him out from the long shadow of Bill Parcells. But a Belichick-coached team still shared many of the earmarks of his former boss, and that included a general distrust of star quarterbacks. During the Patriots 1994 training camp, Parcells bellowed at Bledsoe: "Just remember one thing: I don't want a celebrity quarterback on my team. I hate celebrity quarterbacks. You understand?" While Belichick didn't exactly share the same dogmatic approach with Brady, he was still generally wary of placing too much on the shoulders of his young signal caller, even if he appeared at times to be an extension of the coaching staff. In the system the Patriots were building, no one player was more important than another. The first guy on the roster was just as important to the success of the team as the fifty-third guy. "The strength of the wolf is the pack," said Kipling, a belief that was key to the success of the Patriots, and the idea of a superstar quarterback seemed to run counter to that plan.

But there was something different in the Brady-Belichick association, something different than the traditional coach-quarterback pairing of years past. The relationship between Brady and Belichick was completely unique in the modern NFL. The two had achieved success individually, but together they were borderline unstoppable. It brought to mind the relationship shared by Bart Starr and Vince Lombardi: The legendary coach had to learn to let go of the reins and trust the preternatural young quarterback. Both were great, and both brought a great skill set to the table, but in the end both realized they needed the other if they were going to succeed. "If Lombardi fretted that the quarterback position was too important in football, at least now he had a quarterback who was loyal in every way, who would carry out his game plans flawlessly, who opened up his brain and let Lombardi pour his knowledge in," write David Maraniss in *When Pride Still Mattered: A Life of Vince Lombardi*. "Murray Warmath, who had worked with Lombardi on Red Blaik's staff at West Point, came down from the University of Minnesota to watch the Packers and concluded that Starr was the perfect athlete to run Lombardi's huddle. 'He and Vince,' Warmath reflected decades later, 'were hand in glove.'" In much the same fashion Lombardi fretted about placing too much weight on the shoulders of Starr, Belichick was cautious in much the same manner with Brady. But at the same time, if he had to let go of the reins and trust someone, he was able to do just that with the lanky young quarterback. In turn, Brady was completely loyal to the coach and what he was doing, and he carried out the coaching staff's game plan flawlessly. He clearly trusted that each week the coaching staff, to paraphrase Maraniss, was going to open Brady's brain and simply pour that knowledge in. And just as Belichick learned how to delegate authority and trust his assistants to handle the smaller details in his first two seasons in New England, Brady gave him the peace of mind that would ultimately allow him to do the same with his offense. It helped that Belichick had, in a sense, discovered a stronger, taller, faster version of himself, one who could execute on an NFL playing field in a way that Belichick could never hope to do. "He can do all the things that Belichick thinks," Perillo said of Brady.

Led by Belichick and Brady, the Patriots were a feel-good story, a red, white, and blue success set against a post–September 11 backdrop that caused many football fans to rethink the idea of America's Team. To top it all off, they had a brand-new stadium. CMGI Field—renamed Gillette Stadium after CMGI went under in the dot-com bust—was a state-of-the-art football venue. The Patriots became the first team in the history of the league to move into a brand-new facility the year after winning a Super Bowl. Five years after being vilified as the man who rode Bill Parcells out of town and tried to move the franchise to Hartford, the Krafts were riding a wave of positive publicity. Football was king in Massachusetts, and the Patriots were the champions of the NFL. At the heart of it all was New England's first sports hero of the twenty-first century, Tom Brady.

And none of it would have happened if not for Dick Rehbein.

Since the April afternoon in 2000 when the Patriots drafted Brady, the story of Dick Rehbein has taken on an almost mythical quality among New England sports fans. Because he was associated with the Patriots for such a short time—eighteen months, actually, as their quarterbacks coach—and so little is known about him, he remains mostly a blank slate, save for the information found in the Patriots 2001 media guide: After a lengthy career bouncing from city to city as a professional assistant (which included stops in Green Bay, Minnesota, and New York), he accepted a job as the Patriots quarterbacks coach on February 9, 2000. "In Rehbein's first season in New England, Drew Bledsoe threw a career-low 13 interceptions while passing for over 3,000 yards for the seventh consecutive season," his bio says. By all accounts, he was a popular figure with the players. He spent less than two seasons with the Patriots as their quarterbacks coach, before succumbing to cardiomyopathy on August 6, 2001.

But if it wasn't for Rehbein, it seems highly unlikely that Tom Brady would be a member of the New England Patriots. Prior to the 2000 draft, Rehbein had made a trip out to the University of Michigan to watch Brady work out. And while several other teams had watched Brady and come away relatively unimpressed, Rehbein returned with a simple statement for his bosses. "Draft him," he said.

Rehbein had grown up as a Green Bay Packers fan, a feverish devotee of Lombardi and Starr, and saw a lot of the former Green Bay quarterback in Brady. The two were not overnight success stories; each had to contend with several obstacles on his way to the NFL. Like Starr, Brady had struggled for playing time with over-hyped underachievers: Starr learned the lesson growing up playing football at Sidney Lanier High in Montgomery, Alabama, where he battled his way past several other youngsters who had the backing of the coaches in order to eventually win the starting job. Brady engaged in a similar fight at the University of Michigan, where he was forced to spend time behind Drew Henson, a highly touted athlete and hometown favorite who was a two-sport star coming out of Brighton High in Brighton, Michigan. And as collegians, both had their paths blocked again by coaches who, in hindsight, seemed determined to do all they could to prevent their ultimate success. At Alabama, Starr had a passable junior season, but he suffered an injury and was benched by head coach J. B. Whitworth as a senior. He sat and watched another quarterback guide the Crimson Tide to an 0–10 season, the worst record in Alabama football history. And at Michigan, Brady sat for the first two years of his college career, falling as low as seventh on the depth chart before working his way to the starter's role as a junior and senior . . . only to be overshadowed by Henson. As a senior, Brady suffered ignominy as Wolverines head coach Lloyd Carr platooned the two quarterbacks, even though Brady won twenty of the twenty-five games he started in his college career.

Forget the skinny body, said Rehbein. Forget the subpar foot speed. Get him. His teammates liked and respected Brady, and wanted to succeed for him. And as a result, when Brady commanded a huddle, the players listened and followed him. There was something in the way Brady carried himself—his aura and leadership—that appealed to Rehbein. "Twenty years from now, people will know the name Tom Brady," he told his wife.

But the odds were against Rehbein. Heading into the 2000 draft, the Patriots faced all sorts of issues. Offensively, they had just one running back gain more than 300 yards the season before, and were twenty-first out of thirty-one in total points scored. They had a woefully inadequate offensive line, one of the oldest in the league. Defensively, they were as good as almost any team in the AFC, but were getting older at many key positions, including defensive line. Really, they appeared to need help in any number of places—with the *exception* of quarterback. Drew Bledsoe was a three-time Pro Bowler whose spot in the annals of New England sports lore was secure. Compounding their problems was the fact that they were short their first round pick, which was awarded to the Jets in compensation for Belichick. In all, it was going to be a long day for the new brain trust.

If they were going to take a quarterback, many reasoned, it would be sometime in the later rounds with the express idea of providing depth at the position, a relatively undiscovered talent who could spend a few years as a redshirt sitting behind Bledsoe. That was a good thing. Unlike a year before, when three quarterbacks were taken with the first three picks in the draft—and five with the first twelve picks overall—the 2000 draft was shaping up to be a bad one for any team in the market for a premier quarterback. As draft day approached, it was clear that Marshall's Chad Pennington and Louisville's Chris Redman were two quarterbacks who, in the right system, could flourish in the National Football League. The reasoning around the Patriots was that they wouldn't have to focus on Pennington or Redman; they'd be long gone by the time New England got to the later rounds and was looking for a future backup to Bledsoe.

The rest of the group appeared, on the surface, to be good fits for the Patriots. These candidates included Tim Rattay of Louisiana Tech, Marc Bulger of West Virginia, Hofstra's Giovanni Carmazzi, Joe Hamilton of Georgia Tech, and Michigan's Tom Brady.

For many years, most fans and sportswriters believed that the Patriots somehow lucked into selecting Brady, that some sort of thunderbolt from the football heavens just happened to materialize him on New England's doorstep. But a closer look reveals that, even without the benefit of hindsight, Brady appeared to be a good fit for New England and the Belichick system. They were looking for someone who didn't have to come in and start right away, someone who was coachable and could grow into the role of starter while working with Bledsoe and new offensive coordinator Charlie Weis on the Patriots' offense. That someone had to be smart. Just as Belichick asks a lot of his linebackers on the defensive side of the ball, there was even more asked of the quarterback in the New England offense. But perhaps the most important trait they were looking for couldn't be qualified within the pages of a scouting report or seen on film. They demanded football intelligence, a high football IQ. They were looking for a player who knew that sometimes the biggest play of the game wasn't necessarily the seventy-yard touchdown pass but a three-yard gain they used to set up the defense the play before. In baseball parlance, the Patriots had stopped looking for home run kings and started looking for .400 hitters. Brady was one of those players. While there was a constant negative buzz about his size and strength, no predraft scouting report questioned his intelligence or his leadership qualities.

With that context, it was clear who wouldn't make the first cut. The first two, Rattay and Carmazzi, played in wide-open, quarterback-friendly systems in college, and that lessened their chances considerably. There was a lot to like about Carmazzi—he was smart, a Rhodes scholar, and had a big arm—but he was part of a run-and-shoot offense while at Hofstra, which made him a home run hitter. And even though Rattay worked out for the Patriots many times, clearly there were some doubts. While Belichick had come a long way since his conservative offensive style with the Browns (one former Browns player remembered his offensive play calling in Cleveland as "maniacally conservative"), he still wasn't about to bring a run-and-shoot quarterback into the NFL. Other than Warren Moon with the Oilers, no run-and-shoot offenses had succeeded in the pro game, and he wasn't about to try and break new ground there, not with a rookie quarterback anyway. As for Hamilton, he was on the smallish side, and there were plenty of doubts about his arm strength.

That left Bulger and Brady as the only feasible options. Both were smart, tough quarterbacks who were willing to spend that redshirt season sitting behind a starter in hopes of learning the system. Bulger was smart, and did a good job managing a game. He was clearly tough. After a stellar junior year (31 touchdowns, 3,607 passing yards), he had lost almost all of his weapons on offense, and in his senior season with the Mountaineers, he took a terrible beating, throwing 11 touchdowns and 13 interceptions and finishing the season with just 1,729 passing yards.

And then there was Brady, the young quarterback out of Northern California who ended up platooning with the much-heralded Drew Henson during his senior year at Michigan. He finished his collegiate campaign with good numbers, including a 62.8 completion percentage rate, 20 touchdowns, and just six interceptions. But Brady was on the skinny side, checking in at six foot four and just 195 pounds by the end of 1999. And there were questions about his arm strength and his foot speed. Renowned draft expert Mel Kiper was highly critical of Brady. "At the pro level, his lack of mobility could surface as a problem, and it will be interesting to see how he fares when forced to take chances down the field." In addition, his role as a platoon player hurt his chances, especially with the 49ers. San Francisco offensive coordinator Marty Mornhinweg worked out Brady individually and didn't deem him draftworthy, but did secretly hold out hope that San Francisco could land him as a free agent. He had his doubts: "He never really was 'the guy' at

Michigan for two years, and that makes you wonder. Secondly, with quarterbacks it's very, very difficult to evaluate because you don't know about the gut instincts. They're difficult to evaluate. Third, it's tough to make the transition to the NFL from college; to see someone like him make the transition almost seamlessly is unusual."

While many questioned his body, no one was questioning his mind. He was smart—the Wonderlic certainly proved that. The infamous test is a twelve-minute, fifty-question exam to assess aptitude for problem solving. Administered to pro football prospects since the mid-1970s, it was a quick way for personnel men to determine how a player might do under pressure. For quarterbacks, an average score is in the mid-twenties. Brady finished with a thirty-three. And then there was his ability to play well under pressure. He had finished his college career on as high a note as he could, with a masterful performance in the Orange Bowl, leading the Wolverines to an overtime victory against Alabama with 369 passing yards and four touchdowns.

But that performance did little to silence the doubters. As draft day approached, not much had changed. In the eyes of many pundits, Brady remained, at best, a second-day pick. Meanwhile, back east, Rehbein was doing all he could to convince the Patriots that Brady was the one they should go with. He didn't want a repeat of what had happened to his beloved Packers. In his first year as an assistant in Green Bay, legendary Packers scout Red Cochrane pushed hard for the franchise to draft Joe Montana. "I've seen him; all he does is win," Cochrane told his bosses, most notably Green Bay head coach Bart Starr. Instead, Starr went with two obscure players from Maryland in the second and third rounds, prompting Cochrane to walk out of the draft room and slam the door.

As the draft began, the quarterbacks started coming off the board. Pennington was selected in the first round by the Jets, the only quarterback taken in the first two rounds. At the start of the third, the 49ers went with Carmazzi. Former San Francisco head coach Steve Mariucci and former offensive coordinator Greg Knapp were high on Carmazzi, and player personnel guru Bill Walsh liked Carmazzi enough to draft him (although many Bay Area writers later believed Walsh might have been simply deferring to the coaches). In addition, Knapp was close with Carmazzi's high school coach in Sacramento. It seemed like a good fit for the 49ers, who, with the thirty-eight-year-old Steve Young on the verge of retirement, had found their quarterback of the future. "The Niners have a tradition of knowing the quarterback position," Carmazzi said shortly after being drafted. "It's an honor for me to be considered to maybe someday be one of those guys." Mariucci was similarly enthused. "What intrigued us about Gio is his size, his arm strength and the fact that he was a Rhodes scholar," said Mariucci. "He's a real high-energy, workaholic kind of guy. And we really like his mobility."

(It was a crushing blow for Brady, who had followed the 49ers his entire life. He grew up idolizing Joe Montana, and was in the stands in January 1982 when Montana threw the pass to Dwight Clark that won the NFC championship and launched the 49ers onto their dynasty. "You're always hoping for the hometown team [to draft you]," Brady said a few years later. "I was always hoping for the Niners. That was a dream. How quickly that turns when they pick another quarterback three rounds before you, and then they become the team you probably dislike the most.")

Redman was selected midway through the third round by Baltimore. Tennessee's Tee Martin went at the end of round 5 to Pittsburgh—a bit of a surprise—but they were hoping to add another quarterback in the mold of do-everything signal caller Kordell "Slash" Stewart. Bulger went with the second pick of the sixth round to New Orleans. (Bulger would go on to a successful NFL career of his own. After bouncing from New Orleans to Atlanta to St. Louis, he became the backup to Kurt Warner, and was on the sidelines while Brady led the Patriots to a win over the Rams in Super Bowl XXXVI. A year later, after an injury to Kurt Warner, he stepped up and took the starter's job, winning it for good in 2003. And remarkably, early in the 2006 season, he reached 1,000 completions, faster than any quarterback in NFL history. Bulger got there in forty-five games, two games sooner than any other quarterback.)

Meanwhile, New England took a pair of offensive linemen (Adrian Klemm in the second round and Greg Robinson-Randall in the fourth). Running back J. R. Redmond came off the board in the third round. They went with tight end Dave Stachelski and defensive tackle Jeff Marriott in the fifth round, and cornerback Antwan Harris in the sixth round. After each one of the picks, Rehbein grew more and more nervous. He called his wife frequently (his wife estimated it was between ten and fifteen times a day) and fretted that Brady would slip through the Patriots' fingers—until the sixth round, when Rehbein relayed the good news to his wife. There would be no repeat of Red Cochrane. When Rehbein left the room, there was no slamming of the door behind him, only a happy phone call. "We got him," Rehbein gleefully told his wife. "We got him."

No one realized it then, but the drafting of Brady represented a seismic shift in the way the Patriots would be run under Bill Belichick. According to those who worked with Parcells, the head coach would listen and work with assistants and scouts, but once he had settled on a player, he would not be budged. With Belichick, the assistants and scouts were encouraged to speak their minds, to fight for a player to be drafted, and to openly question authority, whether in the draft room or anyplace else. It was a potpourri of ideas, one that Belichick brought with him from Cleveland. Belichick cultivated debate with assistants and scouts, drawing as many different opinions as he could into a forum. As a result, the franchise had become a true meritocracy, and it was a liberating experience for many. In the same way Rehbein viewed Brady as something other than just another quarterback who struggled to win the starting role, scouts and assistant coaches were encouraged to think nontraditionally when it came to evaluating a player. And so, in a profession where assessing a prospect's chances often comes down to measuring a vertical leap, time in the 40-yard dash, and bench press, it was a liberating thing for a scout to make a push for a prospect who might not have the best numbers, but could still manage to contribute in ways a head coach hasn't come up with yet. Tom Brady didn't have the speed of Tee Martin, the passing yardage of Marc Bulger, or the overall statistics of Tim Rattay or Chris Redman. But his selection represented the triumph of the new approach put in place by the New England front office. Don't always just look at the measurables. Trust your scouts, your personnel men, and your assistants who have seen the prospect operate. You were smart enough to hire them. Have faith in the fact that they know exactly what they're doing.

"Sometimes, you just have a *feel* for a player," said Armey, who has worked in NFL front offices for almost twenty-five years. "One of the rules I've always had was that when a scout or assistant coach has a strong commitment to a player, you have to investigate to the fullest extent, because when these guys have an instinct and a strong feeling for a player—and they've been doing it for a long time—you have to respect their opinion.

"We've become such a 'measurable' league. We just look at a capsule and if it doesn't quite fit the 'measurables,' we try to find a guy that does, because that's a good starting point," Armey added. "That's just the way the league works. Sometimes, you think you get the guy you think is going to be an absolute savior—Ryan Leaf, for example—and he can't do it. And then, sometimes, you find a guy like Brady."

Of course, there was also a certain amount of luck involved as well. Every generation has their story of a great quarterback who slipped through the cracks, falling through the draft before becoming a legend as a pro. In 1956, Starr—like Brady—was the 199th pick overall, a seventeenth-rounder. In 1979, the 49ers found one of the game's best quarterbacks in the third round when they selected Montana. And in 1987, they were able to trade a pair of draft picks to Tampa Bay for a United States Football League retread named Steve Young.

After forty years of front-office boobery, it was finally New England's turn to get lucky.

"You would never see a team that would have more bad luck come its way," Perillo said of the sudden turnaround. "From the time they lost that playoff game in 1976 they had no business losing—it was stolen away from them with some ridiculously bad officiating. In 1978, they have another team that's as good as any in football, and the owner is so cheap that the head coach decides to leave and take a college job and it rips the team apart as they're preparing for the playoffs. Right on down the line. There are countless examples.

"Every time they took a step forward, they got slammed by a truck. If any franchise deserved a stretch of good luck, it was the Patriots."

To remind him of just how lucky they got, Pioli still has a football card on his desk. On the upper left corner of the card is a picture of one of their fifth-round picks, Dave Stachelski, a tight end from Boise State. On the bottom right corner is a picture of Brady. (Stachelski did not make it through training camp.) "If we thought he was going to be this good, I don't think we would've waited for the 199th pick to take him," Pioli would say of Brady years later. "We definitely don't have things figured out. Trust me."

"You cannot expect to find one of the ten best quarterbacks to ever play the game in the sixth round," said Aaron Schatz of Football Outsiders. "You can't even expect to find him in the third round, which is why it was hard to copy the Bill Walsh 49ers. Everyone and his brother can run the West Coast offense. Not everyone is going to find one of the greatest quarterbacks who ever lived in the third round in Joe Montana, and then have another one of the greatest quarterbacks who ever lived fall into their laps because of the USFL, and then he was terrible in the two years he was in the NFL before, [in] Steve Young. That stuff just doesn't happen to most teams." ·

The news of Brady's arrival was greeted with a collective yawn. Following Belichick's statements on the Patriots' second-day selections—which included Robinson-Randall, Stachelski, defensive tackle Jeff Marriott, cornerback Antwan Harris, defensive tackle David Nugent, linebacker Casey Tisdale, and running back Patrick Pass—there were four questions that were asked by the local media, none of which were about the quarterback out of Michigan. After all, why would you need to ask a question about Brady? Bledsoe was firmly entrenched as the No. 1, and it didn't look like he would be moving out of that spot anytime soon.

Patten was one of the first players to suspect that Brady could be something special. Between the 2000 and 2001 season, Brady told him during a break in the weight room how to adjust some of his routes on the fly. Patten, who had spent several years in professional football with the Giants and Browns, as well as the Arena Football League, was stunned. "You just don't hear that coming from a backup," thought Patten at the time. "What if he were *starting?*" The ownership soon got the same feeling. Kraft got a taste of Brady's confidence during training camp in 2000. "I was leaving late one night, and this tall, skinny kid approached me holding a pizza box. I said, 'I know who you are. You're Tom Brady, our sixth-round pick out of Michigan.' And he replied, 'And I'm the best decision this organization has ever made.'

"I was stunned," Kraft added. "The amazing thing is, he didn't say it to be cocky or arrogant. He was sincere."

"Tom carried himself like this was his team," said Patten of Brady's first months in the league. "I thought, 'If he's this confident as a backup, I can only imagine how he'll be running the show.'"

Bill Parcells and Bob Kraft, shortly before Super Bowl XXXI. It would be Parcells's last game as head coach of the Patriots. The lessons Kraft learned from his relationship with Parcells would prove invaluable when it came to dealing with Belichick. (Robert Sullivan/AFP/Getty Images)

Shortly after he was hired by the Patriots as head coach in January 2000, Bill Belichick and his hooded sweatshirt became a well-known image to New England football fans. (Rick Stewart/Getty Images)

Tedy Bruschi and Mike Vrabel were just two of the linebackers who helped provide the defense with the spark necessary to turn the Patriots from also-rans into Super Bowl champions. (Glen Cooper)

Adam Vinatieri connects on the game winner that helped beat the Raiders in the 2001 postseason. It was the clutch kick that helped jump-start his career —he would go on to be viewed by many as the best big-game kicker of his generation. (Matt Campbell/AFP/Getty Images)

Troy Brown went from being an afterthought—an eighth-round draft pick that was just lucky to make the team—to indispensable Pro Bowl wide receiver and return man. (Glen Cooper)

Belichick and Tom Brady celebrate the Super Bowl XXXVI victory over the Rams. (Jeff Haynes/AFP/Getty Images)

The Patriots became the only franchise in NFL history to move into a new stadium the year after winning a Super Bowl. Opened in 2002, Gillette Stadium represented a major upgrade from the often dank and depressing conditions at Foxboro Stadium. (Glen Cooper)

Tedy Bruschi has shared a close bond with New England fans throughout his long career with the Patriots. His emotional, heart-on-your-sleeve approach easily made him a crowd favorite. (Glen Cooper)

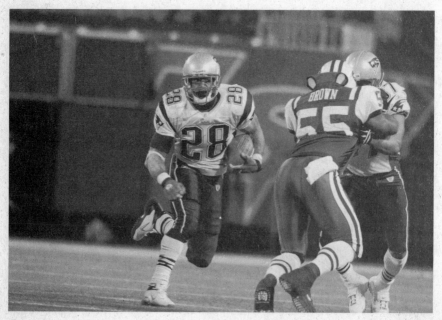

The trade for Corey Dillon before the start of the 2004 season signaled a departure from the Patriots' usual approach to acquiring talent. (Glen Cooper)

By the middle of the decade, Brady had started to be more at ease

The success of the franchise would not have been possible without (from left) Scott Pioli, Bill Belichick, and Robert Kraft all working in concert, taking great pains not to overstep their bounds. (Glen Cooper)

In the early days of the twenty-first century, victory parades celebrating another Patriots' title became a regular event in Boston. (Glen Cooper)

While it was Lewis's hit on Bledsoe that kick-started the magic carpet ride of 2001, the 2002 season needed no such spark. With former president George H. W. Bush and Japanese prime minister Junichiro Koizumi in attendance for the first regular-season game at Gillette Stadium—and a national television audience looking on—they embarrassed the Steelers in a rematch of the AFC Championship Game, 30–14. They then proceeded to rattle off two more wins to start the year 3–0, running their overall win streak to twelve.

To this point in his career, despite the fact that he already had a Super Bowl ring on his finger and a Super Bowl MVP trophy on his mantle, Brady was still incapable of drawing respect in some corners of the football world. In the minds of critics, he was an acknowledged charismatic figure, but not the sort of quarterback who could single-handedly dissect a defense, like Peyton Manning or Dan Marino. His statistics certainly weren't overwhelming. As a rookie, he had just four games where he went for 250 passing yards or better, and was at the helm of an offense that managed just three touchdowns in the 2001 postseason (only two of which were delivered by Brady). At that point, opponents weren't game-planning to stop Brady. They were far more concerned that the Patriots were going to beat them on special teams, or with a defensive takeaway or two. As odd as it sounded, Brady was referred to almost derisively a good game manager, someone the defense didn't necessarily have to key on when it came to stopping the Patriots.

But even stranger, the game seemed to be moving away from an emphasis on the quarterback. In truth, since the dawn of the salary cap era, several of the better teams in the league were winning without a marquee quarterback, preferring instead to spend their money on a game manager. The Baltimore Ravens (winners

of Super Bowl XXXV), the Tampa Bay Buccaneers (eventual winners of Super Bowl XXXVII), the Atlanta Falcons (the 1998 NFC
champions), the New York Giants (the 2000 NFC champions) and
San Diego Chargers (the 1994 AFC champions) had all reached a
considerable level of success with either veterans on their second
or third stop around the league, or flat-out bona fide journeymen
under center. Trent Dilfer, Brad Johnson, Chris Chandler, Kerry
Collins, and Stan Humphries were all considered game managers
who did just enough to put their teams in position to win.

But in the early stages of the 2002 season, the perception of
Brady changed rapidly. Through the first three games of the season, Brady was nothing less than brilliant, throwing nine touchdowns and guiding the New England offense to an average of
thirty-eight points per game. He appeared to have truly come of
age under Belichick and Weis on a warm September afternoon
against Kansas City, when he threw for a career-best 410 yards and
four touchdown passes in a 41–38 overtime win. In those games,
Belichick was able to keep the Patriots remarkably free of any
traces of Super Bowl hangover. As an assistant coach with the Giants, he had seen it ruin the 1986 team, the one that had steam-
rolled its way to Super Bowl XXI. That team was considered one
of the best in league history—they would ultimately be recalled as
the thirteenth-best Super Bowl champions in an NFL Films
retrospective—but their undoing came quickly when they lost
their focus. Seven players on the team ended up writing books,
and they approached the 1988 season with a decidedly laid-back
attitude, believing they could simply flip the switch on the intensity level when the games began. They ended up finishing 6–9 and
out of the playoffs.

Chief among the players who kept the Patriots vigilant against
that sort of backsliding early on was Brady, who managed to keep
his teammates on point throughout September. It was simply the
latest example in a long line of incidents that helped illustrated the
fact that the head coach had found a partner in crime in his young

quarterback. They were of one mind on almost every topic related to football, and that included their dealings with the media. Throughout his coaching career, Belichick has always been extremely cognizant of staying on message when discussing an upcoming opponent, usually sticking to a series of talking points he would hit on throughout the week when speaking with reporters. He wants his players to do the same thing. On several occasions, he has stood in the middle of the locker room with news clippings of what other players are saying around the league, saying, "This is what we're *not* looking for." And even in his first full year as a starter, it was clear Brady understood those rules of dealing with the media and clearly followed Belichick's lead, even if it meant engaging in a good cop, bad cop routine that frequently had reporters rolling their eyes. By midway in the 2002 season, the two had their routine down. Most mornings, Belichick addressed the media before they had a chance to speak to Brady—or any other players, for that matter. The head coach would play the bad cop, offering precious little in the way of information about game plans or injuries, schemes or technique, steering clear of any sort of specifics. In contrast, the genial Brady would play the good cop. When he addressed the media on Wednesdays, reporters would ask him for specifics here and there. He would simply stand there, smiling and talking, smiling and talking, smiling and talking. Pretty soon, he would be flashing that grin, a grin that would say, "I want to tell you guys. I *really* do. But coach would kill me if I said anything."

Despite his reticence to go any deeper than simple generalities, Brady generally received a pass from the media and fans through his first season as a starter. His first real PR challenge came after an ugly home loss to the Broncos on October 27, 2002. It was the fourth consecutive defeat for the Patriots, who had suddenly slipped to 3–4. After the game, he publicly called out many of his teammates, challenging their desire. "I like the guys in this room, don't get me wrong," said the twenty-five-year-old quarterback.

"But it might need to be a little more important to 'em. . . . You look at these last four games, you see the other guys playing like it really means something. We've got to figure out how much this means to people. You've got to play like your life is on the line. Maybe guys aren't playing like it's their livelihood. Certain guys play like that every play—they try to make their mark. When there's balls on the ground, you've got to get 'em. You've got to make the perfect throw, the perfect catch, the perfect block. You can't walk out of here and say, 'I played pretty good.' We didn't do it good enough and we didn't do it often enough."

For a young quarterback to be challenging the oldest team in the league—especially after going 15-for-29 with 130 yards and no touchdown passes—didn't sit well in many corners of the locker room, especially a year after those same veterans went out of their way to protect him from the media prior to his first start. And it was another indication that the era of good feeling in Foxborough had come to a close. Despite the continued growth and maturation of Brady, it was clear that the 2002 Patriots were still a deeply flawed football team. Among their many deficiencies, the bend-but-don't-break defense that had carried them through the rough times in 2001 snapped in 2002, as several teams enjoyed career days against the Patriots. Much of that success against New England came on the ground. At the end of the season, they were thirty-first in the league in run defense. (They had been nineteenth the year before.) They had somehow managed to win a Super Bowl by getting almost no production out of their tight end position. (In the eyes of many reporters, the greatest contribution from tight ends Rod Rutledge and Jermaine Wiggins came not from their on-field play, but their comedic interaction off the field. The two spent one afternoon in the locker room arguing about the origins of the Road Runner, the cartoon nemesis of Wile E. Coyote. One believed he was an ostrich, the other believed there was an actual bird called a roadrunner. They ended the argument agreeing to disagree.) And they were also the oldest team in the league. That sort of veteran leadership that helped Brady in 2001 was simply too old and rusty in 2002.

In addition, many of the free agents were unqualified busts, with defensive lineman Steve Martin and wide receiver Donald Hayes serving as the two poster children for the free agent class of 2002. Both were advertised as strong complementary parts, smart and savvy veterans willing to play their part to help the Patriots make a return trip to the Super Bowl. Martin was supposed to be the run stuffer the team had lacked before, a big body in the middle that could clog up space on running downs. But while pleasant and chatty with the media, Martin looked completely overwhelmed at times, eventually getting himself released toward the end of the season. Ditto for Hayes, who was supposed to be the tall, rangy receiver the Patriots lacked in 2001. However, Hayes stumbled out of the gate, and later confessed to *The Boston Globe* he had a learning disability.

Despite the free agent failures, Belichick said the team's overall philosophy wouldn't change. "What Scott [Pioli] and I have always believed in, and continue to believe in, is to try to add quality people and quality players to this football team," said the head coach at his year-end press conference. He also hammered at the "misconception" the franchise appeared to have toward overspending on free agents. "There seems to be a conception, or misconception, that we won't consider or sign anybody that makes a certain amount of money, or has a certain profile or whatever that happens to be. That simply is not a criteria for us. The criteria is to find people that'll help our football team, and if they can do it for the value, then we're interested. If the value is way above what we think it is, then that puts it in a different situation.

"Would we reevaluate our philosophy? Yeah, I don't really think we would, because our philosophy is to be open-minded, and it has been all the way though. I think you still have to be realistic, too. What we're trying to do is find good football players and good people for the football team, and I don't think that's going to change."

But it wasn't just the busts in free agency. There was a different culture in the locker room that season. The all-business approach that was on display most days during media availability in 2001 had vanished. One day late in the season, two players were going head-to-head in Madden '02 on a PlayStation console someone had bought into the locker room. Some blamed the cushy new facility; the locker room was at least twice the size of Foxboro Stadium, and the amenities were off the charts compared to the old place. Some critics believed the Patriots had lost the "eye of the tiger." Like fighter Rocky Balboa at the start of *Rocky III*, the 2002 Patriots were lacking the same hunger that doomed the fictional boxer. They had gotten fat and happy, satisfied with success. The intensity, the hunger, and the opportunism that had marked the Patriots' stretch drive the season before was nowhere to be found in the latter stages of the 2002 season. In 2001, they played every game as if their lives were riding on the outcome, using the perceived lack of respect to keep their intensity levels high. A year later, many of the same players made veiled allusions to intensity and hunger and desire, but the proclamations rang hollow once they got on the field. They limped to the finish with double-digit losses to the Dolphins, Packers, Titans, and Jets. But nowhere was the payback sweeter than in Oakland, when they lost a 27–20 decision to the Raiders in front of a national television audience, who gained a measure of payback for the loss in the Snow Bowl the year before. Oakland dominated from start to finish, and the Raider fans enjoyed hooting profanely at the Patriots as they left the field. "This is a nice punch in the gut to give them a little something back," said Raiders tight end Roland Williams.

Even with all their faults, the 2002 Patriots were in the playoff chase until the final day of the regular season, when they hosted the Dolphins. If New England won and the Jets lost to Green Bay, the Patriots would squeak into the postseason. *Then*, thought many of the fans, *the old magic would surely return*. New England certainly had plenty working in their favor, including the fact that they were facing a Miami team that had traditionally struggled mightily when they faced the Patriots late in the season in Foxborough. And then there were the words of defensive lineman Anthony Pleasant, who delivered a stirring speech based on the Book of Exodus at a captains' meeting before the game. He pointed directly at Brady and boomed, "You are our Moses!" And when the Dolphins managed to cough up a double-digit lead with less than five minutes remaining—with the coup de grace coming on a 43-yard Vinatieri field goal with 1:09 left in regulation to tie the game at 24—it certainly looked like the magic was back. And sure enough, six plays into overtime, Vinatieri's 35-yarder won it.

But the Packers failed to deliver. As almost a thousand members of the Patriots family—including players and coaches—watched television in a 5,000-square-foot party tent set up by the Krafts, the Jets stomped the Packers. Brady, one of the last to leave the party, met a *Boston Globe* reporter on his way out the door. "I think of a lot of plays during the year that we could have done better," Brady said. "Make those plays when we could have, a win here and there, and you know, we're in the playoffs regardless. But when you start to rely on other people . . . well, you don't want to do that. You just keep thinking, 'If we had done some things better when we had the chance.' . . . I wish we had a game here next week to see what we're all about, but now it's over—and we're not going to get that chance."

If they had moved on, some wondered if it would have been Huard getting the start at quarterback instead of Brady, who appeared to have suffered a shoulder injury. There were several occasions when he was battered and bruised by the Miami linemen, and he could clearly be seen wincing after throws throughout the game. Responding to questions after the game about his condition, he shrugged off the idea of an injury by deflecting the story in a typical Belichickian manner. "I'm always hurt after games," he said. "You always have some bumps and bruises, but it's fine. It's not a big deal." But a few questions later, he was asked if he could recall the specific point in the game when he was injured. "Yes." Asked when, Brady stammered quickly and appeared confused before regaining his footing: "Which play? I don't know. Yes, I don't remember. No, seriously . . . it's fine."

That loss marked the end of a long and arduous sixteen-month stretch for Brady. Instead of hammering him for being less than forthcoming about his injury—or taking him to task for failing to get the Patriots back to the postseason—the usually ravenous Boston media instead pleaded with the NFL's newest crown prince to go home and get some rest. "Any number of his teammates are far more banged up than Brady. But no one else on this team has been living the hybrid life of championship athlete and mega-celebrity to the extent Brady has, and he needs a major battery recharge," wrote columnist Bob Ryan in *The Boston Globe* of Brady's whirlwind. "This season was an unbroken extension of last season, but now the entire Super Bowl thing is over. The Patriots officially have become the immediate past champions now, and it is time for Tom Brady to crash. So listen up, kid. Go home. Get out of our sight. We'll see you when we see you, OK?"

The fact that the Patriots had missed out on the postseason gave critics more than their share of ammunition: New England was officially written off as one-year wonders. Doubters knew it all along. *See? The success they had enjoyed before was not sustainable. They had simply caught lightning in a bottle and gotten lucky, faced good teams at bad times, gotten the right calls and ridden a wave of the good fortune all the way to become the unlikeliest Super Bowl champion of all time.* The EKG meter that had fluctuated so wildly in the past when it came to measuring the success and failure of past Patriots teams appeared poised to be making another permanent downturn, and with it, the professional opinions many had of the head coach. At the end of the season, Belichick acknowledged the transitory nature of the "genius" tag he had acquired in the days following Super Bowl XXXVI. In a tongue-in-cheek op-ed he wrote for *The New York Times* the day of Super Bowl XXXVII entitled

"OK Champ, Now Comes the Hard Part," he handed out thirty-seven pieces of advice for the winning coach. He reminded the winner that oftentimes the toughest job he'd have would be dealing with post–Super Bowl hangover. "You'll tiptoe on the line between helping your players forget that they're the champions and helping them remember why they're the champions," he wrote. And he reminded them that, when it comes to coaches, the post–Super Bowl bump can be fleeting. "Remember, the Smart Coach/Moron Coach Meter, which is currently way off the charts in the right direction, can be very moody."

When Belichick and Pioli began team building back in 2000, they looked for players who shared many of the same characteristics. They wanted players who could see the big picture, who valued team over individual and who had a genuine passion for the game of football. With those guidelines in place, they managed to assemble a core of very special players who were the foundation of a Super Bowl champion. But as the 2002 season came to a close, it became clear that, for their purposes, they also needed more than their share of players who were scrappy overachievers who played with a chip on their shoulder. For many, the realization grew out of organic experiences with the 2001 roster. That team was a collection of players who had spent their entire football lives operating as hungry underdogs, guys who had spent their lives scrapping for respect. That spirit was epitomized in players like Brady, who wasn't recruited heavily out of high school and was a sixth-round pick out of Michigan. Bruschi and Vrabel were third-round picks, and Brown was an eighth-round pick. They also had plenty of players that weren't even taken in the draft. Undrafted free agents like Adam Vinatieri made up a large portion of the roster.

That same underdog approach wasn't there in 2002. That Patriots team was wholly unprepared to deal with the trappings that came with success. That year, when they were out in the community, they didn't have to buy a drink. They were asked to appear at openings for grocery stores; they had their numbers retired when they went home that fall for their high school homecoming. A championship-starved populace did nothing but remind them how great they were, how inspiring they were, how much they did to raise the spirits of the region. A player can only hear so many stories like that before he starts believing them, before he starts believing that all he had to do if he wants to return to Super Bowl glory is to flip a switch. *You'll tiptoe the line between helping your players forget that they're the champions and helping them remember why they're the champions.* Despite the efforts of Belichick, there was nothing hungry about their approach to the game through the middle of the season, and by the time they went to flip the switch on the intensity, it was too late. Much to the consternation of Belichick, the 2002 Patriots suffered the same fate as the 1988 Giants.

The cofounder and former chairman of Intel, Andy Grove, once said, "Success breeds complacency. Complacency breeds failure. Only the paranoid survive." If they were going to return to football greatness in 2003, the level of complacency the Patriots had lulled themselves into throughout much of the 2002 season had to go. The front office had to shake things up a bit. As they did when Brady took over the starting job in 2001, they needed to inject a little paranoia into the locker room again and shake up some of the veterans. And under their new plan, no one would be safe, not even the guy who had come to be identified as Belichick's favorite player.

# CHAPTER SIX

# THE BUSINESS

I can't say everyone here loves Bill. Some really don't know him that well.

—*FORMER PATRIOTS CORNERBACK TY LAW,*
*PITTSBURGH POST-GAZETTE, JANUARY 22, 2005*

In the summer of 1975, twenty-three-year-old Colts assistant coach Bill Belichick had been given the least palatable job on the coaching staff—the role of the Turk. It was a thankless job, especially for a coach who was younger than three-quarters of the players on the roster. Raised in the culture of football with a father who played and coached at the highest levels, he understood the bottom-line aspect to the process. If you were a football coach, releasing a player was simply part of the game. Not everyone is cut out to be a football player, after all. But seeing it up close was something else in entirely. That summer, Belichick got the nickname Billy Bad News. While he wasn't the one who ultimately did the deed, it was his first real taste of the most thoroughly unsavory side of coaching in the NFL. If you're going to succeed as a coach, you can either be a coach or a friend. If you want to be good at one, you're probably not going to be good at the other.

Not many coaches can stomach the job, but over the course of his career, Billy Bad News proved he was up to the task on multiple occasions. In many cases, he was utterly fearless and unblinking when it came to dealing with the aftershocks that can come with the release of a popular player. In 1991 as the head coach of the Browns, he didn't blink when he cut favorite son Bernie Kosar, sparking a regionwide riot that began with the release of Kosar and ended with the team moving to Baltimore. After the 1999 season, he and the rest of the organization decided the Patriots wouldn't re-sign popular Pro Bowl tight end Ben Coates, as well as perennial Pro Bowl offensive lineman Bruce Armstrong. And on the morning of September 2, 2003, Billy Bad News was back when he announced the Patriots had cut loose veteran safety Lawyer Milloy in a contract disagreement.

The idea of tossing a high-priced veteran overboard in a salary dump was nothing new. The new NFL economy only amplified the lesson he learned as Billy Bad News: If you let your personal feelings for a player color your evaluation, it could lead to an unrealistic new contract, and could ultimately end up hamstringing the franchise for years.

And even after Super Bowl XXXVI, the feeling of wariness between the coach and his players prevailed. They were friendly, but never *friends*, each for the most part keeping the other at arm's length emotionally. There were captains' meetings once a week in which the head coach had the opportunity to gauge his team through the eyes of the players, and the captains had the opportunity to feel Belichick out on a number of topics. Overall, they respected him, but many privately confessed they didn't know more about their coach than what they read in the media guide. One player reacted with surprise when he found out that Belichick's father was a former college coach and scout whose relationship with football went back a half century. And in the wake of a big victory, there would be hugs and platitudes and niceties, but afterward, both player and coach would return to the business at hand.

While Belichick may not have cozied up to his players like other

NFL coaches, he did, at least publicly, respect them. Longtime reporters couldn't recall a single episode where he belittled one of his own players in the press, a rarity in NFL circles. But most of the time, it was all business. (However, many players believed that Belichick's approach did deepen the bonds within the locker room. "Coaches don't have [the] relationships with players and the management doesn't know what guys are like," Brady would say a few years later. "In that sense, it's probably tougher for players to see players go because we hang out. We're buddies. It goes far beyond the football field.")

In this context, it was hardly surprising what he did when he was faced with the case of Coates. Much like Milloy, Coates had ingratiated himself with the fan base over a number of years, and had become what many figured was a key part of the New England offense. Moves like these were like playing a high-stakes game of chicken with an agent. *They're not going to cut you. Cutting you would be a public relations embarrassment of the highest proportion. They'll blink. They can't afford to lose you.* But the two sides were unable to agree on a new contract, and the Patriots released him. For many close to the team, it was a prime example that Belichick was not going to let personal feelings stand in the way of his team-building technique. "To me, the one move that he made early that told me Belichick was not going to be sentimental about things was letting Ben Coates go," said longtime radio voice Gil Santos. "Ben Coates had been a great player for this team. But his age caught up with him, and Bill did not hesitate in moving him off the club because it was too big a contract to pay for a player who was at the tail end of his career. That said to me, 'Whoops, this guy doesn't mess around.' I thought that was a key move early on, to show or solidify the fact that he was very much in charge."

Milloy and Coates shared many of the same traits—both were veterans who had been with the team for a number of seasons, and both were considered integral to the overall success of their unit—

but they were, in truth, far different cases. Coates had prospered for many years in New England, but he didn't share the history that Belichick and Milloy had. Milloy came of age as a professional under Belichick. The two had worked closely when Milloy was a young safety and Belichick spent his one season with the Patriots under Parcells as the coach of the secondary. And when the franchise was cutting loose several established veterans like Coates and Armstrong in salary-related moves prior to the 2000 season, one of the first things the New England front office did was award Milloy a new seven-year, $35 million deal, per Belichick's instructions. "He has all the attributes I'm looking for in a football player," said Belichick at the press conference to announce the signing. "I know this is a big commitment by the organization to Lawyer and it's one I think is deserving. . . . He's the type of player I want to commit to and I'm proud to commit to."

The two reached pro football's summit a year later when, in the moments immediately following Adam Vinatieri's game-winning kick in Super Bowl XXXVI, it was Milloy who quickly raced to join his coach in the postgame celebration. NFL Films captured the moment between the two, when Milloy lifted Belichick off the ground in celebration and planted a kiss on his cheek. While many of his teammates were sharing their greatest professional moments in a variety of ways with a variety of different people, Milloy chose to celebrate with his head coach. Moments after that, a third figure entered—Belichick's daughter, Amanda. The three held each other in a tight embrace. The three of them stayed like that for close to fifteen seconds. It was curious and touching scene—Belichick and his daughter, joined by the emotional defensive back who had become very close to his head coach.

In September 2003, it was a far different story. In the three-plus years Belichick and Pioli had been at the controls of the Patriots, they had done a brilliant job at manipulating the salary cap. It played a huge role in their team-building approach. A good chunk of their roster was made up of pliable veterans who didn't mind having their contracts reworked from time to time in hopes of finding an extra dollar or two here or there, all of which was in the name of finding more room for the team to maneuver under the cap. While many of the players who occupied the middle and lower spots on the roster had little problem with it, history would show that a few of the real stars—like Milloy, and later kicker Adam Vinatieri and linebacker Willie McGinest—would be less willing to accept redone deals. (Brady would have his contract redone, signing a six-year, $60 million deal in 2005 that was well below market value.) And when Milloy wouldn't acquiesce to a redone deal that included a pay cut, he was released. The lesson was clear. On a Belichick-coached team, there are no sacred cows. There are no untouchables. Sentimentality is for losers. Your friendship with a coach, whether real or perceived, is not enough to protect you. *Anyone can be released.* No matter who you are, no matter what position you play, no matter how long you've been around, you are never completely safe unless you keep producing.

Lawyer Milloy was a talented player who appeared to have a great working relationship with the coach and his staff. He was beloved by fans and teammates; he had played in New England for many years. But in the end, even that wasn't enough to save his job in New England. The bottom-line approach to winning would spare no one, especially when it came to dealing with the economic realities of the NFL salary cap.

Saying the move was simply part of life in the new NFL, Billy Bad News stood before the cameras that morning and announced the release of one of his favorite players. Forty of the forty-five questions during that morning's press briefing were about the Milloy transaction, and Belichick stood before the media crowd, unblinking, and answered every one. "This is a player and a person that I have immense respect for, and means a lot to this team and this organization. It is just unfortunate that this was kind of a casualty of the way the system is right now," Belichick said. "In the end, the timing is obviously not good, not what we would be looking for. I think it is a reflection of the fact that we tried. Both sides tried all the way to, truly, the eleventh hour, to try to find a way to make it work but in the end we just weren't able to get to that point. That is basically the situation there." Belichick closed with the following: "Of all of the players that I have released in my career this easily would be the hardest. It's an unfortunate situation all the way around, but one that we've made and we will have to move forward with."

Belichick stood poised to take a beating in the media, which was magnified a week later when Milloy signed with Buffalo and led the Bills to a 31–0 rout of New England. "New England coach Bill Belichick, an NFL head coach or assistant for 27 years, should have been smart enough to know the consequences of waiving a leader as popular as Milloy at the 11th hour. . . . Ultimately, Milloy's abrupt change of address may have shifted the balance of power in the AFC East in the Bills' favor," wrote Peter King in *Sports Illustrated*. "[Belichick is] an arrogant oaf," said Kevin Mannix, veteran football writer for the *Boston Herald*. The worst came from ESPN's Tom Jackson, a studio analyst, who said: "Let me say this clearly: they hate their coach," on *NFL Countdown. Remember, the Smart Coach/Moron Coach meter, which is currently way off the charts in the right direction, can be very moody.*

Milloy was just one of many old faces who had been jettisoned. Most of the change that took place between the end of the 2002 season and the start of the 2003 season came in the secondary. The statistics revealed no major precipitous drops in the New England pass defense from 2001 to 2002. (They actually stayed level or improved in many areas, including net yards passing allowed, average passing yards allowed per game, and total first downs, passing.) But there were a series of very ugly performances for the secondary over the course of the 2002 season, including a December loss to the Jets in which the Patriots allowed Chad Pennington to complete his first eleven passes and end up with three touchdowns and 285 passing yards.

Just as Belichick and Pioli had radically remade their linebacking corps in a few short moves prior to the start of the 2001 season, their team-building approach dictated that they now do the same with their secondary. And just as the change they brought about at linebacker two years before, many of the moves were made quickly, using cash they had saved by not gorging themselves at the free agent buffet. Their economic efficiency, which they had begun practicing a few seasons before, was now paying off. That foresight allowed them to move quickly, landing several talented new defensive backs. In the spring of 2003, the Patriots signed veteran safety Rodney Harrison, then traded veteran safety Tebucky Jones to New Orleans for a third-round draft pick. And a few weeks after that, at the draft, they selected a pair of highly rated defensive backs in Asante Samuel and Eugene Wilson. In one eighteen-month span, the Patriots had almost completely turned over their secondary. Gone were Jones, Victor Green, Otis Smith, and Terrell Buckley, as well as part-time defensive backs Matt Stevens and Terrance Shaw. In their place were Harrison, Samuel, Wilson, and veteran Tyrone Poole. The salary difference was negligible, and the changes gave them plenty of new faces by the start of the 2003 season.

But the moves left veteran cornerback Ty Law as the last man standing, the last remaining link to a secondary that had dominated Super Bowl XXXVI. In the eighteen-month stretch since then, every defensive back he had played with since New England beat the Rams that night in New Orleans had come and gone. In fact, most of the defensive backs he had played with *the previous December* had already come and gone. "The last time we played Buffalo, there was Victor Green, Otis Smith, Lawyer, Tebucky Jones, Terrell Buckley, and me," said Law quietly. "This team is going in another direction. They're all gone but me."

In all, there were eighteen new players brought in between the end of 2002 and the start of 2003, an astounding total for a team that tied for a division title. But when it came to overall impact, no one could match the addition of Harrison. In his first week of training camp with New England in the late summer of 2003, he ended up in a shouting match with Brady, hit running back Kevin Faulk so hard that Faulk had to be restrained from going after him, and traded punches with the laid-back Troy Brown. Economic impact aside, the move from Milloy to Harrison was representative of a massive shift in the Patriots' new approach. They were no longer the rough-and-tumble underdogs, the scrappers who made do with the dingiest facilities in the league. Now, to go along with the upscale surroundings, there was a more businesslike feel in the locker room. The day Milloy was released, Harrison called the younger players together out of the glare, away from the media. He reassured them, telling them the move was simply part of the game. "Take care of your money. It's a hard business," he told them quietly.

Harrison had become a dominant figure in other areas of the New England locker room. He became a go-to guy for the media, eventually moving into Milloy's old corner locker and replacing Milloy's heart-on-your-sleeve approach with a quiet intensity that many of the other players started to pick up on. If many of the same players who were with the Patriots from a season or two before were still there, it would have been unthinkable that any new player—even a veteran with the cachet of a Rodney Harrison—would have taken that sort of leadership role that quickly. But Harrison's understated approach and steady hand behind the scenes in the early stages of the 2003 season helped guide the Patriots through one of the toughest stretches of the Belichick era.

Harrison was just one of several new faces who would make their impact that season. While the heart of the 2001 team was made up primarily of veterans who had been around Foxborough for a few years, the 2003 team would find much of its identity in the new faces. There was Harrison and Eugene Wilson, Ty Warren and Ted Washington, Dan Koppen and Tyrone Poole. But the new face the Patriots had the highest hopes for was linebacker Rosevelt

Colvin. After a season in which he finished with 10 ½ sacks and emerged as one of the premier pass rushers in the NFC, it was originally thought New England wouldn't be able to afford him, even though it was clear Belichick was enamored of Colvin. In the week leading up to the Patriots-Bears game the season before, the New England head coach gushed over Colvin without even being asked about him. "That guy is really a good fast football player," Belichick said of the linebacker, three days before New England would sneak past the Bears in a thriller, 33–30. "He is probably one of the smallest rushers in the league, but also one of the most effective. He has got tremendous quickness and even though he plays end in a lot of cases as well as linebacker, again this is a guy that has big-time speed off the edge, pass rush ability, is very, very instinctive. People try to run plays on him, you know draws, screens, shovel passes, stuff like that, to take advantage of his up-field speed rush and they just can't get him. This guy is really good."

The Patriots front office clearly loved Colvin, who was going to be an unrestricted free agent. When it came to landing free agents, the sales job had become a lot easier than it was a few years previous when they had a hard time attracting the Adrian Murrells of the world. When Harrison was being wooed, they took him to Ground Round—a family-style steakhouse—for dinner. Colvin got much the same treatment, a one-hour interview with Belichick and a quick tour of the stadium.

On the surface, the job they had trying to convince a player to sign with the Patriots was pretty easy: They had a shiny new stadium. They already had one Vince Lombardi trophy under glass and had a pretty good shot at getting another one. And they did have some money to spend. They could afford to appear to be blasé. They didn't have to try and do backflips in order to impress the free agents, bowing and scraping in embarrassing fashion as some teams were forced to do. In Detroit, Colvin saw his name on a Lions jersey. He went to Arizona and enjoyed a limo ride to a five-star restaurant. He got the same sort of treatment when he made visits to the New York Giants, Houston, and Jacksonville. The Patriots? Well, there would be none of that. If there was any sales pitch, it would be considerably understated. *We like you,* they seemed to say. *If you want to come here, we think you'd be a good fit. If not, well, good luck somewhere else.*

Colvin was a terrific talent, a pass-rushing demon who could alter the course of a game. Any team would be lucky to have him. But early in his visit, he quickly learned one of the most basic principles of a Belichick-coached team: It's not about collecting talent. It's about assembling a team. And while Belichick would be more than happy to have Colvin's talent, he wanted to make it clear he was not coming to New England to be the centerpiece, but another piece of a puzzle. "It was not a glamorous visit," Colvin recalled later in an interview with *The Boston Globe.* "I went to Bill's office and talked to him for an hour. Then Scott came in, and we talked another hour. Bill asked if I wanted to see the locker room. He opened the door a crack and said, 'There it is.' There were no lights on. He took me to see the club seats—in the dark.

"The whole place was deserted. There was nothing to see. Just a bunch of sand, dirt, and snow."

Colvin was another undersized collegian lineman who made the switch to pass-rushing linebacker with ease, à la Bruschi and Vrabel before him. And he certainly appeared ready to step in and become the latest weapon in Belichick's arsenal. In the season opener, he played well, registering a sack and four tackles in the loss to the Bills. But in the second quarter of the Patriots-Eagles game in Week 2 of the 2003 season, the twenty-six-year-old linebacker had bent down to scoop up a fumble, and he felt something . . . wrong. There was pain in his left hip, pain like he had never felt before. The injury was far worse than anyone had realized. Eight days after he hurt himself, the Patriots placed him on the injured reserve list, ending his season. It was the latest in an amazing string of injuries to open the year. Linebackers Ted Johnson (broken foot) and Mike Vrabel (broken arm) were out of commission by the fourth week of the season, as was nose tackle Washington (broken leg). Vrabel and Washington were hurt in a win over the New York Jets the week after the win over the Eagles. In addition, guard Mike Compton (foot) had been lost for the season at that point, while receiver David Patten (leg), cornerback Ty Law (ankle), and fullback Fred McCrary (knee) were all question marks.

In that context, any talk of a return to the Super Bowl seemed ridiculous, especially when you consider the fact that they were hosting the Titans that Sunday. Tennessee was a just a few years removed from a trip to the Super Bowl—they had suffered a narrow loss to the Rams in Super Bowl XXXIV—and quarterback Steve McNair was in the midst of a season that would see him go on to become a co-MVP. The Patriots? At this point, missing almost half their starting defensive unit, they were simply hoping to stay healthy against one of the most physical teams in the league until Vrabel, Washington, and Johnson were well enough to return.

And so, on a clear and cool October afternoon, New England met Tennessee. As New England held on to a four-point lead late in the fourth, Ty Law's lobbying skills took over. The cornerback was well known on the sidelines as someone who wouldn't shut up. ("[Ty] talks to the receivers; he talks to the coaches. It's hard to keep Ty quiet," Belichick once said with a grin.) And late that afternoon, Law spent the bulk of his energies trying to convince Belichick that his injured right ankle, which he had dinged up two weeks before against the Jets, wasn't all that bad, and that he was ready to go. "It was kind of like two weeks ago in the Jets game where he was on the sideline saying, 'Put me back in, Coach, put me back in.' So he made the right call on that one," Belichick said after the game. "They told me he couldn't go back in. He just came over to me and said, 'Coach, I can go back in. I can finish the game if you need me.' So I said, 'OK. Are you sure you're all right? Are you sure you can [Cover] Two?' And he said, 'I'm OK on that.'"

Late in the game, he lined up against rookie Tyrone Calico. Calico had been enjoying the best afternoon of his young career, catching three balls for 92 yards, including a seven-yard reception against Law that had gotten Tennessee to the New England 40-yard line with 2:01 remaining. But Law had lulled Calico into a false sense of complacency, and, on the next play, the youngster took the bait. The veteran cornerback jumped in front of a down-and-out route, picking off the pass and limping the better part of the 65 yards needed for a touchdown, assuring the Patriots of a 38–31 win.

It would be a full twelve months before the Patriots would lose again.

They started winning and kept winning. The opponents changed—from the New York Giants to the Miami Dolphins to the Cleveland Browns—but the outcome was the same each and every time. By the end of the season, there was a curious *Groundhog Day* quality to the streak, which had reached twelve straight to close out the regular season. In none of the victories were the Patriots particularly dominant. With the exception of the 31–0 blowout of Buffalo in the season finale, none of the wins were by more than twelve points. And just three of them—the overtime victories against the Texans and Dolphins, as well as a win over the Colts that was decided on a goal-line stand late in the fourth quarter—were what you might consider dramatic.

In 2001, critics believed the Patriots' success was based on some level of harmonic convergence. Belichick and his team were able to take advantage of a whole lot of questionable decisions at just the right time, had a roster full of players who had the best seasons of their career, and were blessed to have kicked over a rock and found Tom Brady. In the 2001 postseason, they took advantage of Walt Coleman's interpretation of the tuck rule and they took advantage of the fact that Bill Cowher and the Steelers didn't put much of an emphasis on special teams. And in Super Bowl XXXVI, they benefited from the fact that Mike Martz and the Rams decided against trying to take advantage of the Patriots' nickel defense most of the game. There was none of that in 2003. After their October win over Tennessee, there was, most of the time, a stunning inevitability to every game. It was as if the Patriots spent week after week facing the Washington Generals. Sure, a team could hang around New England for the better part of the afternoon. But in the end, they just couldn't hang with the Patriots, who would either make a key play at a certain time or wait for their opponents to make a mistake.

That sense of the inevitable wasn't an accident. New England's team-building approach dictated that while the 2003 Patriots might not have had as much talent at the top of the roster as some of the other teams in the league, they were considerably stronger through the middle and at the bottom of their roster than almost every other team in the NFL. While other teams that had spent too much on top-tier talent were faced with a crisis, they turned to unproven or woefully inadequate backups. In New England, they faced the same challenges that every other team went through, including injuries. The only difference was that the Patriots were able to fill that empty spot with a better than average player whom they were able to attract by dangling a slightly above average contract—thanks to many of the bigger stars signing cut-rate deals to stay in New England. As a result, when the Patriots needed to go to the second and third spots on their depth chart, they were always able to find someone who was better prepared, better conditioned, and smarter than the player he was facing on the other side of that line. And over the course of the season, there wasn't a single player who didn't have at least a passing moment in the spotlight. (Because of injuries, they were forced to use forty-two different starters and sixty-five players in the regular season. Five players who started in the opener finished the season on injured reserve.)

Making his first pro start against Philadelphia, rookie wide receiver Deion Branch had six catches for a game-high 89 yards and a touchdown in the first win of the season. Against the New York Giants, veteran linebacker Roman Phifer made 19 tackles in a 17–6 win. Against Houston, it was little-used tight end Daniel Graham making a great catch in the end zone to force overtime. Against Miami in overtime, it was Troy Brown running a perfect route on a touchdown pass to help New England gain a rare win in South Florida. In a win over Jacksonville, cornerback Tyrone Poole was the star, picking off a pair of fourth-quarter passes from Byron Leftwich in a win over the Jaguars. Against the Jets, the defense had five interceptions and much-maligned running back Antowain Smith rushed for 121 yards in a 21–16 victory over their division rivals. And in the season finale against the Bills, it was linebacker Larry Izzo picking off a pass in the end zone as time ran out to preserve the 31–0 shutout of Buffalo and help bookend the season with an amazing symmetry: They had began with a 31–0 loss to the Bills at Ralph Wilson Stadium, and ended with a 31–0 blitzkrieg of Buffalo at Gillette Stadium.

And prior to the 2003 AFC Championship Game, Belichick hoped it would be Damon Huard's turn. When Huard arrived in New England prior to the start of the 2001 season, it was believed he would serve as the No. 2 quarterback behind Drew Bledsoe. But he was quickly supplanted on the depth chart by Brady, and spent much of the year as the No. 3 man, failing to see any game action. Despite that, he was a celebrated figure in many corners of the locker room. His ability to broker a cautious and delicate peace between Brady and Bledsoe in the quarterback meetings in 2001 made him more Kofi Annan than Dan Marino, and his constant good nature made him a favorite of many of his teammates.

Prior to the 2003 AFC Championship Game, Belichick gave Huard the job of playing the role of Manning in practice the week before the game. Manning could be a maestro at directing traffic when he came to the line, and his presnap signals could confuse even the most talented defense. But Huard's masterful imitation paid dividends, as the Patriots were able to shut down the high-octane Indianapolis offense. Manning finished the game with a season-low passer rating of 35.5 (the third worst of his career at that time) as he completed 23-of-47 pass attempts for 237 yards with one touchdown, four interceptions (three by Law), and four sacks (2 ½ by defensive lineman Jarvis Green). Belichick—as well as the rest of the team—rewarded Huard's effort with a postgame shout-out and a game ball. It was a rarity for a backup quarterback who never actually took a single snap on game day. "I also thought that one of the most valuable players in the game for us didn't play, and that was Damon Huard," Belichick said afterward. "I thought the look he gave us in the scout team for our defense was fabulous."

"Let's talk about Damon Huard," Bruschi said after the 24–14 New England victory. "The first thing Bill mentioned was that the guy that had a big hand in this victory didn't even play. I don't know if he took acting classes or anything like that, but it was like Peyton was on the other side. Damon gave us a great look. Just throwing the ball, he was on fire at certain times. That really got us prepared."

This time, things were different. This time, there was no red, white, and blue backdrop. This time, the Patriots were not the scrappy underdogs going against the big, bad Rams. This time, they were the favorites, meeting a group of overachievers from Carolina in Super Bowl XXXVIII. After a stagnant first half—the game was scoreless for the first 26:55—the game quickly turned into a shoot-out between Brady and Carolina quarterback Jake Delhomme, one that was tied at 29-all with under two minutes to play. It appeared the Panthers were in great shape heading down the stretch, while New England was struggling. Late in the fourth quarter, Rodney Harrison had broken his right arm while trying to tackle DeShaun Foster. In addition, Eugene Wilson ripped his groin, and the Patriots were an injury away from going to emergency defensive back Troy Brown.

But just as it had happened so many times over the previous three years, fate smiled on the Patriots. Carolina kicker John Kasay booted it out of bounds on the kickoff, giving New England the ball on its own 40 with 1:08 left and all three time-outs. On the sidelines, Ty Law turned to Harrison, who had snuck back onto the field after having his right arm x-rayed and put in a cast. "Rodney, we're not going to lose this game," Law said. "You know why? Because we have Tom Brady."

"It was like a thousand pounds of brick being taken off my chest," said Harrison, recalling the moment later.

As Brady and the Patriots maneuvered downfield on a drive that was eerily similar to the one two years before, long snapper Brian Kinchen started to sweat. Kinchen, who had been brought in to replace incumbent Lonie Paxton after Paxton went down with an injury, had accidentally sliced open a finger earlier in the day. When he told Vinatieri what happened, the normally unflappable kicker was stunned. "I think he ended up cutting his hand on a piece of bread with a butter knife or a steak knife or something," Vinatieri recalled later that year. "It was kind of a fluke thing. We're all going: 'What in the heck are you doing, man?'" It had been a bad week of practice for Kinchen, who, even as a veteran, seemed overwhelmed by the largeness of the game. "I was playing mind games with myself," Kinchen confessed. "I was scaring [Belichick] half to death. I just couldn't compose myself." Kinchen bounced a snap to punter Ken Walter, and Vinatieri did miss two field goals earlier in the game—a 31-yarder was wide right and a 36-yarder was blocked—but he later said those were not the fault of Kinchen.

As the drive continued, Brady found Troy Brown for thirteen yards and Deion Branch for seventeen, steering the Patriots to the 23. It would make it a 41-yarder for Vinatieri, who had missed four of his previous thirty-five indoor attempts, all of them inside Houston's Reliant Stadium. And so, with nine seconds left, as the Patriots lined up for the game winner there were some doubts in the back of the minds of the folks on the New England sidelines. "He struggled a little bit in practice," Vinatieri said of Kinchen. "But ultimately, when it came down to that last one at the end of the game, he was money. It was a perfect snap." And once again, it was a perfect hold. And again, it was a perfect kick. For the second time in three years, the Patriots were Super Bowl champions. They'd won fifteen in a row to close out the season, a monumental effort in the era of free agency and the salary cap.

"It was a great team effort," Belichick said. "We've done it fifteen weeks in a row. This team met all comers this year, fifteen straight. There's been some heart attacks, but they came out on top."

As another blizzard of red, white, and blue confetti gently fell around him, Kraft addressed the crowd. "Fans of New England, we waited forty-two years for our first championship; we waited two years for the second. The fifty-three players, seventeen coaches and the head coach, the heart and soul of our team, showed us what the concept of teamwork is about; and that when that's combined with perseverance and commitment, great things happen. League-high injuries were overcome and we won fifteen games in a row— because of the concept of team.

"In . . . today's era, people celebrate individuals and individual accomplishments; but my family and I are proud of this man, Coach Belichick, who instilled the values of power of TEAM. And because of that today . . . we have seen a true team and a true champion."

Afterward, Vinatieri was whisked from postgame interview to interview, swept along by a group of men in suits that resembled something out of the Secret Service. Rosevelt Colvin became the world's most highly paid cheerleader, handing out championship T-shirts to teammates as they came off the field. And just as Brady had been immortalized two years before, holding his head in disbelief as confetti gently swirled around him in the wake of the Patriots' win in Super Bowl XXXVI, this time it was Harrison. The sight of the veteran safety crying, his left arm extended in a victory salute, was the image that stuck with many Patriots fans for years to come. In many ways, it was an appropriate image. Just as Brady's disbelief came to be readily identified as the image of the franchise in the wake of Super Bowl XXXVI, it was Harrison's postgame image from Super Bowl XXXVIII that remained the face of the 2003 Patriots—bruised and banged up, but utterly resilient in the face of trauma.

Almost four years to the day after Belichick and Pioli started trying to change the climate in Foxborough, they were coming home with their second Vince Lombardi Trophy in three years. They had the league's No. 1 quarterback, the best big-game kicker of his generation, a peerless defense, and a state-of-the-art facility. They had become the gold standard, the measuring stick for every one of the other thirty-one teams in the NFL in terms of how to do business.

"There's a culture that's been created here now," Pioli said after the game, "and everyone knows what to expect, and they respond to it."

The same people who were digging the professional grave of Billy Bad News at the start of the season were now praising him as one of the finest minds in the game. "Around the league, teams were examining Bill Belichick and his system with fresh eyes, looking beyond his reputation as a defensive mastermind to the method behind his personnel decisions, his draft strategy, his symbiotic partnership with personnel director Scott Pioli, the series of crises and responses that made the Patriots one of the more compelling stories in recent memory," wrote author Michael MacCambridge in *America's Game: The Epic Story of How Pro Football Captured a Nation*. "There was also a genuine sense of awe over the Patriots' ability to run off a string of fifteen consecutive wins against a brutal schedule, in the most competitive era in league history. The accomplishment was, in its context, every bit as impressive as the Dolphins' perfect season of 1972."

Americans hold a special place in their hearts for the underdog. We love the upstart, the little guy who has a puncher's chance of knocking out Goliath. "The pleasure of rooting for Goliath is that you expect to win. The pleasure of rooting for David is that, while you don't know what to expect, you at least stand a chance of being inspired," wrote Michael Lewis of the scrappy Oakland A's in *Moneyball*.

After the 2001 season, the Patriots were the plucky little engine that could. In the wake of September 11, they were the football team that everyone could get behind, the very symbol of can-do American fortitude that anyone could appreciate. They pulled off an upset against a team that had the brashness to call itself the Greatest Show on Turf. They did it by trusting in a smart coach, an all-American quarterback, and banding together to create something bigger than themselves. Small wonder that President George W. Bush invited them to the White House and lauded them by saying, "They came out as a team, and now, all of America knows that. . . . I thought that was a pretty good signal to America that teamwork is important; that the individual matters to the team, but the team is bigger than the individual. . . . I remember watching all the experts talk about the Super Bowl; no one thought they'd win. They learned what I learned—that in politics and sports, the experts are often wrong."

Of course, not all football fans felt that warm and fuzzy about the Patriots. Belichick, who was still Public Enemy No. 1 for what happened to Cleveland after he left, was still being hammered on message boards by fans who blamed him for everything from the state of the Browns to the environment around Lake Erie. And Raiders fans, with the memory of the 2002 divisional playoff defeat fresh in their minds, still considered themselves the AFC's rightful representatives to Super Bowl XXXVI. For the rest of the country, the Patriots' shelf life as a lovable sporting Cinderella ended sometime shortly after they beat the Panthers in Super Bowl XXXVIII for their second title in three years. After spending forty or so years as David, it had taken then just three years to morph suddenly into an NFL Goliath. And as Wilt Chamberlain once said, "Nobody roots for Goliath." It was clear that their success had bred a level of contempt.

New England *did* accelerate the process a bit, much to Belichick's chagrin. In 2002, the San Diego Chargers privately accused the Patriots of doing more than a little trash-talking during San Diego's 21–14 win in late September. And in a move some Patriots said was simply good fun, New England's four former Dolphins (Huard, Izzo, Buckley, and offensive lineman Grey Ruegamer) sent photos of themselves to their former teammates in South Florida, with their Super Bowl rings on their middle fingers—and with their fingers extended upward. Publicly, Belichick was mum on the topic, but privately, he was furious and fined the players. The Dolphins posted copies of the picture in their practice facility, and wide receiver Oronde Gadsden said they used it to their "advantage" the following week, a 26–13 win over New England in South Florida. And in 2003, there was more. In the wake of Super Bowl XXXVIII, an impressive feud began to percolate between the Patriots and Panthers. On the first play of Super Bowl XXXVIII, Poole jammed Smith, busting his lip. On the second play of the game, Smith strongarmed Poole to the ground. According to Smith, soon after that, Poole spit on him. "Then he started calling me names. He's a Christian and he wasn't cursing at me, but he was just calling me some names that in my book was cussin' still. So I said, 'Look here, Dog. You're gonna shut up and

I'm gonna make you shut up,'" Smith told Sirius Satellite Radio. "I was hot, I was very hot. There's a lot of people I have respect for. Tyrone Poole, he's not [one of them]. He's like Nike and I'm like Reebok. I don't talk to him. I got nothing to say to him."

It wasn't just Steve Smith. The Patriots' success had started to ruffle some feathers. But nothing got their critics worked up more than the idea that they were a dynasty. Critics argued a *real* NFL dynasty had to cut a swath through the league like Hannibal through the mountains. A real dynasty had to not only win, but shred the competition with style. This New England team had won a pair of Super Bowls—and was on its way to another one—but they had won both by the narrowest of margins, by a combined total of six points. Stacked against the dynasties of the past, their less-than-dominant performances on the big stage left some feeling flat. After all, the Steelers had rolled to four fairly easy Super Bowl wins by a total of 30 points—including double-digit wins over the Rams (a 31–19 win in Super Bowl XIV) and Vikings (a 16–6 victory in Super Bowl IX). With the exception of Super Bowl XXIII—a 20–16 win over the Bengals—the 49ers of the 1980s were even more dominant, winning their four title games by a total of 76 points, a streak that included the biggest blowout in Super Bowl history, a 55–10 victory over the Broncos in Super Bowl XXIV. And the Cowboys of the 1990s were no less impressive, winning their three title games by a total of 62 points, with the high-water mark coming in 52–17 blowout of the Bills in Super Bowl XXVII. There were no such blowouts by New England.

There was also another argument against the Patriots, an argument that made absolutely no sense: In addition to being dominant on the field, a dynasty also had to have a larger-than-life persona off the field. Sure, they had to drub the opposition and render the rest of the league meaningless, but they had to do it in a sexy, stylish fashion. In the NFL, dynastic teams loomed large and partied hard, like the Cowboys of the 1990s and the Raiders of the 1970s and early 1980s. Colossal characters like Michael Irvin, Deion Sanders, and Kenny Stabler were the stuff of legend. Love them or hate them, *these were the sorts of players who stirred genuine emotion in fans*. They were polarizing figures who got people talking about the league. They were easy to root for or root against. Compared to those teams, the Patriots were mostly a vanilla-bland group. In New England, there were no colorful fat guys willing to dole out goofy quotes. There were no roguish characters who filled notebooks. There were no outlandish touchdown dances or rap albums or tell-all books. And with the occasional exception of Brady, there was no real star power. They were simply a collection of fairly emotionless football players who appeared to be happy to keep their names out of the newspaper. It left people scratching their heads. In the me-me-me world of professional sports, the Patriots were an anomaly. They achieved success, but publicly, they appeared to show little appreciation for their accomplishments.

It left some cold, and a healthy amount of Patriots haters sprang up everywhere, hammering the franchise on everything from Belichick's wardrobe choices to their know-it-all attitude. In an online poll, ESPN.com would anoint the 2001 Patriots the "worst team sports champion of all time," narrowly beating out the 1997 Florida Marlins and the 1984 Brigham Young football team. "I hate the Patriots because they are detached and disdainful," read one 2004 post from a Pittsburgh-based football fan site. "They're the machine in Lang's *Metropolis*. If Capra were directing the NFL, the Patriots would be. Mr. Potter or D. B. Norton." (The same site added another shot across the Patriots' bow, this one at ownership. "I hate Patriots owner Bob Kraft because he wears those ridiculous Pauly Walnuts shirts with the white cuffs and collars. I wish they'd 'make' him like Joe Pesci was 'made' in *GoodFellas*.")

"The metronomic, death-by-a-thousand-cuts offense. Coach Bill 'Genius' Belichick's ratty sweatshirt. Linebacker Tedy Bruschi's 7-Eleven clerk bangs. That ridiculous mascot. The blah uniforms.

The incessant: 'We're the ultimate team in the ultimate team game' platitudes. Snore," wrote slate.com's Robert Weintraub in an essay about the Patriots entitled "The Lamest Dynasty in Sports."

"Yes, the Patriots are a great team and their fans will obviously trade compelling play for victory after victory. But I think I speak for the rest of us when I say: Bring back the Jimmy-Troy-Emmitt-Irvin-Deion-Jerry Cowboys."

"I think balance is needed," said commissioner Paul Tagliabue when asked if the Patriots' dynasty was good for the NFL. "I think the history of pro sports, especially pro football, shows that if you have weak sisters, that if you have weak links in the chain, that you are going to have Sundays that don't matter. You want every Sunday to matter. You want every one of those sixteen games to be a big event and a competitive event."

Regardless of the critics, it was certainly a good *time* to be a dynasty. The great teams of previous eras always had another team to measure themselves against. The Pittsburgh Steelers had the Oakland Raiders or Dallas Cowboys, while the Cowboys of later years would enjoy a spirited rivalry with the 49ers. The Patriots had very little competition in that regard. "Once you got around to the 2000 season, the Dallas dynasty had died off, and you had no other dynasty out there, so Belichick came along at a good time," said ESPN's K. C. Joyner. "If he had come along at a time in the NFL where there was a power team, another dominant club, I don't know if New England wins. They probably still win a Super Bowl, but I don't know if they become a dynasty at that point. If he was facing a team that had a great collection of players like the Cowboys or the Niners. . . . I don't mean to knock the New England players, but he built a different kind of team than if they were going against a powerhouse team, I don't know if they would have had the same level of success."

As the Patriots began to win with greater frequency, that resentment would build across the country, first among fans and then among other players and into the media. Belichick would use that resentment to help New England achieve the next level of success. Call it Motivation 101.

In the early days, motivating the Patriots was easy: Simply preach the values of teamwork. In that context came the Patriots' first night at the movies. On the night of August 1, 2001, Belichick decided to give his team a break from the rigors of training camp, and the New England head coach piled everyone in buses and spent $800 of his own money to rent out a local IMAX theater that was showing *Shackleton's Antarctic Adventure*. After seeing the film at Boston's Museum of Science earlier that year, Belichick believed the story would have a positive effect when it came to showing examples of perseverance and togetherness. The movie is based on the experiences of Sir Ernest Shackleton, who attempted to become the first explorer to lead an expedition across Antarctica, and the 1914 voyage of the *Endurance*. The ship became trapped and crushed in the ice, forcing Shackleton and his twenty-six-man crew to suffer through seventeen months of hunger, frigid temperatures, and tedious monotony before making their way to safety. Everyone on the *Endurance* survived. The lesson got through. "That told you that there are always going to be obstacles in the way," Brady said afterward. "You have to keep your faith, keep believing in each other, keep working together, even if you think you're never going to make it."

Late in the 2001 season, Belichick again reached into his bag of tricks for more motivation. He pulled out a tape of the Breeders' Cup, and showed the players a race involving a horse that was pulling out of the pack for the victory. He stopped the tape at the start of the stretch and asked his team if they knew who would win. At the time, the Patriots were locked in a four-way race for the AFC East title and packed among many other teams battling for playoff spots. The lesson? It doesn't matter who's ahead at any given point in the season. It only matters who's ahead at the finish.

"Your team gets tired of hearing you say the same thing day after day," Belichick shrugged when asked about his horse race.

"You have to find a different way to get the message across, so you come up with a different flavor."

A year later, it was more creative motivation. Before the start of the 2002 season, Belichick invited Celtics' legend Bill Russell to address the team on a number of issues—including the difficulties in defending your title. It was the latest in a long line of training camp seminars that were geared toward teaching and motivating, a process that began when Belichick was the head coach in Cleveland and would invite Jim Brown in to speak to the players.

"We've had different speakers, like we do with the rookies; guys would come in and talk with the rookies. We did that in Cleveland, too, former players, coaches, or athletes from maybe a different sport," Belichick said. "When I talked to Bill and listened to Bill, I understood one of the reasons why [the Celtics] were pretty successful. He had a lot to do with it. He is pretty perceptive and understands how a team is supposed to win. I've learned a lot from listening to him."

While the opponents for the big games changed—from the Steelers to the Rams to the Panthers and back to the Steelers—there was no team that consistently managed to give Belichick more fodder than the Indianapolis Colts. On the field, they were the only consistent measuring stick the Patriots had. The Colts were a curious team. They were without peer on the offensive side of the football. Quarterback Peyton Manning, wide receiver Marvin Harrison, and running back Edgerrin James formed the nucleus of one of the most feared offensive attacks in the league. Head coach Tony Dungy was one of the most respected coaches in the game. And season after season, the Colts were able to put together teams that were among the best in the AFC. But throughout the early stages of the twenty-first century, they made an annual habit of saying and doing the wrong thing at the wrong time.

Bill Polian was pissed. And whenever Bill Polian got pissed, profanity was sure to follow.

It was the 2003 AFC Championship Game, and the Indianapolis team president was sitting in the middle of the Gillette Stadium press box. Indianapolis came into the game loaded for bear. They had scored a combined seventy-nine points in their first two playoff games, causing Indianapolis tight end Marcus Pollard to say that if the Colts keep playing that well, "they might as well give us the rings." But once the game got underway, there was no more talk of rings, at least on the Colts' sideline. On the field, the Patriots linebackers and defensive backs were having their way with the fleet Indianapolis wide receivers, blasting the Colts over and over again. For Colts fans, two plays near the end of the game stood out. Manning was within a touchdown of tying the score at the two-minute warning. On consecutive plays, passes to tight end Marcus Pollard fell incomplete after New England linebacker Roman Phifer impeded Pollard beyond the five-yard zone. Polian raged at officials, saying, "Throw the fucking flag" after New England defenders committed one perceived infraction after another against Colts receivers on the way to a 24–14 win.

(After that game, Indianapolis officials were particularly peeved at Belichick. After a Manning interception on a pass meant for Harrison, Harrison went sliding out of bounds. He tried to get back into the play after Ty Law picked off the pass, but Belichick clearly stepped in front of Harrison, preventing him from making a tackle on Law.)

That summer, in a move that was widely perceived to have been sparked by suggestions from Polian, the league would institute tougher rules when it came to pass defense, cracking down on illegal contact and defensive holding. Polian sat on the league's competition committee that met several times to rectify what had become lax enforcement of the illegal contact and holding rules. "You can't deny that it took place in the championship game," Polian told reporters two months after the game. "You've got guys grabbing shirts and pulling guys down. But that's not the reason for the rules [clarification]. As I said in the committee meeting, that took it to its nadir, to its zenith."

(Polian would continue to sit in the press box at Gillette, and would gain a small level of satisfaction a few seasons later when the Colts came to New England and blasted a hobbled Patriots team that was without Tedy Bruschi or Rodney Harrison. During the game, there were plenty of histrionics, including pounding the table and cursing under his breath. In the waning moments of the game, backup quarterback Doug Flutie was rolling out, away from an Indianapolis pass rush, and Polian yelled out "Break his leg!")

By the start of the 2004 season, games at Gillette Stadium began to look like a spectacle out of the Roman empire, and the season opener was particularly grandiose. The NFL was looking to kick off the season in style, and had a one-hour on-field pregame special lined up that included bands, comedians, and remotes from Foxboro, as well as Jacksonville, the home of Super Bowl XXXIX. While they understood the routine, none of this was going over well with the Patriots. "The circus is in town," muttered Belichick when talk of the pregame festivities—which featured several bands, including Mary J. Blige, Destiny's Child, and Elton John, as well as the unveiling of the Super Bowl Champions banner—was initially brought up. Was he concerned that the pregame spectacle, dubbed the "NFL Opening Weekend Kickoff," would be a distraction? "If the players want to watch Mary J. Blige sing, then I'll get them a good seat in the stands and they can watch it to their heart's content," Belichick said.

One person who Belichick knew wouldn't be distracted was veteran Willie McGinest. Drafted in 1994, the veteran linebacker had seen plenty of these pregame shows. Off the field, he was part of a dying breed in the New England locker room. By the start of the

2004 season, there were just a handful of players who remained from the Parcells era. McGinest, Bruschi, Ty Law, Adam Vinatieri, Ted Johnson, and Troy Brown were the last link to the Parcells regime, and all of them carried considerable gravitas with their teammates as a result. But among those veterans, it was McGinest who exerted the most influence in the locker room. The six-foot-five, 270-pound linebacker was an intimidating presence, and he wasn't above using it to his advantage. A big, booming voice made it easy to see why teammates called him the Regulator. He had the locker next to one of the exits to the field, and nothing got past him. If you were a rookie who spent too much time with the media—or tried to shirk your rookie duties of offering to carry the shoulder pads and helmets of your fellow veteran position players—he noticed. And if you were a newcomer who was unfamiliar with dealing with the New England media corps—and needed an occasional reminder that the team's problems were never aired through the newspapers—he noticed.

"He was like the grandfather in the locker room," Brady said of McGinest. "Willie would regulate the locker room. He'd regulate the airplane. He'd regulate the hotel. There was nothing that ever got by Willie. I was scared of Willie. Every time I looked at Willie, I was like, 'Man, I never want to mess with Willie.' And he's one of my best friends. I think every player that came here . . . Willie was there to say 'Listen, this is how we're going to do it.'"

On the field, he had played many different roles with New England. Under Carroll, he had played the vaguely defined role of "elephant," a role out of the 49ers' system in which a pass rusher constantly moves around on the line of scrimmage, looking for a crevice through which to attack the quarterback. And Belichick frequently moved him around from spot to spot. It was not uncommon to see him move from outside linebacker to down lineman.

There was some talk that McGinest would be exposed in the expansion draft at the end of the 2001 season. He had started a career-low five games that year, which left some wondering if there was anything left in his tank. But McGinest returned in 2002, and, by 2003, he had returned to his familiar role as a pass rushing force off the end, making the Pro Bowl in the process. What he lacked in pure speed he made up for by coming up big in big moments, especially against the Colts. The season before, he had led the Patriots goal-line stand against Colts running back Edgerrin James, blasting James on the one-yard line as time ran out in New England's 38–34 victory.

And so, in the first game of his twelfth year in the NFL against his old nemeses, it was no surprise to see McGinest in the middle of things. Down the stretch, the Patriots clung to a 27–24 lead. Manning and the Colts were at the New England 17-yard line, facing a third and eight with 49 seconds left to play. With Indianapolis in scoring range, Manning and the Colts came to the line looking to take one more shot at the end zone. If they missed, they would likely turn things over to their kicker, Mike Vanderjagt. The occasionally irascible kicker had made forty-two straight field goal attempts, an NFL record, so they felt pretty good about their chances. But as Manning dropped back to pass, McGinest came screaming off the edge unblocked as part of an outside blitz called by defensive coordinator Romeo Crennel. The Indianapolis quarterback went scrambling, back, back, back. McGinest kept coming, eventually catching him at the 29-yard line. The Patriots called time out with twenty-four seconds left. It would be a 48-yard attempt for Vanderjagt, who rubbed his fingers together at the New England sideline—indicating that he was "money"—as he lined up for what would be the game-tying kick.

But Vanderjagt missed, pushing the ball wide to the right, giving New England a narrow win and adding another chapter to McGinest's legacy. "I remember hearing I was done," the veteran linebacker said after the game. "But I love the game, and I wasn't ready to leave it then, and I'm not ready to leave it now. I got a lot of passion. They're going to have to kick me out. When they kick me out, I'll go home. But they're not going to be doing that to me for a while."

"It seems that Willie always seems to be there when we need him," Belichick said.

From a team-building perspective, the 2003 and 2004 teams were far different than the 2001 team, with the major difference being the fact that the 2001 team was formed almost completely by players who could have been had by any other team in the league through the draft or free agency. In particular, the Patriots of 2004 were suddenly stocked with plenty of top-tier talent, thanks to some smart trades and key free agents. Along with Colvin, the Patriots boasted Harrison and Ted Washington, a pair of key free agent acquisitions the season before. While Washington would sign elsewhere before the beginning of the 2004 season, the team quickly added to their stable of top-level talent with the off-season acquisition of running back Corey Dillon, acquired from the Bengals for a second-round pick that spring.

On the surface, the acquisition of Dillon appeared to be a highly risky maneuver. Dillon was known in many circles to be the ultimate NFL malcontent. In 2003, he lost his starting job to Rudi Johnson and openly lobbied for a trade. He went on TV shows and called teammate Willie Anderson "a bum." And at the end of the season—after tossing his equipment into the stands after the final regular-season game against Cleveland—he cleaned out his locker and asked to be traded. "They don't need me," Dillon told reporters at the time. "They've been winning, quote unquote, without me." Dillon hardly appeared to be model Patriot.

There *were* acquisitions that the Patriots had made over the years that could be construed as questionable. When they got linebacker Bryan Cox prior to the 2001 season, he was coming off a checkered past that included thousands of dollars in fines and a reputation as a troublemaker. But Belichick had a past with him and knew the sort of player he was getting—Cox had played for Parcells and Belichick with the Jets. Cox had a wild reputation, but he cared deeply for the game of football. There were no such guarantees with Dillon, whose public persona was that of angry malcontent.

Belichick and Pioli held a clandestine meeting with Dillon and his agent in a Foxborough hotel. "These two men think you're a bad guy," Feldman said to Dillon in an exchange later recounted in *ESPN: The Magazine*. "Tell them why they're wrong." Dillon unloaded, saying he was a good person, but had just gotten sick of the losing, and sick of being the star asked to carry the load for a team that had given him no support. The pitch worked. The Patriots acquired him for a second-round pick. And just as the drafting of Brady represented a significant shift in the way the Patriots went about judging talent, the acquisition of someone like Dillon was equally illuminating. Despite Dillon's pleas, no one was sure how he would react to New England's team-first mantra. But whatever happened, it was clear the front office saw the infrastructure in place—on the coaching staff and in the locker room—that could support the presence of a potentially combustible individual like Dillon. If Dillon decided to go off the rails as he did in Cincinnati, there were enough veterans around who would put him back on the straight and narrow. Many of the regulators who were present in 2001 were still around, guys like Willie McGinest who patrolled the locker room on a daily basis, making sure nothing got out of hand. For his part, in a symbolic move designed to make people forget about the past, Dillon shaved his head the night before training camp, eliminating his cornrows, and, with it, his bad reputation. During training camp, Dillon did all he could to fit in. In his first year with the Patriots, he acquiesced to interviews. He was a model citizen. In the words of one reporter, that year, "He always drank his milk all the way to the bottom of the glass, and always said 'Please' and 'Thank you.'"

The rest of the season passed in much the same fashion as the end of the year before. The defense remained at the top of its game, while the offense, suddenly powered by the "bell cow" of a running back in Dillon that Belichick had spoken of so covetously in years past, was held under twenty points just once all season. And with a 24–10 win over the Dolphins on October 10, 2004, they broke the record for consecutive wins, pushing their mark to nineteen in a row. They had become a model of efficiency, rolling through opponents into the history books. "The Patriots achievement is not only unprecedented but also remarkable when you consider how competitive our league is today," said Tagliabue in a statement issued after the game. But other than a brief postgame aside from a Gatorade-soaked Belichick—"You've done something no other team in the NFL has done," he told his team after the game—it was back to the grind. "I told the team they should be proud," Belichick said. "No other team in pro football has done it.

"That being said, our goal is not winning four games in a row."

Just as in *Groundhog Day*, the script remained the same. The Patriots beat Seattle and the New York Jets before their ride finally came to a screeching halt on Halloween against the Steelers in Pittsburgh. It was a rough, physical game—not unlike most Steelers-Patriots games since 2001—and, in the end, Pittsburgh picked up a fairly easy 34–20 win. But the Steelers spent much of the final quarter woofing at New England, and NFL Films picked up footage of several players, including linebacker Joey Porter, on the sidelines saying there was no way the Patriots were in the same class as the Steelers.

While there was plenty of respect between Belichick and Pittsburgh head coach Bill Cowher, that same feeling didn't extend to the players. There was a brutishness to the Steelers' game that seemed to be the polar opposite of New England. The Patriots of 2003 and 2004 didn't win games, they won chess matches. They wanted to outthink their opponent, to work and work and work, and then take advantage of that one key moment when the defenses were down. In many ways, they were a team that was perfectly at home in Massachusetts, home to a number of world-class colleges and universities. The Patriots played smart football, outthinking the opposition. With Pittsburgh, there was none of that. Instead of chess, the Steelers engaged in brutal hand-to-hand combat. They were all about aggression and intimidation. And while the Patriots had more than their share of that on their side, the Pittsburgh style of play was somewhat distasteful. And when it came to Porter? Well, that was another matter entirely. Many New England players openly despised Porter and the "dirt-kicking" routine he pulled after every sack. "What an (expletive)," one unnamed Patriots player told the *Boston Herald* afterward. "I mean, what has he *ever* won?"

Porter may have spent much of the afternoon kicking dirt on the Patriots, but they were by no means dead. New England responded to their first defeat in twelve months with a 40–27 gutcheck win over the Rams, a funky game that featured Vinatieri throwing a touchdown pass to Brown on a fake field goal, and Brown coming in to play defensive back. Because of an injury to Law in the loss to Pittsburgh, as well as injuries to other defensive backs, Brown would continue to play cornerback much of the season. He wasn't the only player forced to play out of position in 2004. Special teams ace Don Davis, a linebacker by trade, saw plenty of time at safety, while linemen Dan Klecko and Richard Seymour routinely lined up at fullback in short-yardage situations. In addition, linebacker Mike Vrabel would play tight end. In the end, it all worked, as the Patriots entered the 2004 postseason with a 14–2 mark.

By this time, the professional relationship between Brady and Manning had reached Russell-Chamberlain proportions. Brady was seen as the guy who didn't have the gaudy numbers, but in the end somehow always ended up the winner because of his knack for rising to the occasion on the big stage. As for Manning, he had the fantastic numbers—including a record-setting forty-nine touchdown passes that season—but was never able to get past Belichick, Brady, and the rest of the Patriots. Like Russell and Chamberlain, they were friendly off the field, working together to get new quarterback-friendly rules passed. And while people flocked to the Russell-Chamberlain matchup to see the two stars do battle, it was frequently the supporting players who were the difference. To that end, if Damon Huard, Ty Law, and Jarvis Green were the difference in the 2003 AFC Championship Game, it would be Dillon who would make the difference in the 2004 divisional playoff against Indianapolis.

That, and Mike Vanderjagt. Almost a year after the 2003 AFC title game, the Patriots were preparing to meet in the 2004 AFC divisional playoffs. Belichick stood in the middle of the Patriots locker room with a copy of the *Boston Herald*. The headline across the back page screamed "VANDERJERK," and the story discussed Indianapolis kicker Mike Vanderjagt's recent comments about the Patriots on a local Indianapolis television station. "I think they're ripe for the picking," Vanderjagt said shortly after the Colts throttled the Broncos to set up a rematch of the 2003 AFC Championship Game. "I think they're not as good as the beginning of the year and not as good as last year."

It was not the first time Vanderjagt had said something that drew the ire of other players. A few years earlier, he said Indianapolis quarterback Peyton Manning should show more emotion and Indianapolis head coach Tony Dungy was too mild-mannered to be effective—calling out two of the most respected people in the game. Manning later responded by calling Vanderjagt an "idiot kicker" during an interview at the Pro Bowl, and Dungy said Vanderjagt should have come to him with his complaints instead of airing them on a Canadian cable television show.

Publicly, Belichick was curt when it came to discussing Vanderjagt's comments. "I don't have any comment on what Vanderjagt did or didn't say," he said with a small smile in the days leading up to the game. "I'm sure he'll be out there a few times in the game to do his one special thing. We got a kicker and we'll put him out there and he'll do his one special thing." Behind the scenes, he was pleased that the Colts were able to provide some tangible ammunition for his team. It was the sort of thing he used to keep them hungry and humble. Many times, the disrespect was something manufactured, some perceived slight he was able to use to his advantage. As the week continued, it was clear his team was using the comments as fuel for their fire.

"He should focus on making the field goals, not worried about what we're doing over here, OK?" said safety Rodney Harrison. "I mean, he has to be a jerk, Vanderjerk, if he sits there and criticizes Peyton Manning and Tony Dungy, one of the best quarterbacks in the game and one of the best coaches in the game. And then for him to put his foot in his mouth again just shows what type of character he has."

Belichick went looking for more incentive and found it when he discovered that an Indianapolis official had ordered an extra 1,500 tickets from the Steelers for the AFC Championship Game the following week. Despite the fact that several teams around the league viewed the move as a common practice, it was another perceived slight for the Patriots to feed off of. What had been a friendly rivalry had devolved into a bitter feud.

In the game, the one sure way to beat Manning was to keep him off the field. To that end, the Patriots hit the Colts with plenty of Dillon—the running back picked up an astounding 144 rushing yards (the second-highest total for a playoff game in team history), helping New England maintain an astounding edge in time of possession (the Patriots controlled the ball for almost thirty-eight of the game's sixty minutes) and imposed their will on the Colts. "Third-down conversion after third-down conversion after third-down conversion," explained Belichick when asked about the secret of their offensive success against Indianapolis. On the other side of the ball, without starting corners Law and Poole, as well as Pro Bowl lineman Richard Seymour, the Patriots were physical with the fleet Colts receivers. When Manning was on the field, a variety of defensive looks the Patriots threw at him were enough to keep him off balance all afternoon long on the way to a 20–3 win for New England. At the end, fans gleefully taunted Manning with cries of "Cut that meat!"—a reference to his MasterCard commercial.

After the game, the New England players taunted Polian and the Colts, believing they were behind the changes. "I'm just trying to think of what excuses they'll be saying in the locker room right now," said Bruschi after the game. "I wonder what rules they want to change now. Maybe it will be we can't play a game in the snow. I don't know, but they will think of something. I was just tired of it. I was tired of hearing this and that, them talking about the last game [a 27–24 Patriots victory in the season opener] and how we didn't win the game, that they lost the game by giving the ball away. [That afternoon], we just took it away from them."

In the AFC Championship Game, the Patriots were forced to return to Pittsburgh, the scene of their ugly Halloween loss to Porter and the Steelers. This time, New England wouldn't go right at the physical Steelers, but outthink them by using Pittsburgh's aggression to their advantage. Setting the tone on their first play from scrimmage, they faked a handoff to Corey Dillon off left tackle and instead gave the ball to Deion Branch on an end around to the right, gaining 14 yards and setting up a 48-yard field goal by Adam Vinatieri. Later in the first quarter, a flu-ridden Tom Brady got Pittsburgh to bite on another fake, this time a play-action to Dillon. The Steelers' secondary fell for it and, combined with a mistake in coverage by Pittsburgh safety Troy Polamalu, gave Branch just enough separation from him to make an over-the-shoulder grab on a sixty-yard pass play to make it 10–0. Shortly afterward, Brady hit David Givens for one touchdown, and a Harrison 87-yard interception return for a touchdown tacked on seven more, making it 24–3 at the half. They coasted to a 41–27 win.

"Those players have met strong challenges every week from all of our opponents, none more so than the Steelers, and I give them all the credit in the world for their mental and physical toughness, their resiliency and their ability to play well under pressure," Belichick said afterward. "We made a lot of big plays today. The players just did an outstanding job, and they deserve all the credit for this one. They made the plays when they had to make them and we didn't turn the ball over. We were able to hold them to few enough points on defense to come out on top. We're very excited and happy to be representing the AFC in Jacksonville. "

There was less than a minute to play in Super Bowl XXXIX when Philadelphia quarterback Donovan McNabb led the Eagles to the line of scrimmage. Philadelphia was buried deep in their own end, facing third and nine from their own five-yard line with seventeen seconds left. The Eagles quarterback was in the shotgun, hoping to conserve as much time as possible, and he received the center snap cleanly from Hank Fraley. The pass rush closed in around him, and both Bruschi and Jarvis Green came within a few feet of the Philadelphia quarterback. But he was still able to get the pass off, a nice tight spiral that floated down the middle of the field.

Belichick watched the play develop on the New England sidelines. The game had a distinctly different feel than their other two Super Bowl apperances (see also entries in Part 2 and Part 3). In their two previous trips to football's final game under their head coach, New England was in control of their destiny as the clock ticked down. In Super Bowl XXXVI, with the score tied at 17 against the heavily favored Rams, the Patriots had the ball with 1:30 left. As John Madden told a national television audience that Brady and New England should play for overtime, the quarterback— without any time-outs—led the Patriots on a drive that became the stuff of legend, a drive that ultimately culminated in a 48-yard field goal by Vinatieri to win the game with no time left. And in Super Bowl XXXVIII, it was more of the same. Late in the fourth, Brady conducted another drive into the heart of the Panthers' defense, allowing Vinatieri to deliver a 41-yarder with four seconds left that stood up as the difference on the 32–29 win over Carolina.

However, this one was different. After Vinatieri banged home a 22-yarder, New England held a 24–14 lead with just over eight minutes remaining, and it looked like, for once, Belichick would be able to enjoy the final few moments of a Super Bowl. But after the Patriots went three-and-out on their next possession, the Eagles were able to draw to within three when McNabb hit wide receiver Greg Lewis for a thirty-yard strike with 1:55 remaining. And when the Patriots were unable to run out the clock, Philadelphia was able to regain possession with 55 seconds left. Even though New England punter Josh Miller pinned the Eagles at their own four-yard line—and even though Philadelphia was only able to muster a single yard over their first two plays of the possession (a one-yard pass from McNabb to running back Brian Westbrook)—there was a vague sense of unease among many of the Patriots who had made the trip to Jacksonville. After all, New England was firmly in charge down the stretch against the Rams in Super Bowl XXXVI. And while there were some anxious moments down the stretch in Super Bowl XXXVIII, it was Brady who had the ball as time ticked down. This time, the Eagles had the ball. And even though the Patriots had plenty of faith in their man Brady, they knew as long as McNabb had the football in his grasp, he remained one of the most dangerous threats in the game.

McNabb's spiral continued its path. Roughly ten or so yards downfield from McNabb, Philadelphia tight end L. J. Smith was being shadowed by Patriots linebacker Roman Phifer. Smith saw it was headed in his direction, and was able to shake Phifer for a few moments and turn to reach for the football. But it glanced off his hands ever so slightly and continued floating, end over end through the chilly Jacksonville evening, before landing in the hands of New England defensive back Rodney Harrison. The veteran safety—a part of so many bad teams for so many years in San

Diego before Belichick and the Patriots took a chance on him prior to the start of the 2003 season—smiled broadly and started celebrating.

Belichick jumped in the air, pumping his fist several times. As Brady kneeled down on the football and the clocked ticked to :00 on the Alltel Stadium scoreboard, the New England sideline erupted. Super Bowl XXXIX was the first time Belichick was able to enjoy the actual celebratory moment—the other two games had been decided in the final frantic seconds—and he was enjoying himself. In Super Bowl XXXVI, the postgame moments were spent with his daughter Amanda. Three years later, he shared a moment with his father, Steve, a quick embrace that ended when Bruschi dumped a bucket of water on the two of them. He also shared a moment with offensive coordinator Charlie Weis and defensive co-ordinator Romeo Crennel, holding the pair tight in an embrace that lasted for nearly a minute. After several years together, it would be the final game together for the three of them. From East Rutherford, New Jersey, to Foxborough, Massachusetts, the trio was together for almost twenty years, helping bring football success to the Giants, Patriots, and Jets. They had developed a unique bond. The three of them, out from under the large shadow of Bill Parcells, had managed to craft a team that had now won three Super Bowls in four years. However, it was time to say farewell. Weis has already taken the job as head coach at his alma mater, Notre Dame, and Crennel would be in Cleveland the next day to discuss the Browns' head coaching job, a position he would take a few days later.

"I think the world of those two guys," Belichick said later that night. "They've done a tremendous job. I don't know what the future holds for Romeo, but I'm sure, in my opinion he certainly deserves an opportunity to be a head coach in this league, or wherever he wants to do it. And Charlie has done a tremendous job, especially the last few weeks, especially with his responsibilities. I was thrilled to be able—for the three of us to be able to hug each other. We've been together a long time, all the way back to the Giants. It was a good feeling."

When they rolled out the podium to present the Vince Lombardi Trophy, Robert Kraft took the moment to salute the fans, as well as the Belichick belief in team over individual. Raising the Vince Lombardi Trophy over his head for the third time in four years, he said: "Fans of New England: The best fans that any team could wish for. This is your third Super Bowl in four years. This great accomplishment happened because we are blessed to have smart and talented players, a brilliant, tireless coach in coach Belichick and his entire staff; and a great personnel department led by Scott Pioli.

"The NFL is the great leveler of all sports. And the Super Bowl is the highest form of competition. Competition is the foundation of what made this country great. And I am proud that we were able to win this Super Bowl with stressing team, and not individual accomplishment. We're honored to be here."

Taking his turn at the podium, Belichick was his usual succinct self: "These players have just played great all year. They've played their best in the big games, and they deserve it. They really deserve it."

Ultimately, the NFL is a lot like Hollywood. If one formula works, everyone tries to come up with a variation on the same theme. And so in the days after Super Bowl XXXIX, the indisputable evidence that the Patriots' team-building approach was now the next hot thing in the NFL could be seen in the way many football organizations conducted their business. On the basest of levels, many went directly for the obvious—the surest way to get a fresh apple is to make sure it's picked directly off the tree. So Notre Dame and the Cleveland Browns lifted the Patriots' coordinators, with Weis taking the New England offense to South Bend and Crennel trying to turn around Cleveland by using a dose of the Patriots' system.

But for most other teams, changes were more subtle. Since 2000, many teams had slowly begun to forsake the traditional front office look—the head coach making all the calls on personnel issues—in favor of a more egalitarian approach involving at least one other person, usually a de facto general manager. But with the triumph of the New England system, that process began to accelerate, and by the end of the decade, traditional NFL thinking dictated that the head coach and general manager had to be completely in sync when it came to any and all personnel matters or the franchise would ultimately fall short of any real success.

Like New England, the really successful front offices were seen as the ones that arrived with a big picture plan as to how to win. Within those front offices, the people in charge did all they could to cultivate a debate in the meeting rooms and coaches' offices over prospects and encouraged nontraditional thinking when it came to approaching traditional meat markets like the NFL Scouting Combine. The new head coach did not work alone. Instead, he had in place a support staff he trusted. He delegated properly, finding loyal assistants, trusted scouts, and assistant coaches, who set out to find players who were not only able to see the big picture needed to achieve real team success in the NFL, but were passionate about the game to boot.

In addition to overall changes in the way coaching staffs and front offices handled themselves, there were other indications that teams were looking to copy the Patriots' blueprint for success. More and more, the successful owners were seen as the ones who scaled back their involvement in personnel issues or dropped out of the spotlight altogether. *Commit to a front office, let them pick the coach, and then get out of the way* was the way things were supposed to go, and successful owners like the Rooney family in Pittsburgh, Paul Allen in Seattle, and Jeffrey Lurie in Philadelphia did just that. Small wonder that in the same time the Patriots have won three Super Bowls, those three teams have won several conference championships. For some owners, it was painful to step out of the spotlight, but when they considered the financial gains they could accumulate as a result, the process was made considerably easier: In the months after Super Bowl XXXIX, the Forbes 2005 National Football League team value rankings estimated the worth of the Patriots at $1 billion.

Of course, not all of these changes were a direct result of the Patriots success, but the idea that they happened in a vacuum is naïve. With three titles in four years, many of the other teams openly confessed to looking to New England as the model for how to run their franchise. As the middle of the decade loomed, it was clear that New England's team-building approach was now the next big thing in football circles, and the other thirty-one teams would be doing all they could to try and copy their approach. If Belichick and the Patriots wanted to keep their edge, they had to start looking elsewhere for their advantages.

# CHAPTER SEVEN

# THE PIPELINE

I'm not really surprised by what any of them have done. Outstanding group of coaches and people. I think time has shown that was a
pretty capable and competent staff.

—BILL BELICHICK, DECEMBER 24, 2004,

ON HIS COACHING STAFF WHILE IN CLEVELAND

It was Draft Day, 2005, and the Patriots were on the clock.

The draft is Belichick's favorite team-building exercise. You
can restock your roster in two ways: through free agency and
through the draft. And when you traditionally exercise caution in
free agency, as the Patriots had done, it places greater emphasis on
that two-day exercise in April. Along the way, your team has a
chance to get younger, and you're able to acquire cheap labor
that's easier to control than a veteran free agent. Of course, if you
are going to restock your roster via the draft instead of free agency,
that leaves a very small margin for error when it came to picking
your talent. If you swing and miss on a draft completely, it can set
the entire team-building process back for at least a year, maybe
two. A reliable feeder system is key when it comes to assembling a
team.

To that end, through his first five years as head coach in New

England, Belichick and the Patriots had always managed to come out of the draft with at least one major contributor. It was a good percentage. Drafting most of the time in the mid to late stages of the first round, most teams would be lucky to get one impact rookie on the roster a season. But New England hit on a good run throughout the early years of the twenty-first century. In 2000, it was Brady. In 2001, it was defensive lineman Richard Seymour and left tackle Matt Light, both of whom were full-time starters by their second season. In 2002, tight end Daniel Graham, wide receiver Deion Branch, defensive lineman Jarvis Green, and wide receiver David Givens all became key contributors.

But it was the 2003 draft that will likely go down as Belichick's finest hour when it comes to talent evaluation. It yielded riches, and will stand alongside 1976 (which brought future Hall of Famer Mike Haynes and fellow defensive back Tim Fox to New England, along with center Pete Brock), 1977 (defensive back Raymond Clayborn, wide receiver Stanley Morgan, running back Horace Ivory, and tight end Don Hasselbeck were all eventual starters taken in the first two rounds that year) and 1995 (defensive back Ty Law, linebacker Ted Johnson, and running back Curtis Martin) as one of the great drafts in franchise history. That spring, New England chose defensive lineman Ty Warren (first round), defensive back Eugene Wilson (second), cornerback Asante Samuel (fourth), offensive lineman Dan Koppen (fifth), and linebacker Tully Banta-Cain (seventh). The 2004 draft was also impressive— nose tackle Vince Wilfork and tight end Ben Watson were taken with the first two selections—but it was the 2003 draft that remains New England's finest hour when it came to personnel evaluation, for several reasons, not the least of which was that so many of those players appeared to be NFL-ready their rookie season. Of that group, the only player who didn't play in all sixteen regular-season games was Banta-Cain, who ended up playing in nine. Afterward, Belichick paid tribute to the scouting department, headed by Larry Cook. "They go through literally thousands of names and times and all different sorts of information, medical, player evaluations, and otherwise," Belichick said. "All their history and draft research on all these players and it all comes together for just a handful of guys. In the end, it seems like a lot of work gets thrown away with all of the hundreds or thousands of guys that you end up not drafting. It's just part of the process, and I think those guys did a really good job, and of course, Scott [Pioli] as well. I thought they were really well prepared. It really made it easy for me to go through the information because they sort a lot of it out."

In that context, when the New England front office settled into their bunker deep within the confines of Gillette Stadium that April weekend in 2005, there was plenty on the line. With the continued health issues surrounding linebacker Tedy Bruschi—the linebacker had suffered a stroke less than a month after Super Bowl XXXIX, and his professional future was in doubt—they could try and get younger at that spot. There were also several other possibilities: Questions about depth in the secondary arose year after year. The franchise wanted to keep wide receiver Troy Brown from another year of having to play as an emergency defensive back. And with the chance that veteran Ty Law would leave via free agency, the need for help in the secondary was also readily apparent.

That afternoon began predictably enough, as most of the big-name linebackers and defensive backs were quickly taken. Cornerback Pacman Jones went No. 6 to Tennessee, while cornerback Antrel Rolle went No. 8 to Arizona and fellow DB Carlos Rogers went No. 9 to Washington. Then, the run on linebackers began. There were five taken between No. 11 and No. 17, including DeMarcus Ware (to Dallas at No. 11), Shawne Merriman (San Diego, No. 12) Thomas Davis (Carolina, No. 14), Derrick Johnson (Kansas City, No. 15) and David Pollack (Cincinnati, No. 17). But as they started to get closer to No. 32, the first and only selection of the first round for New England, there were still several linebackers available, including Channing Crowder out of Florida, Nebraska's Barrett Ruud, and Lofa Tatupu from USC, three players who had been linked to the Patriots in several mock drafts as potential targets.

However, the Patriots had their eye on one player—Logan Mankins. Mankins was a versatile offensive lineman, having suited up at guard and tackle while at Fresno State. However, most predraft publications had him listed as a second- or third-round choice. On the surface, the move seemed especially odd for New England, as the offensive line didn't seem to be the sort of position the Patriots should be placing a priority on. But Mankins had one thing going for him that several other available players didn't. As a collegian, he played for Pat Hill, a former assistant coach under Belichick in Cleveland in the early 1990s. And when a former Belichick assistant gave his thumbs-up on a player, the New England head coach knew the recommendation spoke volumes. The Patriots picked Mankins.

"I have a lot of respect for Pat," Belichick said after Mankins was selected. "I think that Pat is a really good football coach. He obviously has spent the majority of his career coaching the offensive line and his players are always fundamentally sound and they are very well coached. I think that Logan has certainly developed a good playing style, a good fundamental base to come into this league similar to some of the things that we said about [Dan] Koppen playing for [Tom] O'Brien at [Boston College]. I will let Pat speak for himself. Suffice it to say that Pat recommended Logan."

That weekend, New England selected another FSU player, the relatively anonymous safety James Sanders in the fourth round. Why would the Patriots take a pair of players from an 8–5 team? The selections of Mankins and Sanders continued a trend that had been building since 2002: When Belichick has an opportunity to go after a collegian who plays in a system coached by a former Belichick assistant, he'll often choose that player ahead of another player who has equal value on the board. Between 2002 and 2005, seven of the thirty-one players drafted by the Patriots in that span came from schools where a Belichick assistant or close friend was the head coach. In 2002, New England selected quarterback Rohan Davey and defensive lineman Jarvis Green, both of whom attended Louisiana State University and played football under Nick Saban, a defensive coordinator under Belichick with the Browns from 1991 to 1994. That draft class also saw the addition of running back Antwoine Womack, who played for the University of Virginia under Al Groh. Groh also served on the same Cleveland staff, working as the linebackers coach under Belichick in 1992. (Groh would go on to work with Belichick and Parcells in New England and the New York Jets.) In 2003, the Patriots chose center Dan Koppen in the fifth round out of Boston College. Head coach Tom O'Brien had never worked with Belichick on a coaching staff, but the roots between O'Brien and Belichick were deep. O'Brien is an ex-Navy man, and also had ties to the coaching staff at the University of Virginia, having worked there as a head coach prior to Groh's arrival in December 2000. (That year also saw the addition of another LSU product when the Patriots added undrafted free agent cornerback Randall Gay—another product of Saban's intricate defenses at Louisiana State. He would go on to become a key part of New England's defense, eventually getting the start in Super Bowl XXXIX and making eleven tackles in the win over the Eagles.) In 2004, the tradition of plucking talent from former Belichick assistants continued when New England selected defensive lineman Marquise Hill with a second-round selection out of Louisiana State. And when Mankins and Sanders were taken in 2005 out of Pat Hill's program at Fresno State, that list got even longer. They added to that in 2006 with the selection of offensive lineman Dan Stevenson, a product of the Charlie Weis system at Notre Dame. In 2007, two more products of Belichick-style systems were selected in Notre Dame cornerback Mike Richardson and Iowa offensive lineman Mike Elgin.

Some of the moves make plenty of sense: Players like Koppen, Green, and Gay were almost instant starters. Some have been head scratchers: Womack and Hill struggled in New England's system, and Davey, despite several chances, never seemed to make it with the Patriots. But the idea remains the same. The complicated New England schemes put in place by Belichick can be solved by players who already have some background in the system. "I think the combination of guys who play in systems like his and will therefore understand the terminology," said football statistician Aaron Schatz. "I'm guessing that's a lot of what it was with Randall Gay. If Pat Hill vouches for a guy, he knows Pat Hill isn't goofing with him. He's been talking to these guys about these kids since they were sophomore or freshmen."

Few coaches have the network of former assistants that Belichick has. Seven individuals who have served as assistants under Belichick are now head coaches in the NFL or in college: Kirk Ferentz (Iowa), Al Groh (Virginia), Pat Hill (Fresno State), Mangini (New York Jets), Nick Saban (Alabama), Crennel (Cleveland Browns) and Weis (Notre Dame). In addition, several others who have worked with Belichick are running NFL front offices, including Phil Savage (GM, Cleveland Browns) and Ozzie Newsome (GM, Baltimore Ravens). All of them are graduates of what some have started calling Belichick University, an ever-growing network of former assistants that, as each one moves on to a bigger and better job, continues to expand. While Belichick and his contemporaries in the pros share an understandably cautious relationship, things are much different when it comes to the college game. He's managed to make many of those former assistants who are now guiding college programs his unofficial eyes and ears when it comes to scouting. And while he will always sing the praises of his scouting department, a thumbs-up from a graduate of Belichick University will almost always put a prospect over the top.

Many of those graduates were schooled under some of the most difficult of circumstances, in the nightmarish season of 1995, when the Cleveland Browns were falling apart. Owner Art Modell, angry that he had not received the public funding necessary to build a new stadium, announced in November that he was moving the team to

Baltimore. The decision, coming in the middle of the season, threw the organization into chaos. The area went into a full-scale rebellion. Virtually all of the team's sponsors immediately pulled their support, leaving Cleveland Stadium devoid of advertising during the team's final weeks. Over a hundred lawsuits were filed by fans, the city of Cleveland, and a host of others, most of which were later settled in their favor. Congress held hearings on the matter. Modell was forced to resign his membership (and in many cases, leadership positions) in local civic and charitable organizations, and would literally be forced to leave the city—never to return. None of it mattered. The Browns were moving, and the city was powerless to stop them.

Against that backdrop, the Browns coaching staff was charged with the nearly impossible task of keeping the players focused on the job at hand—namely, winning football games. And while Belichick became inexorably tied to Modell and his legacy, he was fortunate enough to have a talented collection of coaches to work with in hopes of saving the season. Saban was the defensive coordinator, and under his guidance, the Browns went from allowing the most points in the league (462) in the NFL prior to his arrival to allowing the fewest points (204) in the league in 1994, the sixth-fewest points surrendered in NFL history at the time. In each of Saban's four years in Cleveland, they never permitted an average of more than 19.2 points per game, and Saban clearly earned Belichick's respect. When someone asked Belichick about what things were like when he *had* Saban as an assistant, he quickly cut off the questioner. "I didn't *have* him anywhere. We worked together. I didn't have him anywhere," he said. "Things that we run, he understands because he did them. Things that he runs I understand them because I've done them at some point. We talk from time to time. . . . It's a good relationship. I have a lot of respect for him as a person, as a friend."

Losing coaches from your system can be a double-edged sword. Since the end of the 2004 season, the Patriots have been forced to replace two defensive coordinators (Crennel and Mangini) and one offensive coordinator (Weis). Belichick's approach is so admired that anyone associated with him—even a thirty-four-year-old with limited experience—is in demand. Why go after a Belichick guy? "He's been a major contributor to a very successful organization," said Jets CEO Woody Johnson after New York hired Mangini. Mangini had spent one year as New England's defensive coordinator. "He's won sixty-eight games in the last five years, three Super Bowls, I think that's well documented. But the most important thing is he demonstrated to us a passion for football, passion for teaching, and I think he knows something about the culture of football that appeals to us in this building."

It's part of the price of success in the NFL: If you are successful, people will want to try to replicate your system by poaching the people who had a hand in developing the franchise's success. In New England, that means continually trying to find new assistant coaches. Belichick confessed at the start of the 2005 season that's just part of life in the NFL. "This is a game of change," he said. "Even if the same people are in place, it still changes from year to year. It changes from week to week for that matter. I think that's inevitable. You play different opponents. You have different people. At some point you just say, 'Hey, we have to move on,'" he added. "I don't think you can go out there and run the same thing for ten years in a row."

But at the same time, coaching turnover allows those who are familiar with the Belichick system to fan out across the football world, both in the NFL and in college. That allows a collegian who has been schooled in a Belichick-style system to be able to step right in and flourish when he arrives in Foxborough. That was certainly the case with defensive lineman Jarvis Green, who played under Saban at Louisiana State and learned the Belichick-Saban system as a collegian. That made it all the easier to plug him into the Patriots' system, a system that started while Belichick was with the Giants, but really started to flower when Belichick and Saban were together in Cleveland. "I'm only slightly exaggerating, but Belichick got a new view of how to make a Cover 2 scheme (two deep safeties, each taking half the field) morph into a Cover 4 (four deep DBs, each taking a quarter of the deep secondary) from Saban . . . because he's not afraid to change, and thus, not afraid to fail," wrote *Sports Illustrated* football writer Peter King.

"Coming to New England, there was no difference at all," said Green, who finished fourth in LSU history with twenty career sacks. "There were some differences in terms of learning the new system. I had to get through that. But just adjusting to the game was a lot easier. Coach Saban talked about the NFL and the way it is and how it's a business and what you have to expect. So the transition was easy."

Green recalls being able to sniff out many of the details of the Patriots' complicated defense because he was schooled in the Belichick-Saban system at LSU. It wasn't a breeze, but he remembers being able to say, "I remember this from college," in his rookie year in New England, and that allowed him to get a leg up as a rookie, an experience he's still thankful for today. "It was like that," he said. "But I still had problems learning different things . . . the size of the playbook and the speed as to how fast coaches expect you to learn the game. For me, it was tough coming in, even though I learned a lot of different things under Coach Saban. There was still some adjusting I had to deal with. But I think the more you do it over and over again, you get the hang of it."

When an NFL team thinks nontraditionally when it comes to acquiring talent, they'll find someone like Stephen Neal. A big guy with a quick smile, the six-foot-four, 305-pound Neal was a legend in high school and college wrestling circles throughout the late 1990s. As a high schooler in San Diego, he was fourth in the state with a 45–2 mark at 198 pounds and picked up a win over future Heisman Trophy winner Ricky Williams. At California State, Bakersfield, he became a star on the college wrestling circuit, winning a pair of NCAA Division I titles, a world title, a medal in the Pan-Am

Games and closing out his collegiate career with an 88-match winning streak. (Among wrestling aficionados, he's best known as being the guy who beat future WWE star Brock Lesnar 3–2 to help give CSBU a national title.) But in a story with *USA Today* his senior year, he told a reporter that if wrestling didn't work out, he'd love to give football a try. After graduation, he decided to give agent Neil Cornrich a call, and Cornrich got him seen. The Cleveland-based Cornrich—who has done a lot of legal work for Belichick—got him a shot with New England. The NFL is populated with several high school wrestling champions, like Baltimore middle linebacker Ray Lewis. The skill set needed to succeed as an NFL lineman is the same for a great Greco-Roman wrestle: strength, footwork, leverage, balance, explosion, and hand-to-hand combat. But the fact that there was no college football in his background was a major strike against him. There was only one notable ex-collegiate wrestler who had made it to the NFL after not playing a single down of college football: Carlton Haselrig, the winner of three Division I wrestling titles in the late 1980s and early 1990s, ended up becoming a Pro Bowl offensive lineman with the Steelers.

While there was no doubt about Neal's athleticism—he competed in five sports in high school, including tennis and swimming—the Patriots' front office and coaching staff remained dubious. There wasn't a month that went by when they didn't receive a videotape from a weekend warrior who believed he could make it in the NFL.

"I could show you a thousand tapes a year of guys who send in stuff," recalled Belichick. "'I can play. I was great in high school flag football. This Thursday league that I play in . . .' We get a thousand of those, maybe more than that. Are there any of them out there? More than we have time to deal with.

"Some of those are just classics. The guy has his girlfriend out there throwing passes to him. He's the receiver. 'I ran a 3.8 in high school.' You can imagine. You can imagine."

When Neal arrived for a workout, New England put him

through a traditional workout, using the usual measures that help gauge a prospect's ability, including the forty-yard dash. Neal ran the forty in five seconds, an immense disappointment for him, but an eye-opener for the Patriots, because most world-class offensive linemen are in the same neighborhood. The results of the workout were good enough for Belichick and Pioli, who signed him as a defensive end, and invited him to his first camp in 2001. But when he arrived, Belichick first realized how steep the learning curve for Neal would be. "When I tell you he didn't know where the field was, he didn't know where the field was," Belichick said with a smile when discussing Neal's first days in camp. "He didn't know how to put his pads on. He didn't know where to line up. We're starting from below scratch."

There was something there, enough for New England to keep him around until the final cuts before letting him go. Belichick confessed to quietly pulling for Neal. "The game was simple for him with two people and not twenty-two. This is like me trying to learn Chinese. In two days you're not going to have Chinese down," Belichick said at the time. "But Steve's got good balance from being a wrestler. He can handle other big guys being on him. He knows how to bend his knees and he can get good leverage, and keep from getting pushed around. Fundamentally, he's got a long way to go, but for three days, and for someone who hasn't played football for six years, not bad."

He was snapped up by the Eagles, who placed him on their practice squad. A few months after that, the Patriots signed him to their active roster. Injuries to others forced him into the starting lineup in 2002, and privately, many Patriots officials were keeping their fingers crossed that the experiment would work. New England was going up against a tough Green Bay defense, and the idea of starting Neal—who still hadn't played a meaningful game of organized football above the high school level—made plenty of people nervous. However, he played well and earned Belichick's praise in his first start. In an October 2002 loss to the Packers, the

THE BLUEPRINT

Patriots were down 7–3 late in the second quarter when Brady attempted to dump the ball off to Kevin Faulk on a pass that looked like it could have been a lateral. Faulk couldn't handle the ball, and as it rolled to a stop on the soggy turf, he and several other Patriots stood around watching and wondering whether the ball was a lateral or a forward pass . . . until massive Packers defensive end Kabeer Gbaja-Biamila fell on it, giving Green Bay the ball deep in New England territory. Just one Patriot went for the football.

"One guy—Stephen Neal," Belichick said the next day. "One guy."

In the process, Neal suffered a shoulder injury, and was sidelined the rest of the season. But that moment of hustle was enough to keep him on Belichick's radar screen for the foreseeable future. New England placed him on injured reserve, and he missed the rest of the 2002 season as well as the entire 2003 campaign. Belichick was certainly not in the business of handing out roster spots to charity cases, but Neal began to flourish. He rewarded Belichick's patience in 2004 by becoming a regular starter on an offensive line that paved the way for Corey Dillon to set the Patriots' single-season rushing record, with 1,635 yards. In addition, he put together a streak of forty-one consecutive starts that started early in the 2004 season and didn't end until he suffered an injury midway through the 2006 season. For his efforts, the Patriots rewarded him prior to the start of the 2006 season, with a sizable multiyear contract that reportedly featured a signing bonus in excess of $3 million. Not bad for a former wrestler who wasn't sure how to put his pads on during his first day in training camp.

"It is a wonderful story about a guy that with hard work, dedication, overcoming the setbacks of the injuries and the lack of playing experience, has turned into, really, a good football player," Belichick said.

"You have to be amazed at him," said teammate and fellow offensive lineman Dan Koppen. "When you look at him on the field . . . especially when you see his wrestling tapes, you know what kind of an athlete he is. And he shows it out there on the field. He's more athletic than any other lineman that we have out there right now, bar none. I have no problem saying that. He just loves to work. He gets in there and he studies and just wants to do better every day. When you have a guy like that with that athleticism, it's hard to hold him down."

Around the same time Stephen Neal was starting to find his footing as an NFL offensive lineman, Belichick came across something called the Bellman equation. Or, specifically, "It's Fourth Down and What Does the Bellman Equation Say? A Dynamic-Programming Analysis of Football Strategy." It was a study by a professor at Cal-Berkeley, thirty-three pages long, complete with references and tables detailing its argument. On the surface, it certainly didn't look like the sort of thing an NFL coach would use to better his team. It didn't contain a revolutionary blocking scheme or an untapped series of pass patterns. There was no new approach to the draft or a unique look at the scouting process. Instead, David Romer, a University of California, Berkeley, professor of economics, used NFL box scores from the 1998, 1999, and 2000 seasons to attempt—along with mathematical, statistical and economic tools—to debunk the idea that when it comes to fourth down, it's better to kick than to go for a first down or touchdown.

The findings of Romer's analysis included:

- A team facing fourth and goal within five yards of the end zone is better off, on average, trying for a touchdown.
- At midfield, on average, there is an argument for going for a first down on any fourth down within five yards of a first down.
- Even on its own 10-yard-line, a team within three yards of a first down is marginally better off, on average, going for it.
- Of the 1,575 fourth downs in the sample in which the analysis implied that teams were, on average, better off

kicking, teams went for it only seven times. However, on the 1,100 fourth downs where the analysis implied that teams were, on average, better off going for it, they kicked 992 times.

In the NFL, the application of the Bellman equation to football was greeted with a collective yawn. Conventional wisdom suggests that going for it on fourth down is not the sort of move that most coaches would try, at least coaches who are interested in holding their jobs past next week. In most quarters, Romer's analysis was dismissed by many in the NFL as just another offering from someone who has never played the game. Giants head coach Jim Fassel called it something out of "Cal-Berzerkely. . . . What does the professor coach? Maybe he needs a few more classes to teach. Too much free time?" Others said that it's easy to sit and apply numbers, but it's another matter to be walking the sidelines on Sunday with 70,000 fans screaming for you to kick it away. "There's so much more involved with the game than just sitting there, looking at the numbers and saying, 'OK, these are my percentages, then I'm going to do it this way,'" Steelers head coach Bill Cowher told reporters. "That one time it doesn't work could cost your team a football game, and that's the thing a head coach has to live with, not the professor. . . . If we all listened to the professor, we may be all looking for professor jobs."

But much to Romer's surprise, Foxborough showed a willingness to use something other than the traditional statistics. Belichick confessed to having studied the risk-versus-reward approach of the Bellman equation (when Romer heard Belichick had read his paper, his jaw dropped; it certainly hadn't been widely advertised, and was only available through a small Web site run by Cal-Berkeley) and was able to put it into practice on several occasions.

"I think I understand some of the points that were made in there, and I think he has some valid points," Belichick said after reading Romer's study in the summer of 2002. "There's sometimes an emotional aspect, and momentum, if you will, to those decisions, but I'm not sure how to calculate that. One of the points he was making was that if you go for it, particularly when you're inside the opponents' twenty, even if you come up short, you've got them backed up, they got eighty, ninety yards to go. Do the mathematical percentages of them scoring in that situation versus you getting the ball, and so forth and so on, and that's a valid point. On the other hand to go down there and get nothing out of it, psychologically there's an impact there on your team.

"I understand the points that he's made, I don't understand all the mathematical equations how he got to those points, but I think that some of those are legitimate points and you just have to evaluate the situation to your team, the team you're playing," he added. "I see where a lot of that's coming from. Nobody ever said we were smart, just trying to do the right thing."

The most notable instance came in the 2004 AFC Championship Game, when New England, on their first drive of the game, was facing a fourth and one against the Colts at their own 44-yard-line. Conventional wisdom said the Patriots should punt the ball away, but figure 5 of the Bellman equation illustrates that the potential benefit of keeping the drive going at that point of the field outweighs the cost of giving the opponents good field position. Tom Brady kept the ball on a sneak and gained two yards for the first down.

There are many variables involved—strength of the defense, ability of the kicker, and the overall look of the opposing offensive and defensive schemes. But in an era when teams routinely admit to following the conventional wisdom because it's what they've always done, the Patriots' approach is a radical one. Just by their acknowledgment that something like the Bellman equation exists—while so many other teams disregarded the idea—is another example of how the Patriots have managed to succeed by looking at the game in a slightly different way than the rest of the NFL.

It was not the only time New England had turned to the academic world for guidance. After Rutgers statistician Harold Sackrowitz was quoted in *The New York Times* as saying teams go for two-point conversions more often than they need to, he received a phone call from the Patriots, who asked him to critique their "go-for-two" chart, a common in-game tool for coaches when they have to decide whether they want to kick the extra point or try a two-point conversion. "Nobody had any real interest other than the Patriots," Sackrowitz told the *Times* when they asked about his chart, but it was clear the Patriots liked what they saw: they did not try a single two-point conversion that season.

Even though the Patriots' 2005 and 2006 seasons came to an end earlier than they had hoped, their model continues to be studied by the rest of the sports world. "The Patriots have been successful in this market. I'm not saying that we'll adopt all of their practices, but it's hard to quibble with their approach," Red Sox general manager Theo Epstein told reporters in early 2006. "You know those bracelets people wear that say, 'WWJD—What Would Jesus Do?'" Marc Ganis, a Chicago-based sports consultant, told *The San Diego Union-Tribune* in 2005. "After last season, people in the NFL were asking, 'WWPD—What Would the Patriots Do?' Everyone's trying to emulate their business model."

It's not just at the professional level. Rutgers football enjoyed a renaissance in the fall of 2006, and Scarlet Knights head coach Mike Schiano used the Patriots blueprint when it came to turning around the program. "What we're looking for, No. 1, is guys who have a love of the game of football," he said in late 2006. "I know one thing, a guy that loves game is going to do the right things socially and academically, because he doesn't want to risk not playing. These guys want to be in my office, meeting, studying on their own, doing all the things that can make them better.

"I study the Patriots very closely, and they do an incredible job of identifying guys that fit their system. They're not the most talented. In fact, I think they're middle of the pack from top to bottom. But because they have that system, and they recruit guys that fit into it, it works. The more you figure it out, it's not so much who's highly touted, it's who fits what you do in all phases."

In hopes of trying to make people look at football in a different way, Schatz—as well as a collection of numbers crunchers—has discovered that when it comes down to using the numbers in hopes of gaining an edge on their opponent, no one does a better job of it than the Patriots.

"The Patriots are better than any other team at using the stats to break down where their opponents' strengths and weaknesses are, and then attacking those weaknesses," Schatz said. "Philadelphia is the best team at approaching it from an economic perspective. But it's the Patriots' in-game strategy that sets them apart."

Many believe the Eagles are as close as you're going to get to the Patriots, and, to a lesser extent, the Steelers. The Rooney family in Pittsburgh and Jeffrey Lurie in Philadelphia operate in much the same manner as the Krafts. Each ownership group remains financially committed to creating an environment that allows their team to succeed. They have overseen the building of state-of-the-art new venues, each of which allows the team to gain a competitive edge by any means. They are passionate about their product and remain active in league affairs. However, they are hands-off when it comes to personnel decisions, trusting their front office to make the right call. Those front-office people have managed to work the cap to their advantage, creating a situation where they have been able to remain competitive over long stretches of time. And both the ownership group and front office have remained committed to stability, both in the front office and on their coaching staffs, not an easy feat considering that both markets operate in the demanding, football-frenzied market of Pennsylvania. "I think the Eagles franchise, starting at the top with Jeff Lurie, Joe

Banner, and Andy Reid, down to the coordinators, the players, the way they have managed the cap, the team by integrating young players into their system, I think they have done a fantastic job," Belichick said shortly before New England and Philadelphia met in Super Bowl XXXIX. "It's a team we look at very closely in the off-season and when we have to evaluate how they manage their team, I think they are one of the model franchises."

"I think the Eagles are the same as the Patriots," said Perillo. "I think Pittsburgh does the same kind of stuff. They try to keep their own guys, but they won't overpay their own guys and they're constantly losing in free agency. You never see those teams go out and make a huge splash.

"They sold their soul to the devil with Terrell Owens once, because they were desperate to get over the hump, and they got over the hump and got to the Super Bowl—they just didn't win it. Now, I think their model . . . Andy Reid, in terms of how he wants to build his team from a personnel standpoint, is a clone of Belichick. Now, his personality and all, that's much different. But how he believes in team building, I think it's very similar to the way Bill does it."

Ultimately, the question remains: Will the Patriots become victims of their own success? Because they stick to a hard line in negotiations, they have lost many key contributors over the last few years—kicker Adam Vinatieri, linebacker Willie McGinest, and wide receivers David Givens and Deion Branch all departed between the 2005 and 2006 seasons. They have managed to take many lower-round players and undrafted free agents and shape them into stars. Will this feeder system continue? As long as they keep following the blueprint—in particular, thinking outside the box when it comes to approaching the draft—they'll keep achieving success.

"As long as they continue to scout *those* kinds of guys, then they'll get more. If they continue to scout, they'll keep getting useful low-round players," said Schatz.

"The other thing is that players who fit this specific defense and offense system and [that] other teams go after, they're just not there anymore," he added. "There are other guys: I remember constantly hearing, 'Well, this guy is one of those guys who's a smallish defensive end in college who will probably move to a linebacker in the 3–4,' and he'd be taken by Cleveland. I think that's where [Belichick] the victim of his own success—because so many teams are playing a similar defense now. I don't know if offensively it's quite so much of a big deal. Everyone and his brother is playing a two tight end set now. I think that because you're getting a lot of those 3–4 tweener-type dudes getting picked up by teams in the draft before they fall to the Patriots."

"The thing I worry about the most with the Patriots is not necessarily the fact that they can make stars for the other teams, but their valuing flexibility and adaptability over other characteristics," said ESPN's K. C. Joyner. "There's an upside to that, and there's a downside to that. They get injured an awful lot. And they get injured a whole lot because they say, 'Yeah, we've got flexible guys.' Another team might go for toughness, saying, 'We want durability. We want guys who can play every single game.'"

Others believe it's Belichick's ability to game-plan that will help keep the Patriots ahead of the pack. "I would say Belichick's ability to game-plan—and this is hard to quantify, because you can't really see game-planning—but I think his ability to game-plan and nitpick and find every little detail as to what an opponent does . . . there's no one who's on a level with him," Perillo said. "You never beat the Patriots because you do something they didn't expect or they get outfoxed or anything. I think the Patriots do that to a lot of teams. I just think their ability to prepare is unmatched, and their mental toughness is unmatched. I think that's coaching."

But the one thing that everyone can agree on is that the Patriots have hit upon a perfect convergence, a balance between the coaching staff, the front office, and the ownership that few have been able to replicate. "It's like the separation of church and state. It's a marriage of convenience," said football writer Dan Pires. "My opinion is that the Krafts and Belichick don't have such a rosy relationship. They kind of swoon over one another, but I think there is some genuine tension there. But from a business perspective and a coaching perspective and a sports perspective, they put all that aside because it all works.

"They've actually mastered it. They've got it all down to a science. 'Bill is doing his thing; we won't screw with him.' Then, you have Jonathan [Kraft] and Bob [Kraft] doing the marketing, and then they have all these other entities in the middle doing their own thing. But they're all working toward a collective goal. They all understand they have a collective goal and purpose in this whole grand scheme of things. And it all works out. The thing is, they left no stone unturned. If there's a speed bump, they find a way around it or over it."

# EPILOGUE: JANUARY 21, 2007

*I*t *was over.*

That was what Tom Brady kept thinking. As the Colts started their pigpile on top of backup cornerback Marlin Jackson and the biggest party Indianapolis had ever seen was breaking out everywhere around him, Brady walked slowly to the sidelines and removed his helmet, with the same phrase rattling around in his head, time and again. *It was over.*

On January 21, 2007, the Colts had finally gotten over on the Patriots. The team that had been reduced to a postseason punchline at the hands of Brady, Belichick, and the rest of New England so many times finally got the last word, winning the 2006 AFC Championship Game against the Patriots in a shootout for the ages, 38–34. (The game ended when Jackson picked off a Brady pass with less than a minute remaining and the Patriots driving for what would have been a game-winning score.) By this point, Indianapolis had beaten the Patriots fairly soundly in a pair of regular season meetings since the start of the 2005 season, but this was the first time the Colts had beaten New England in what could pass for a big game. In the days following the loss—and as New England fans watched Indianapolis celebrate a Super Bowl title two weeks later with a win over the Chicago Bears—some wondered if Brady's statement didn't just apply to the game, but also to New England's dynastic run of success over the previous six years.

The Patriots were a far different team than the one that burst upon the national scene in the fall of 2001. They were no longer the lovable little outlaw rogues who had risen up to snatch a title from the rest of the league. Owner Bob Kraft had risen to a level of unprecedented power within NFL circles. He was a member of the NFL's most important committees, including the eight-owner group that selects the new league commissioner. He helped negotiate two television deals that helped the NFL reap untold billions, and when Street & Smith's *SportsBusiness Journal* released its fifty most influential people in sports business in 2006, Kraft was No. 14. "The Patriots are consistently one of the top teams in the NFL in terms of revenue," wrote the magazine. "From sponsorship to suite sales, New England is one of the standard-setters in the sport." They had Belichick, who was also regarded as more than just a football coach. His management style had been studied by CEOs and coaches alike, and he had been celebrated as "the Thinker" in a memorable photoillustration in *The Sporting News*. On the eve of Super Bowl XXXIX, *The Boston Globe* penned a lengthy piece surveying local management experts on Belichick's leadership style, and all of them lauded his no-nonsense approach. And the Patriots had the league's marquee talent, a quarterback who made everyone around him better.

But in the two years between their win over the Eagles in Super Bowl XXXIX and their loss in the 2006 AFC Championship Game to the Colts, the Patriots were dealt plenty of setbacks. First, both coordinators departed. Defensive coordinator Romeo Crennel left to become the head coach of the Cleveland Browns, while Fighting Irish alum and offensive coordinator Charlie Weis took over at Notre Dame. Second, there was the sudden and shocking stroke of linebacker Tedy Bruschi. One of the last remaining links to the pre-Belichick era, Bruschi was the emotional centerpiece of the locker room. He would eventually return midway through the 2005 season, but in the days leading up to training camp that summer, veteran linebacker Ted Johnson suddenly retired. Two of the most important players at the most important position on a Belichick-coached team were suddenly gone. And third, a year later, there were the losses of key figures like kicker Adam Vinatieri, line-backer Willie McGinest, and wide receivers David Givens and Deion Branch, all of whom left because of money issues. The de-parture of Branch was particularly crippling. The diminutive wide receiver had developed a close relationship with most of the locker room, but was unhappy about his contract situation, and had forced a trade to Seattle. And while his departure didn't register at the seismic level like the Milloy release or Bledsoe deal, it still rattled many of his teammates. The day the deal went down, the locker room was almost completely empty, save for Mike Vrabel and Richard Seymour. "I don't think any of us envisioned some-thing like this happening. It took the air out of me. It really did," Seymour said. "When you look at Deion Branch, he embodies everything we want in a football player. Everything we talk about, the kind of guy we want on this football team, he did as good a job as anybody of embodying that.

"It's a tough day for a lot of guys on this football team, especially guys like myself who came in with Deion Branch," he added. "To not have No. 83 in a Patriots uniform definitely hurts."

Brady was close to both Milloy and Branch. But almost three full years after his emotional farewell speech after Milloy's release, this time, he saw it for what it was. "It's tough because you develop relationships with players," he said a few days later. "We hate to see players like Deion go. We hate to see Willie [McGinest] go and Adam [Vinatieri]. [But] the list goes on for the last three or four years."

In that context, many wondered just how long the window of opportunity could remain open. No team had enjoyed a run of this magnitude in the salary cap era. They had won three titles in four seasons. The roster had been turned over at several positions—sometimes three or four times—since Belichick and Pioli first arrived, and they had surpassed the dreams of even the most optimistic of Patriots fans. Realistically, how could they be expected to keep winning?

On the surface, one of those basic team-building points that eluded them in 2005 and 2006 was keeping a general sense of roster balance. Since Belichick and Pioli arrived prior to the 2000 season, the Patriots had managed to keep a good blend of talent. With the exception of a precious few players like Brady and Richard Seymour, the great majority of their fifty-three-man roster contained younger players who were either on their first contract or older guys on their last contract who had not won a title. (Traditionally, these two types are the hungriest of players.)

You wanted young players for many reasons: The young players were looking to put up the sort of numbers that could get them that big payday with the second deal, the one most NFL players considered as their best chance at making the big financial splash. And in the new NFL economy, another of the advantages to stocking your roster with young talent was that it would come relatively cheaply. With the Patriots, as was usually the case, they would be able to find a way to make that cheap talent even more inexpensive. Over the years, they had managed to get many of their early picks to agree to contracts that were longer than the industry standards. Consequently, they were able to hang on to their young talent for an extra year or two longer than most other teams. The best example appeared to be Ben Watson: a tight end who was taken with the thirty-second pick in the first round out of Georgia in 2004. His agent Tom Condon wanted him to sign a five-year deal, but New England held firm to a six-year contract. (Watson eventually fired Condon and signed for six years.)

As for the other end of the roster, most of the older players they went after shared three common traits. For one, they were familiar with Belichick through a series of events (they had either played for him in a previous location or were recommended to

New England by someone who had played for Belichick); two, they were already financially secure; and three, they had yet to win a title. With the Patriots dangling that sort of carrot, an established veteran hoping to win a title on his last go-round found it easy to sign for short money. Over the years, the Patriots would turn out to be the final stop for players like Bryan Cox, Roman Phifer, Rodney Harrison, Doug Flutie, Vinny Testaverde, and Junior Seau, all of whom signed with the Patriots late in their career in hopes of winning a title before they called it a career.

But for all the successes they enjoyed, it wasn't always the Bradys, Seymours, and Dillons who made the difference, but the middle part of their roster, their complementary players. No matter the age, from 2000 through 2004, the success of the Patriots depended largely on the fact that the middle and lower levels of the New England roster were stocked with better talent than other teams. Injury and change was always inevitable. Belichick and Pioli always wanted to make sure that when that happened, they were prepared to replace that starter with a player who was at or near the level of the starting player. And for most of the first five years, Belichick made sure the backups were just as prepared to play as the starters. No one on the fifty-three-man roster was considered more important than another. Each player would eventually be called on to contribute at one time or another; it was just a matter of when. And that level of preparation for emergency situations was one of the reasons they were able to achieve success. In 2001, when they lost Drew Bledsoe, it was Tom Brady. Throughout the 2002, 2003, and 2004 seasons, there was a constant shuffling of the offensive line, but Dan Koppen, Stephen Neal, and Russ Hochstein all stepped in when called upon to play, and all played well. At defensive back in 2004, veterans Tyrone Poole and Ty Law yielded to Randall Gay and Asante Samuel, and the secondary didn't miss a beat. At wideout, at the start of the 2004 season, Givens stepped in and thrived. In each case, it was a younger, more inexperienced player making the most of his opportunity.

THE BLUEPRINT

But by and large, throughout 2005 and 2006, those success stories were few and far between. Over the course of those two seasons, there would be many of those types of players who would go
on to have great success in the New England system, including defensive back Artrell Hawkins and rookie offensive lineman Logan
Mankins. But others the Patriots called upon for support in those
seasons—nicknamed "the Replacements" by some members of the
media—were failures. It became clear that the problem with the
Patriots was not at the top of their roster, but in the middle. Many
of the players who dominated the middle of the roster over those
two seasons—the same types of players who had given the Patriots
their edge in years past—did not respond as they had hoped. Instead of backups stepping in to become key figures as a result of
injury to a starter, they instead were forced to go with a series of
JAGs, transitory players plucked off the waiver wire who were
asked to fill in at key positions. To replace Bruschi after his 2005
stroke (and provide depth after the unexpected retirement of Ted
Johnson), the Patriots hurriedly signed Monty Beisel and Chad
Brown, both of whom were miserable washouts in New England.
(Beisel looked especially overwhelmed, both on and off the field.
After a rough stretch, he ripped into a reporter in the locker room,
saying, "Why do you have to come by my locker and rub it in?
That's your professionalism? You slash me in front of everybody?
What kind of shit is that?") The same was true for cornerback Duane Starks, who was embarrassed in a brutal prime-time loss to
the Colts in 2005. Starks, who was a part of the record-setting Baltimore defense in 2000, struggled in New England's system, and
was placed on injured reserve midway through the 2005 season,
and very quietly released. (Ex-teammates later ripped Starks, calling him "garbage.") Kick returner and wide receiver Bethel Johnson had a strong rookie season in 2003, but he was clearly a source
of annoyance by the midpoint of his second year in New England.
Prior to the 2006 season—and with the Patriots lacking any sort of
real depth at wide receiver—he was practically given away for

overweight defensive lineman Johnathan Sullivan in a swap of un-derachieving draft picks. (Sullivan was later cut.)

When the backups in 2005 and 2006 didn't make the same sort of leap as backups had in previous seasons, things slowly slid downward. They didn't suffer the same sort of EKG spike and drop of previous Patriots teams. They still made the postseason in 2005, eventually losing a divisional playoff game on the road to the Broncos. And while his 2006 was considered statistically subpar when compared to his usual level of success, it was, perhaps, the finest season of Brady's career. Forced to turn to traditional back-ups like Jabar Gaffney and Reche Caldwell at wide receiver, the twenty-nine-year-old quarterback was asked to do more with less than at any other point in his career. Working with a patchwork re-ceiving corps, Brady lifted the offense on his shoulders, carrying the Patriots past the upstart Jets in the wild-card round, a superior San Diego team in the divisional playoffs, and into the AFC title game.

But those weaknesses in the middle and lower levels of the ros-ter were on display for all to see that night in Indianapolis, in par-ticular at the linebacker position. Eric Alexander was burned on a key pass play late in the game, and Tully Banta-Cain was flagged for a costly roughing the passer penalty. At wide receiver, despite a fine performance a week earlier in the upset of the Chargers, Reche Caldwell dropped two passes late in the game. By way of contrast, it was the role players—the same sort of "middle of the roster" guys who had made the difference for the Patriots so many times—who ultimately made the difference for Indianapolis. For-mer Patriots lineman Dan Klecko caught a touchdown pass out of the backfield, and offensive lineman Jeff Saturday pounced on a fumble. Joseph Addai, the running back the Colts were forced to settle for after the Patriots drafted Laurence Maroney, scored the eventual game-winning touchdown with a minute left, and backup defensive back Jackson sealed it by picking off Brady on the final series.

But even with all the struggles in the middle and lower parts of their roster, the Patriots were just thirty-five yards from another trip to the Super Bowl, and so it was clear that there was no need for a complete overhaul. They simply needed to regain that edge in the middle and lower levels that had given them the advantage so often in the early stages of the twenty-first century. Much of that change came at the wide receiver spot. Where the 2006 roster was populated in large part by retreads at the receiver position, they made sure that wouldn't be the case in 2007 with the acquisition of dependable veterans like Kelley Washington, Donte Stallworth, and Wes Welker. In particular, Welker was the sort of typical Patriots signing that had the rest of the league shaking its head—a classic overachiever, Welker was an undrafted free agent who ended up making a mark with the Dolphins as a special teams star and slot receiver. (He tortured New England on a fairly regular basis, including a nine-catch game in a 2006 loss to the Patriots.) His versatility and flair for the dramatic on special teams—he was just one of two players in NFL history to return a kickoff and a punt, kick an extra point and a field goal, and make a tackle in the same game—seemed to be a perfect fit for New England. In addition the franchise rededicated itself to making New England the type of place where players wanted to play. They made sure that potential free agents were aware of the fact that management would do the little things for players—like cater to their culinary needs. One morning late in the 2006 season, Testaverde was bragging to reporters about Gillette Stadium being one of the only places he had played where a player could get breakfast if he wanted to. "It's not done anywhere. You're in here and you work out in the morning and you can finish it up with a nice breakfast," said Testaverde, who had spent twenty years in the NFL with the Buccaneers, Browns, Ravens, Jets, and Cowboys. "[Many] places don't serve breakfast. You got to go get your own breakfast, come work out, and you lose a little bit. I think it's an edge that we have over other teams. And it starts with the head coach again. Just the mentality of the type of guys he brings in. Character guys who put the team before individual success. There's a lot of those guys in this locker room."

Players who previously weren't inclined to discuss things that went on far from the eyes of the media were suddenly making sure that the rest of the league knew that the Patriots were allowed conveniences that would have been vetoed on other teams—some of which were as small as getting extra practice T-shirts or socks from an equipment manager, or as large as bringing in a chiropractor to ease the pains of training camp.

But from a PR perspective, the start of the off-season was grim. Less than a month after the AFC Championship Game, former New England linebacker Ted Johnson ripped the organization, telling reporters that Belichick had made him practice in 2002 despite the fact he suffered multiple concussions while with the Patriots. (Many Patriots players have worked with a dentist, Dr. Gerald Maher, who encourages the players to use a specially designed mouth guard that's scientifically proven to cut down on concussions. Among the players who have used it include cornerback Asante Samuel and nose tackle Vince Wilfork.) In addition, Brady was the subject of plenty of fodder on late-night talk shows when it was revealed that, shortly after breaking up with his girlfriend, actress Bridget Moynahan, she was pregnant with their child.

But when free agency opened, the Patriots were the first to strike. Thirty-six hours into the start of free agency, they announced an agreement with linebacker Adalius Thomas. Thomas was a key addition on a number of levels. He made the linebacking corps a little younger, but like Welker his versatility was a throwback to the early days of the Belichick era where versatility was prized above everything else. "I'm a football player. I don't play a position," said Thomas, who became one of the few players in the history of the NFL to play five positions in one game—defensive end, outside linebacker, middle linebacker, safety, and cornerback.

"That's why the Patriots have been so successful here because they don't look at it as position. They look at it as football."

Making an investment of that magnitude in a player like Thomas wasn't completely new. The Patriots had committed big dollars to linebacker Rosevelt Colvin prior to the start of the 2003 season. But the signing represented a significant throwback. Thomas certainly had a Patriots type of pedigree, the kind of player who, on the surface, appears to be a perfect fit in the New England system. He was an underrated prospect out of Southern Miss who lasted until the sixth round of the 2000 draft before he was taken (just thirteen spots ahead of Tom Brady). He operated with a major chip on his shoulder, waiting until he got a chance to start in 2005 and 2006. When he did, he flourished in the Ravens' system, making the Pro Bowl on a pair of occasions. He certainly sounded the part on his introduction to New England. "I think I fit their pedigree of linebackers—guys that can run, big strong guys that play different things, from Vrabel to Bruschi to Colvin," he added. "You have all these guys that are here that are great players. Again, I just try to come in and add to what they already have, because they have a great linebacking corps here."

While the Thomas deal made a big splash, the biggest news of the offseason was yet to come.

While Bill Belichick spent most of his professional coaching apprenticeship with Bill Parcells, his style as a head coach was much closer to that of Bill Walsh. When it came to team building philosophies, Walsh and Belichick are very similar. In creating the 49ers' dynasty, Walsh made sure to never get too close to his players, always keeping them on guard, never letting anyone get too comfortable. He always valued team over individual. And he worked hand in hand with a once-in-a-generation quarterback, building one of the great franchises in NFL history. Fifteen years later, Belichick would bring much of the same style to the Patriots.

But perhaps the most similar thread that ran through the

organizations of Walsh and Belichick was the premium both placed on locker room infrastructure. Their approach was simple: Once you got to where you wanted to be when it came to on-field personnel, you needed to create a functional locker room, one complete with "regulators" that could control any situation that flared up. These guys weren't always the most talented players, but they served their purpose in other ways. They were there to help police the locker room, always keeping potential flareups under control. Both Belichick and Walsh knew that if you had enough of these guys in place, you could take an occasional chance on a player of questionable character.

The approach of the 49ers teams of the 1980s was well known throughout the game—with Joe Montana, Dwight Clark, Roger Craig, and Jerry Rice, they were one of the most businesslike teams in professional sports. But even after Walsh retired following Super Bowl XXIII, the system he helped create—with solid, dependable veterans who kept the peace in the locker room—allowed the 49ers to continue their run of success. With the groundwork in place, they were able to reinvent themselves, acquiring questionable characters (but tremendous talents) like Ricky Watters (prior to the 1992 season) and Deion Sanders (before the 1994 season) to become a swaggering, in-your-face team that picked up the fifth Super Bowl in franchise history with a win over the Chargers in Super Bowl XXIX. They could take a chance on those players because the rock-solid system they had in place allowed them the opportunity to take a chance on questionable guys.

Walsh and the 49ers fully acknowledged they were lucky to be in a place where they could augment their roster with potential All-Pros. But that luck was the residue of design. Not every franchise could afford to take those sorts of risks on a questionable player. If a lesser team had signed Sanders or Watters—say, the Cardinals— their style would have likely thrown an already dysfunctional team into a state of turmoil. But in San Francisco, they had a solid and stable ownership group and front office that fully backed the coaching staff. In turn, the coaching staff and front office found a myriad of well-respected veterans like Rice, Steve Young, Brent Jones, Harris Barton, or Gary Plummer who could keep question marks focused and on-point, schooling them in the 49ers' method.

Belichick used the same approach. Despite the initial pleas of Kraft to avoid players with a sketchy background ("When I hired Bill, I said, 'Just don't bring thugs or hoodlums to New England,'" the owner would later recall of a conversation he had with Belichick in 2000), the locker room infrastructure was sound enough to take an occasional chance on a player who had been labeled as a troublemaker in the past. In New England, it was first put to the test with the arrival of Bryan Cox prior to the start of the 2001 season. The same was true with Ted Washington prior to the start of the 2003 season, and Corey Dillon before the 2004 season. All three were dogged by serious character issues—in Cox's case, he had racked up thousands of dollars in fines before arriving in New England. Washington had a well-known reputation as being ill-tempered. And Dillon was a well-known problem child who had tossed his gear into the stands after his final game with the Bengals. But because of the overall locker room environment that was in place, all three players weren't a distraction during their time with the Patriots.

It wasn't coincidence. Like the 49ers, the Patriots were able to take those gambles because they had worked for many years to get to a spot where they could afford to wager on a player with so-called character issues. They had spent many years building a solid and stable ownership group and front office that fully backed the coaching staff. In turn, the coaching staff and front office found well-respected veteran players who they knew would make sure Gillette Stadium remained a harmonious work environment, both in the locker room and on the practice field. And those well-respected veteran players in place—a group that began with Willie McGinest and would include Richard Seymour, Tedy Bruschi, Mike Vrabel, Tom Brady, Troy Brown, and Rodney Harrison—had managed to inculcate the Patriot Way among even the most questionable of characters. The successes of players like Dillon and Cox with the Patriots marked, perhaps, the ultimate triumph of the New England system: Belichick could bring anyone into Foxborough, no matter how tormented their past, and they would succeed because of the strength of the system in place around them.

But in the spring of 2007, even the biggest Patriots fans had to wonder if Belichick and Pioli had bitten off more than they could chew. They swung a draft-day trade for controversial wide receiver Randy Moss, a player of supreme ability but one who had several run-ins with the law—as well as coaches and teammates in his nine-year career. But similar to the arrival of Dillon, Belichick was confident that Moss was a changed man. "I talked to a lot of people that were all close to him, both teammates and coaches, people that were on his team, they have a lot of respect for him," Belichick said, adding he learned a lot about Moss from Doug Gabriel, who played briefly for the Patriots in 2006 in between stints in Oakland with Moss. "You rely on other people that you know and also how you feel like he fits into your system and whether he'd be productive as a player within your system."

As far as the players were concerned, Moss—like Cox, Washington, and Dillon before him—started in New England with a clean slate. "I'm not going to judge him on anything he's done in the past," Bruschi told *The Boston Herald* shortly after the deal went down. "I'm not going to judge him on what he did on the field, or some instances in the past. Once he gets here, from that point on, that's when he's a Patriot. Then we'll see from then. We bring a player in, we don't consider the baggage he may have. We just consider him once he gets here, the work he puts into the practice and the games."

Throughout the last few years, one of the best and most engaging interviews in the New England locker room has been Rosevelt

Colvin. The thoughtful and intelligent linebacker has always managed to give spot-on analysis on the current state of the team. "The Patriots are like a soap opera," he said in 2005. "You can turn it off. Then, like three years later, you can catch up." In this case, the linebacker was half right: The soap opera madness that dogged them through most of the first forty or so years of their existence no longer exists. It has been replaced with an efficient system that, in many ways, has become the gold standard for the rest of the National Football League. But that doesn't mean the elements of a great daily drama don't remain. There's the constant shuffling in and out of the fringe players, those on the outer edges of the day-to-day drama. There's the supporting cast, complementary players who always give the action some spice. And there are the stars, those players who live in the spotlight and help churn out the always unforgettable storylines.

And at the top, there's Belichick and Pioli. The players and coaches have changed, as has the NFL. But the basic tenets of their team-building approach remain just as true as they were when they first took over the franchise in January 2000. Always value the team above the individual. Consider the short term, but always remember that real success is gained when you consider the big picture. And remember that it's not about collecting talent, it's about assembling a team.

# AFTERWORD: NEARLY PERFECT

Peyton Manning, Tony Romo, and Tom Brady go to heaven to visit God. God decides who will sit next to him by asking the boys a question. God asks Peyton Manning first, "What do you believe?" Manning thinks long and hard, looks God in the eye, and says, 'I believe in hard work, and in staying true to family and friends. I believe in giving. I was lucky, but I always tried to do right by my fans.' God can't help but see the essential goodness of Manning, and offers him a seat to his left. Then God turns to Tony Romo and says, "What do you believe?" Romo says, "I believe passion, discipline, courage, and honor are the fundamentals of life. I, too, have been lucky, but win or lose I've always tried to be a true sportsman, both on and off the field." God is greatly moved by Tony's sincere eloquence, and he offers him a seat to his right. Finally, God turns to Tom Brady and says, "And you, Tom? What do you believe?" Brady replies, "I believe you're in my seat."

—*POPULAR JOKE IN BOSTON IN THE FALL AND WINTER OF 2007*

The greatness of the 2007 Patriots can be traced back to September 11, 2006, when wide receiver Deion Branch, unhappy with his contract and in the midst of a protracted holdout that stretched back through the summer, forced the franchise to trade him. (He was ultimately dealt to Seattle for a first-round draft choice.) In the Bill Belichick era, it was a first—a player ultimately making the team bow to his wishes instead of the other way around. New England received a first-round pick in return, but as was the case at linebacker a few years prior when Ted Johnson retired and Tedy Bruschi suffered a stroke that left him sidelined, the trade of Branch, as well as the departure of fellow wide receiver David Givens in free agency earlier that spring, left the Patriots uncharacteristically unprepared and scrambling to find last-minute replacements. That season, they added career journeymen in Jabar Gaffney, Reche Caldwell, and Doug Gabriel, a collection of receivers who tested Tom Brady's resolve on several occasions. While Brady said all the right things about his new receivers publicly, privately, he was less than pleased with the situation. It took them awhile to get on the same page, and Brady wasn't happy. The bond that had developed between Brady and Branch wasn't something that could be replicated in a matter of weeks—for all his greatness, Brady had not been gifted with a wide receiver who could match his talents. Unlike Montana or Young, who had Jerry Rice, or Terry Bradshaw and Lynn Swann— or even his contemporary Peyton Manning, who had Marvin Harrison—Brady had never had that No. 1 receiver. Branch was clearly starting to mature into that role, but now, he was gone.

The trade of Branch left Brady trying to make chicken salad out of chicken shit at the receiver position, and the quarterback almost pulled it off, making it all the way to the 2006 AFC Championship Game before falling to the Colts. But despite the fact they missed out that season, the long-term effect of Branch's departure would be a positive one. The Patriots had already set aside some cash in anticipation of signing Branch and Richard Seymour to long-term deals once their contracts were up. In the spring of 2006, New England reportedly offered Branch a contract extension that would have kept him in a New England uniform through

2009, and would have given him a $4 million signing bonus and $4 million option bonus payable in 2007, with a steadily increasing base salary that would last through 2009.

And so while Seymour signed a deal that provided a sizable up-front bonus—in all, he received close to $25 million in salary and bonuses in 2006—Branch's decision to hold out and force a trade suddenly left the Patriots with a major line of credit. As a result, the money that had, in effect, been saved for a rainy day was just sitting there. Combined with the money they already had under the cap, the knowledge that there were more than a few players out there who were good fits for their system, as well as the usual cap increase that kicked in for all thirty-two teams across the board, New England decided to spend, altering their usual team-building blue-print. The very specific approach they used in acquiring talent in the past was still there—they just had a little more money to play with. As a result, they stole Miami wide receiver Wes Welker, the most important part of a very bad Dolphins' offense, for a second-round draft pick. They signed linebacker Adalius Thomas to a below-market deal. And they plucked free agents like running back Sammy Morris and wide receiver/special teams ace Kelley Washington from the waiver wires, veterans who didn't have overwhelmingly flashy numbers, but had many of the subtle intangibles that would have almost surely found them a spot on the 2001 Patriots team.

But the most intriguing addition of the off-season was Moss, a supremely talented but controversial receiver who managed to become a Patriot literally overnight. In contrast to their usual delib-erate and meticulous approach to acquiring talent, Belichick later estimated that 90 percent of the Moss trade took just eleven hours from start to finish, from midnight after Day 1 of the draft to 11 A.M. the next morning. It stands as a testament to the fact that when it came to that particular off-season, the Patriots were willing to tweak their general approach in the name of landing someone like Moss, who, if his head was screwed on straight, could provide a unique skill set for Brady and the Patriots. If their previous blueprint for team building called for cautiously seeking out men of character on the cheap who could subjugate their ego in the name of the team, well, the possible acquisition of Moss would mean they would have to change their approach just a bit.

Beginning with his first game as a Raider—against the Patriots at Gillette Stadium in 2005—Moss and Oakland were never a good fit, for many reasons. (That evening, despite the fact that Moss had five catches for 130 yards and a touchdown, aging Oakland owner Al Davis spent much of the night raging at the receiver from his owners box using language so NC-17 it would make Andrew Dice Clay blush.) Mainly, the Raiders were a lousy football team, and weren't likely to get better anytime soon. Moss was unhappy with the team. The team was unhappy with Moss. And so, two seasons later, when the Raiders had the opportunity to discard Moss, they jumped at the chance. By the time the spring of 2007 rolled around, there weren't many serious suitors for the wide receiver, other than Green Bay. (And it turns out that Moss and the Packers weren't all that interested in each other: After speaking with Moss, Green Bay said the wide receiver wouldn't budge on the idea of renegotiating his contract, which had one year left. For his part, Moss later claimed he was put off the Packers after talking with Green Bay management, who told him that Donald Driver, not him, would be the No. 1 receiver. "Donald Driver is the top receiver here, so don't come in and try to step on his toes," is the way Moss later recalled the conversation.)

So around midnight, the Patriots and Raiders started talking seriously. The proposed deal would send Moss to New England for a fourth-round pick. But even in their haste to cinch a trade, the Patriots took their time: For all his talent, this was, after all, *Randy Moss,* who was still considered a third rail by many NFL front-office people, and who was set to make a $9.75 million this year and $11.25 million next year, a cap-crippling amount for a team like the Patriots.

"There were a number of things that had to get done," said Patriots vice president of player personnel Scott Pioli.

The Patriots were one of twenty teams that passed on Moss when he came out of Marshall in 1998. Had he really changed? So, like any potential employer checking out a new employee, they went looking for references. As the Raiders tried to find Moss—he was in Texas—the Patriots called former teammates like Doug Gabriel, a former Patriots receiver who played with Moss in Oakland. Gabriel and others gave Moss a thumbs-up, and so after the Raiders located Moss, New England flew him into Foxborough in the middle of the night for a meeting, one where Moss convinced Belichick and Pioli he would tear up his current contract and accept more of a cap-friendly deal. "Bill and I walked away from that meeting feeling very confident that Randy really wanted to be here and that we really wanted Randy to be here," Pioli said. "It was a good meeting. It was a good, solid meeting."

One more person needed convincing: Robert Kraft. Ten years before, it might have been the sort of moment that Kraft milked, looking to make an imprint on the personnel side of the franchise with a big splash. *There's a new sheriff in town*. But this time, all he did was listen.

"Mr. Kraft, I've made a lot of money, more money probably than I need," Moss told the owner late that morning as they sat in an office at Gillette Stadium. "This is about winning."

It was what Kraft wanted to hear. Moss signed the new deal, a one-year contract with between $2 million and $3 million. Later that day he told reporters, "The Moss of old is back."

On the surface, Moss and Belichick seemed to be unlikely bedfellows, but the wide receiver appeared to be sincere in remaking his career, and figured an alliance with the Patriots would prove to the world he was interested in remaking his image from an "I" guy into a "we" guy. It wasn't completely out of left field: It had worked for Corey Dillon, who was a model citizen through the early days of his career in Foxborough. Why couldn't it work for Moss? One thing that differed, at least early on, was their approach to the media. In his first few months with the team, Dillon went out of his way to speak with as many reporters as he could in hopes of courting public opinion. (This would soon change. A year later, Dillon's infamous line to a reporter: "Don't come by twenty-eight's locker" became a running joke with the media who might have been looking to speak with the running back. Late in his first season, Dillon cut way back on interviews, and eventually stopped speaking with most of the media altogether.) Early in his New England career, Moss assiduously avoided the media. ("One thing that I promise you guys—I'm going to try my best to give you a few short interviews," he proclaimed in his initial conference call with reporters. "But at the same time, I'm going to stay away from it.") But when he did, he was pleasant and insightful. One-on-one interviews were out of the question, but by the midway point of the season, he was speaking with reporters on a regular basis after games.

Immediately, he set to becoming part of the team. Breaking with tradition—the franchise had usually assigned lockers based on numbers, with number 1 lockering next to number 2 and so on—the Patriots placed Moss's locker next to Brady's. He juggled some off-season obligations to make sure he showed up for all the organized team activities that off-season. And he joined the team at the funeral of Marquise Hill, a backup defensive lineman who was killed in a jet-skiing incident on Memorial Day weekend. By the time the regular season rolled around, many of the preconceived ideas that teammates had regarding Moss went out the window.

"He comes to work, ready to work every day, committed to being the best he can be," said tight end Kyle Brady. "The way he practices, the way he plays, the way he prepares, there's been no complaints, by any means. He's been great."

"You never know what you're going to get when you get a guy

like that, that you hear so much about, until he becomes your teammate," Kelley Washington said of Moss, who even lined up at safety in prevent defense packages throughout the season. "Until you get to know them and go to work with them every day, you don't know what to expect until you see it. But, he's a heck of a teammate and a real team player."

Throughout much of the season, there were no major distractions involving the wide receiver. No squirting water on officials. No mooning crowds. No sulking. No strolling off the field during a game. And no talk of paying fines with "Straight cash, homey." There was a relatively minor incident involving a few nasty words exchanged with a photographer from the Associated Press—Moss, unaware that team policy allows still photographers in the locker room, was angry that the photographer took a picture of him while walking to his locker. And there was an incident late in the season involving a possible domestic violence charge which de-escalated when the case was voluntarily dismissed and both sides agreed to submit a claim to Moss's insurance company for medical bills.

After looking good and saying all the right things at the start of training camp, he didn't get on the field throughout the preseason, the victim of an injured hamstring. With each training camp session missed, the questions from the outside grew louder: *He's a dog. Same old Randy Moss. He's going to bring the whole thing down.* But in the season opener on September 9, he announced his presence with style, catching nine passes for 183 yards and a touchdown. His 51-yard touchdown catch was particularly impressive: The Patriots led, 21–7, midway through the third when the quarterback dropped back on a second and six from the New England 49 and let fly. "Randy slipped behind the backup safety and ran behind the defense," said Brady. "I threw it about as far as I can throw it." The football dropped into Moss's hands in full stride, and he simply cruised past three New York defenders into the end zone. The play was so jaw dropping, so astounding, it should have had a cartoon-style exclamation after it. *SHAZAM!*

Just like that, Brady had found his Jerry Rice, his Lynn Swann, his Marvin Harrison. And New England was in love.

"A year ago, this would have been unthinkable," wrote Dan Shaughnessy of *The Boston Globe*. "A week ago it would have been unlikely. But for one week, at least, everything has changed and you are looking at the new Randy Moss, another guy who swallowed the Belichick broth when he signed his contract with New England."

But Moss's introduction—and New England's relatively easy victory—wasn't the biggest story that would come out of that game. A Patriots' assistant had been caught by Jets' security taping the Jets' defensive coaches from the New England sideline, an illegal maneuver that would, in many ways, define the 2007 Patriots. It would come to be known as Spygate.

Deep within Gillette Stadium, Sunday, September 16 was slowly giving way to Monday, September 17. It was almost a week since the Spygate story first broke, and the Patriots quarterback had spent a long week hearing the national media call his team dirty. Brady had seen his coach—the only professional coach he'd ever known—called a cheater. He'd seen his accomplishments and the accomplishments of his teammates called into question. Critics unleashed a stream of vitriol on Belichick, Brady, and the Patriots that would stun New England fans. And all week, Brady stood by and listened. Now, he was tired of listening. The Patriots had just finished vaporizing the San Diego Chargers in front of a national television audience, and he was weary from one of the longest weeks of his professional life.

But this was his chance, so he kept talking.

"If we were to listen to everything that everybody said and respond, there's just too many battles to fight. There's only one battle that I care about, and that's playing football and performing well.

We can control that," he said. "You just can't go out and respond to what everybody says about you. There's not enough hours in the day. Especially after you've been winning for the last six or seven years."

Deadlines were being missed and rides were being held up. But Brady's unvarnished opinion continued.

"Do we have a lot of goodwill built up toward this team? It's funny, because after the first Super Bowl everyone was like, 'Oh, yeah, this is great! This is a great thing to come out as a team.' And then after the second Super Bowl it's like, 'Yeah, all right, you guys are pretty good.'

"And then the third Super Bowl and it was like, 'Oh, we're sick of you guys.'"

And for many, Spygate would give them the ammunition that they needed. The Patriots were an enjoyable little story for a year or two. But dominance breeds contempt, and people had become fed up with Belichick, Brady, and the rest of the New England franchise. They had the perfect quarterback. They had the genius coach in the sloppy gray hoodie. They were perfect team, always so smart and well prepared. And they kept winning. *Enough. Give someone else a shot, already.*

The 2007 Patriots had already been forced to deal with the loss of veteran safety Rodney Harrison, who would be suspended for four games because of a violation of the league's substance abuse policy. In the wake of the illegal videotaping incident in the Meadowlands, Commissioner Roger Goodell slapped Belichick with a $500,000 penalty—the biggest fine in the history of the league against a coach—and the franchise was fined $250,000 and forced to lose their first-round pick in the 2008 draft. "This episode represents a calculated and deliberate attempt to avoid long-standing rules designed to encourage fair play and promote honest competition on the playing field," Goodell said in a letter to the Patriots. The commissioner said he had considered suspending Belichick but didn't, "largely because I believe that the discipline I am imposing of a maximum fine and forfeiture of a first-round draft choice, or multiple draft choices, is in fact more significant and long-lasting, and therefore more effective, than a suspension."

The rest of the league piled on, saying New England wasn't punished enough and wondering about the Patriots and the secret to their success: *How long have they been doing it? I knew there had to be a reason behind all those Super Bowl wins!* San Diego running back LaDainian Tomlinson said the Patriots live by the motto, "If you ain't cheating, you ain't trying." Pittsburgh's Hines Ward and Philadelphia's Reno Mahe openly speculated about postseason losses to New England. And Indianapolis coach Tony Dungy compared Belichick to disgraced home run king Barry Bonds. For all the greatness he and the Patriots had achieved, Belichick had been reduced to a late-night punch line. The week after the game against the Jets, David Letterman produced a football he said was used in the Patriots-Jets game . . . with a camera that popped out of the end. Jay Leno hit on the same theme later in the season: "President Bush is pushing Congress to expand the government's ability to spy on Americans now that the current phone tap bill has expired. . . . In fact, to gain support for a new spying bill, they're bringing Coach Bill Belichick. They're going to name it the New England Patriot Act." Those who thought the Patriots got off too lightly had their moment after the end of the season, when *South Park* would gleefully skewer Belichick. In an episode where Cartman extols the virtues of cheating, he holds up a picture of the Patriots' head coach and says, "This is Bill Belichick, coach of the New England Patriots. He's won three Super Bowls. How? He cheated. He even got caught cheating, and nobody cared. Bill Belichick proved that in America, it's OK to cheat, as long as you cheat your way to the top. . . . If you cheat and fail, you're a cheater. If you cheat and succeed, you're *savvy*."

From the outside, it looked to be a desperately shaky week for the franchise, which was under scrutiny now from not just the national sports press, but the news media as well. Local stations started augmenting their coverage with news teams, many of whom were completely unfamiliar with the game—some of them showed up wearing Patriots caps. (Later in the season with the Patriots poised on the verge of a trip to Super Bowl XLII, there were some embarrassing acts of bandwagon reporting from some of the same reporters who were hectoring the coach earlier in the season. One reporter from Boston's NBC affiliate would appear on camera wearing a Patriots cap as he filed a report from Gillette Stadium.)

But remarkably, the whole thing held together. For many, it was more than a little reminiscent of the 2001 season, where Belichick used the case of British explorer Sir Ernest Shackleton as a metaphor for crisis management. Before that season, Belichick took his team to see a film about Shackleton that detailed how Shackleton and his crew overcame adversity in 1915 when their ship sank after hitting an iceberg during an attempted crossing of Antarctica. It was a study in perseverance, even in the most difficult of circumstances. The film shows that no matter what happened, the crew held together and survived, focusing on the task at hand. They discovered a way to lean on each other to overcome every possible obstacle to return alive. *There's no problem that cannot be overcome as long as you have the support of your shipmates.* Under Belichick, since 2001, the Patriots had faced numerous icebergs of their own: Terry Glenn, the departure of key free agents, the release of Lawyer Milloy, Rodney Harrison's ill-advised fling with HGH, and now, Spygate. And each time, it appeared from the outside that the whole thing might just sink them. But through each incident, the Patriots survived, Shackleton style. In times of crisis, they'd focused on the task at hand. They'd held together, closed their circle even tighter, and leaned on each other for support. These times would demand the same sort of resiliency. *There's no problem that cannot be overcome as long as you have the support of your teammates.*

Belichick did not offer much public comment on the matter

until the ruling came down the following Thursday evening. Then, less than seventy-two hours before their game with the Chargers— a rematch of the bitterly contested divisional playoff game from the previous postseason—the head coach released a statement through the team: "I accept full responsibility for the actions that led to tonight's ruling. Once again, I apologize to the Kraft family and every person directly or indirectly associated with the New England Patriots for the embarrassment, distraction, and penalty my mistake caused. I also apologize to Patriots fans and would like to thank them for their support during the past few days and throughout my career.

"As the commissioner acknowledged, our use of sideline video had no impact on the outcome of last week's game. We have never used sideline video to obtain a competitive advantage while the game was in progress.

"Part of my job as head coach is to ensure that our football operations are conducted in compliance of the league rules and all accepted interpretations of them. My interpretation of a rule in the Constitution and Bylaws was incorrect.

"With tonight's resolution, I will not be offering any further comments on this matter. We are moving on with our preparations for Sunday's game."

The league would continue to look into the matter—the commissioner would summon Belichick to his office to further examine more video, but find no more evidence, eventually destroying the videotapes and saying the matter was closed. But for now, the issue seemed to be behind them, and Belichick had his ammunition, the ideal sort of chip-on-your-shoulder stuff that the Patriots had specialized in for so many years. If they weren't able to play the no respect card, Belichick would fashion a new role for them: *Everyone thinks you guys are cheaters! No one thinks you have the talent to win! What are you gonna do about it?* (One reporter called it "The best $500,000 Belichick ever spent.") And so, starting that night against the Chargers, their offense began a roll of record-setting proportions: In a playoff rematch with San Diego, they dominated the Chargers, 38–14, setting the tone for an epic first half of the season. As time ticked away in the win, there was little doubt as to where Belichick's team stood: one by one, they approached him on the sidelines and hugged their head coach. "He's always had our backs, now we have his," said running back Laurence Maroney of Belichick, who was awarded the game ball by Kraft afterward. "He's like our brother. He's family. We look after family around here."

The Chargers game was just the beginning. There were plenty of teams that gave lip service to the idea of scoring every time they touched the football. However, the 2007 Patriots appeared to be the first team bent on taking the idea *completely seriously.* "Coach says he puts us out there to score every time we touch it, so that's what we're trying to do," Brady shrugged after a 56–10 win over Buffalo. "I think that's the job description for any offense in the NFL—you score. He's not putting you out there to punt, I know that, or go three and out. He puts out you out there, you run your best plays and try to execute as well as you can." To that end, through the first eight games of the season, the New England offense did a better job executing through one half of a regular season than almost any team in the history of the game. Whether it was under the directions of Belichick to keep the points coming unabated or the acquisitions of Moss, Morris, and Welker representing some sort of cosmic offensive convergence, it was an awesome sight. The Patriots were just the second team in NFL history to score at least thirty-four points in each of its first eight games of a season. Brady threw at least three touchdown passes a game in all eight games, and broke his career high for touchdowns in a season at the midway point. Chris Hanson was called on to punt just eighteen times through eight games. And despite the fact that they were in control of every game as it entered the fourth quarter, through the first eight games, the Patriots actually scored more points in the fourth than they did in the first quarter.

At the centerpiece of the whole thing was Brady. In the midst of his first-ever MVP season, the New England quarterback was magnificent. Working with an almost all-new series of options in the passing game, he had forced opponents to, in the words of Cleveland coach Romeo Crennel, "Pick your poison." You could either take your chances by putting Moss in single coverage. Or, as the Browns did, you could choose to focus your coverage on Moss and hope the rest of the pass catchers—Wes Welker, Ben Watson, and Donte Stallworth among them—didn't beat you. "I've always had a saying that Peyton Manning has his wide receivers, why can't Tom have his?" Moss said midway through the season after a 48–27 win over Dallas. "Now that Tom has his, we'll see."

Tom Martinez, a quarterbacking guru from Northern California who has worked with Brady since the quarterback was thirteen, said that while the choice was deadly for opponents, it was a little slice of heaven for the quarterback. "It's kind of like a dinner party," Martinez said of the convergence of events. "You throw a dinner party, and everybody really shows you that you want to be there. And it's a great dinner party because everybody that needed to be there is there. There's nothing missing.

"The blend," he added, "was perfect."

While it was perfect for New England fans, those outside the six-state New England region were fuming. They had cheated, and only received a slap on the wrist for their infraction. The Patriots were now the bad guys. A mock "concert" tour poster made its way around the Internet with a photoshopped Belichick grinning and holding a middle finger toward the camera. On top of a map of the United States, there was a banner headline that read: "Coming soon to an NFL stadium near you: Bill Belichick's 2007 'Fuck You, NFL' Road Show!" Underneath was listed the Patriots 2007 schedule. New England now wore the black hat. They were the bad guys, the ones who reveled in an outlaw persona. Teams started to call them out: San Diego offensive lineman Nick Hardwick labeled Richard Seymour "a dirty, cheap little pompous bitch." Cleveland offensive lineman Eric Steinbach said Mike Vrabel was "classless." And Buffalo quarterback J. P. Losman blasted Vince Wilfork (who would be fined three times that season for a variety of perceived infractions) after a hit from the Patriots nose tackle sidelined him for a few weeks.

The bad blood bubbled to the surface on the afternoon of October 28, when the Patriots dismantled the Redskins, 52–7. Just hours before the Red Sox clinched their second World Series crown in four years with a sweep of the Colorado Rockies, New England completely dominated Joe Gibbs and Washington, scoring on seven of their eleven possessions. But it wasn't so much how much they scored, but how: The Patriots went for it twice on fourth down, once when they were up 38–0, a second time when they were leading 45–0.

"What do you want us to do?" Belichick asked afterward. "Kick a field goal?"

After the game, Redskins' linebacker Randall Godfrey spoke for many around the NFL, who said enough was enough. "I said something to [Belichick] after the game," Godfrey told NBCSports .com afterward. "I told him, 'You need to show some respect for the game.' You just don't do that. I don't care how bad it is. You're up thirty-five points and you're still throwing deep? That's no respect. . . . You look at all the great head coaches . . . I'm just disappointed.

"You gotta show some class, show some respect. Joe Gibbs? We wouldn't have done that. Bill Walsh? You wouldn't see those types of guys doing that stuff. I've never seen nothing like that. Most teams, you get up like that, you sit on the ball, and try to run the time out. They're up thirty-some points and they're throwing deep. That was blatant disrespect. I hope we can see them again, definitely. You don't see Joe Gibbs doing that. You can't even imagine that kind of stuff coming from him. Joe Gibbs. Bill Walsh. Bill Parcells. This isn't like college going for power rankings. This is the pros. You show some respect, show some class."

That October afternoon cemented their place as one of the most polarizing teams in almost the last twenty years. There was no middle ground with this team. If you lived within the confines of the six-state region, you were worshipping the Patriots, marveling at their run toward perfection and their shock and awe approach to the rest of the NFL. *In Bill We Trust. The rest of the league can eat shit.* Outside of New England, they were an infuriating amalgamation of Duke basketball, Notre Dame football, the 1990s Yankees and Cowboys, and the 1980s–1990s Miami football team, all rolled into one maddening package. They were a team you loved to hate, a lightning rod for football fans everywhere. They had stolen signs and gotten away with it, and now, they were kicking opponents when they were down. *Screw Bill Belicheat and the rest of them. They're dirty, and they don't care who they humiliate.* The insane level of national fervor that surrounded the Patriots did make for great television. No team sparked more passion, and that could be found in the TV ratings. Playing an NFL-high six prime-time games in 2007, the Patriots were a boon for network executives. (That year, the Patriots would play in four games that would be the four most-watched programs of that television season. In addition, their late season contest with the Ravens on ESPN's *Monday Night Football* would be the most-watched program in cable television history. And Super Bowl XLII would be the highest-rated Super Bowl of all time, and the second-highest rated TV show in history behind the *M\*A\*S\*H* finale.)

As November gave way to December, the wins kept coming. Even though they weren't blowouts like the first half of the season, the Patriots record climbed to 13–0, 14–0 and 15–0. It all built to a remarkable head in the Meadowlands on the night of December 29 against the New York Giants. The Patriots entered the game 15–0, poised to become the first team since the 1972 Dolphins to complete a perfect regular season.

Picking the best Brady-to-Moss moment of the 2007 season was like trying to settle on a favorite Beatles' album, but for Martinez and many other New England football fans, the unquestioned highlight came in that regular-season finale against the Giants. With just over eleven minutes left, the Patriots were down 28–23, and Moss and Brady just missed on a pass deep down the right sideline, with Moss having to reach back to try and make a finger-tip grab inches off the turf. However, he appeared to simply drop the ball. (Afterward, both said Brady underthrew it.) That set up a key third and ten situation.

"I had to redeem myself," Brady said.

On the next play, redemption was his when he lofted a clean 65-yard strike to Moss down the same sideline. The receiver gathered it in and raced past safety James Butler for the score that gave New England a lead it wouldn't relinquish. The touchdown pass was the fiftieth of the season for Brady (breaking Peyton Manning's record) and the twenty-third touchdown reception of the season for Moss (breaking Jerry Rice's record). "It wasn't exactly the same play, but come back to the same scenario that just didn't work . . . most football teams that call plays just don't do that," Martinez said. "You take a shot downfield or you take a shot at a reverse pass or you run a screen and it doesn't work, then you put that thing in the closet for a quarter and then you come back to it later. But they needed that play, and then for Moss to drop it when that would have won the game, because it wasn't a well-thrown ball, but still, maybe, he could have caught it.

"And then to come back and hit that next play. It was just like, 'OK, we screwed it up, but here we come again.' Then, it was the perfect throw and the perfect route and a great result."

In the postseason, the Patriots had little trouble defeating Jacksonville—in another legendary Brady performance, the quarterback went 26-for-28 in a 31–20 win in the divisional playoffs. (There were elements to that game that were stunning for many, including one sequence where Brady was giving subtle hand signals to his receivers *in the middle of a play*, something many football old-timers hadn't seen before.) New England struggled in the

AFC Championship against the Chargers, but eventually came away with a 21–12 victory. At that point, the perfect season appeared to be an inevitability, especially when the top two seeds in the NFC, Dallas and Green Bay, both lost—the Cowboys were beaten in the divisional playoffs by New York, and the Giants continued their magic carpet ride the following week with a win over the Packers in Green Bay to advance to the Super Bowl.

But the day after the AFC Championship win, things started to change for the Patriots. In their three previous trips to the Super Bowl, they had assiduously managed to avoid the pre-Super Bowl hype, and had done an excellent job keeping any and all distractions at a minimum. As much as a Super Bowl team could avoid the spotlight, they did. As a team, they went deep into the bunker, only coming out for the occasional press conference. But that all went out the window the day after the AFC Championship, when video of Brady hobbling through the streets of Manhattan with a walking boot surfaced. The quarterback was carrying a bouquet of flowers for girlfriend Gisele Bündchen, and was clearly limping. The video was odd, and the whole thing really ran contrary to the Patriots approach. The sight of the New England quarterback wearily hobbling down the street gave away all sorts of material, strange for a team that is so reticent to disclose anything, especially potentially dangerous injury information. Now they were vulnerable, a maddening situation for a coach who guards injury information like it was a nuclear launch code. In addition, it was certainly out of character for Brady: the quarterback had always stressed putting football first during the postseason. The year before, he was plain in what sort of advice he'd offer a rookie when it came to preparing for the postseason: "Try to put everything off that can wait until the off-season, try to put it off until the end of the year," Brady said on January 4, 2007. "Right now, you just put everything aside in your life and try to go out and put everything you can into each week." Brady certainly didn't appear to be putting everything else aside. No matter how big he had gotten—no matter how many magazine covers he graced, no matter how many television shows he appeared on and no matter how many interviews he gave—he always knew what was important, especially in the postseason. It was football first, football last, football forever. And in previous years, once the postseason rolled around, Brady went into hiding, keeping the focus on what was important. He expected his teammates to do the same thing. But now, the Patriots had the sort of distraction on their hands that Belichick despised.

In the days before the Super Bowl, more distractions arose when Spygate was broached again. Matt Walsh, a former Patriots employee who was working in Hawaii as a golf pro, said he had information that could prove potentially damaging to the franchise, eventually disclosing he had more tapes. And the *Boston Herald* had a report saying a member of the team's video department filmed the Rams' final walk-through before that 2002 game, an accusation that New England officials flatly denied: "The suggestion that the New England Patriots recorded the St. Louis Rams' walk-through on the day before Super Bowl XXXVI in 2002 is absolutely false. Any suggestion to the contrary is untrue." And in a bit of naked political grandstanding in the days leading up to the game, U.S. Senator Arlen Specter demanded an explanation as to why the tapes had been destroyed: "The NFL has a very preferred status in our country with their antitrust exemption. The American people are entitled to be sure about the integrity of the game," he told *The New York Times*. "It's analogous to the CIA destruction of tapes. Or any time you have records destroyed."

For what it's worth, Specter hardly seemed to be the type to be lobbing grenades in the direction of the commissioner. According to records, the previous year, Specter had received more than $100,000 in contributions from Comcast, a cable company in a long-running battle with the NFL, as to whether or not the cable giant could charge its consumers extra money to view the NFL Network. Many raised a cocked eyebrow at Specter's statement.

"For the benefit of those of you scoring at home, Specter began his public career by, ah, creatively debunking the notion of a conspiracy to kill John Kennedy and is now ending it by intimating that there is a conspiracy to protect the New England Patriots," wrote Slate's Charles Pierce. "If only Abraham Zapruder had been around to film the signals of the New York Jets, Specter might have been inclined to lay off." Shortly after going public with his dissatisfaction with the NFL, the senior senator from Pennsylvania—a huge Eagles fan—wondered aloud if the outcome of Super Bowl XXIX was on the up and up. The feelings of many were summed up by Jon Stewart of *The Daily Show*: "You became interested after they beat your hometown football team? Well, the implication is clear: The only way we can get him to investigate Guantánamo is to imprison the Phillie Phanatic there."

(The flap around the tapes would drag on until the spring, when Walsh—after months of negotiating immunity—would meet with Goodell and Specter in a much-anticipated sitdown. However, when it came time for the big reveal, there was little surprise: The tapes, said Goodell, were "consistent" with what the league had seen previously from the Patriots. The commissioner pronounced the matter closed. "As I stand before you today, and having met with Matt Walsh and more than fifty other people, I don't know where else I would turn," Goodell told reporters.)

But on that cool night in the Arizona desert, it wasn't the distraction around the tapes that did them in. It wasn't the pressure of the perfect season. It was a Giants team that ended up playing the game of their collective lives, knocking New England for a loop and ruining the perfect season. The Patriots were flat and uninspired for much of the night, and New York took advantage. "It was like watching a different team play," Martinez said of the Patriots. "Some of those things that happened there didn't happen in the Super Bowl. They did it all eighteen games, and then, in the nineteenth game, it was like, 'Is this the same team I've been watching since 2001?' They had an answer in the past, really, for everything anyone tried to do to them during a game. In the Super Bowl, it kind of seemed like they just didn't have an answer. . . . It was just different watching that game, compared to all the other games that you had watched them play."

The Patriots were unable to match the Giants' intensity from the start. New York won the coin toss and put together a steady, sustained drive that lasted just under ten minutes and culminated in a field goal for a 3–0 lead, and the Patriots answered with a drive of their own that ended with a Laurence Maroney touchdown to make it 7–3. However, the offensive shock and awe that had rained down on the heads of New England opponents throughout the season never came that night in the desert. The Giants defense was able to keep the Patriots in check, blasting Brady time after time. (They ended up sacking him five times, the most on the season for Brady and tying a career high.) It stayed 7–3 into the second half in a physical and chippy game that left players from both sides reeling, and appeared similar in many ways to Super Bowl XXXVI: the underdog, on the strength of a superlative defensive effort, stayed in the game long after most believed they could. The Giants held a 10–7 lead late in the second half, but a classic Tom Brady fourth-quarter drive culminated with a six-yard pass to Moss in the end zone with 2:42 remaining to give New England a 14–10 edge. It appeared the Patriots were in excellent shape: New England held a late Super Bowl lead, and its defense, which had allowed just one touchdown over the previous eight quarters of postseason football, was going to rise up for one final stand against a young quarterback in Eli Manning, a signal caller who would surely wilt under the pressure of the moment.

But much like Brady pulled off six years previously on the floor of the Superdome, Manning engineered a last-minute drive at the expense of the New England defense that secured him a spot in the record books, an imperfectly perfect sequence that included three near turnovers. However, his best moment may have come on a third and long, where he slipped from the grasp of Richard

Seymour and Jarvis Green and flung the ball deep downfield, only to have little-used wide receiver David Tyree outjump Rodney Harrison and come down with the ball pinned against his helmet in what would later be described as one of the best catches in Super Bowl history. Four plays later, Manning connected with Plaxico Burress on a harmless floater over cornerback Ellis Hobbs with thirty-nine seconds left to give the Giants a lead. The Patriots were unable to counter, and the game ended with Manning taking a knee and running out the clock while Belichick scooted off the field with one second left.

According to many New York players, the Patriots players were sounding a lot like Ricky "Tonight, the Dynasty Is Born" Proehl during Super Bowl XXXVI. Although none of it was caught by the cameras of NFL Films, New York reported several instances where Patriots players invited them to New England's postgame victory celebration, the sort of thing that would have riled the Patriots of 2001, 2003, and 2004. Giants players—including wide receiver Amani Toomer—said Richard Seymour spent much of the evening telling them to "go home." The final outcome prompted Giants running back Brandon Jacobs to gleefully exclaim to reporters after the game when asked about Seymour: "I'll give you a quote on Seymour. You can write that he's a soft [expletive]. He said we should get ready to go home. Well, now he's on the team that went 18–1."

On the other side, it was regret at a missed opportunity.

"We had an opportunity to be special," Seymour said quietly after the game. "There were a lot of teams that have won a Super Bowl, but none of them would have done it the way we would have.

"We lost the Super Bowl. When all the chips were on the table, we lost the big hand."

"It's not worth talking about it now, because it's over. It didn't happen," said Tedy Bruschi when he was asked about the possibility of finishing off a perfect season with a Super Bowl victory. "We can look back on this year with a positive attitude and some of the things we accomplished. But when you don't finish . . . I mean, that's what we're all about. We're about finishing the task at hand, and we expect to win, because we've had success in the past.

"But when you come up short, I think you just have to tip your cap to the other team. They're a great team. They're the World Champions."

While the rest of the nation celebrated—and the 1972 Dolphins cackled gleefully from South Florida—the defeat was crushing for many New England football fans, who refused to talk about the loss for months. (Critics drew comparisons to the 2001 New York Yankees, another sporting dynasty that ended in the Arizona desert.) Regardless, two days after the Super Bowl, BetUs.com listed the Patriots as 3–1 favorites to win Super Bowl XLIII. And in a conference call with the media two days later, Belichick announced the Patriots were moving on. "The players did a great job all year long," he said. "We played a lot of good football, but we're certainly disappointed about the way it ended. We came so close, but it just didn't work out. It takes a lot to get to this point, but we're starting all over into the '08 season. It's already time to move on. We're into the off-season and that's just the way it is, so we'll start moving ahead toward next year."

In large measure, the continued on-field success of the Patriots would seem to hinge on being able to maintain that harmony between ownership, front office, coaching staff, and superstar, the balance that's been so key to the success of the franchise since 2001. It's a balance that's rare in professional sports today: Knowing your role is difficult. It's not only enough that you have four capable people in those jobs. The slightest step over the line into someone else's neighborhood—whether it's a contract demand, a personnel change, or a free-agent slipup—can send the whole thing off the tracks. One of the only teams that's been able to achieve that sort of sporting nirvana is the San Antonio Spurs. Tim Duncan, Gregg Popovich, GM R. C. Buford, and owner Peter Holt have been able to help lead the Spurs to four titles in nine years thanks in large part to their ability to trust that each of their comrades will handle his responsibilities. Over the years, they have used each other as a role model, so it should come as no surprise that when it comes to listing the most dominant professional teams of the twenty-first century, the Spurs and Patriots are at the top of anyone's list. "To have sustained excellence over a decade is extremely difficult, and the Spurs have done it as well as anyone," Pioli recently told *Sports Illustrated*. "What is really impressive is their player development, the fact that they've brought in so many international players and integrated them into a system."

"Do your job," is a theme that Belichick constantly hammers home to his players—he's been captured on the sidelines saying the same thing, time and again. The same is true in the relationship between the New England players, coaches, front office, and ownership. Keeping that balance between the four power sectors would seem to be paramount to the success of the franchise. And, at first glance, it appears every member of New England's foursome is content with their current role, and is aware of what it takes to keep the franchise successful. Brady, who will turn thirty-one just before the start of the 2008 season, has enjoyed a tremendous level of success for a quarterback of his age. By the time he turned thirty in the summer of 2007, he had accomplished more than many of the greats of the game had at the same age, and Martinez says the quarterback doesn't appear to be slowing down any time soon.

"The things he's in control of—getting ready for the game plan, executing the game plan, working on his own mechanical things that he thinks he needs to do to not only get better, but to stay at the top—he has all that built in, and those are unbelievable traits for a guy that was doing it in his twenties," Martinez said of Brady, who is currently signed through 2010. "Most great quarterbacks like Elway and Montana, most of their success came in their thirties. It took all that time to really put together what Brady was able to put together in his twenties. Moving forward, I don't think there's anyone who needs to tell him anything. I can't believe he will ever change his approach to preparation and getting better and executing what he has to do. When you have that, that far exceeds ability and technique and everything else, because you're going to work your way through problems."

Brady appears to be closer to Belichick than he's even been, and the two remain happy with their working relationship: "We still have a lot of fun coming in and playing for Coach Belichick who—I've said this so many times—I think we're all lucky to play for him because he's the best," the quarterback told the media early in the season. "There's no question."

When it comes to Belichick, the coach remains in sync with his front office and the New England ownership. In September 2007, it was reported Kraft had given Belichick a contract extension that would keep him in New England through 2013. It certainly appears to be an ideal situation for a head coach—there is relatively little interference from the front office and ownership, which appears content to let Belichick run the team as he sees fit. (However, if the head coach does indeed have a deal that would take him through 2013, he would be sixty-one at the end of that contract, a logical age to begin considering retirement when you look at the retiring age of many coaching greats Belichick has looked up to: Paul Brown retired when he was sixty-seven, Don Shula stepped aside at the age of sixty-five, and Bill Walsh retired from the NFL when he was fifty-seven.) When the report was released, Kraft wouldn't comment on possible new deal for Belichick, but certainly did not issue a denial: "The coach and I have had a policy that we don't discuss his contract, but he's made great contributions to this franchise over the last seven years, and myself and all our fans truly appreciate his efforts," Kraft told NBC.

For his part, Pioli has had several offers to leave the Patriots, including a lucrative deal to become GM of the Seahawks, as well as the request to interview for the Giants GM job prior to the 2007 season. But in the days leading up to Super Bowl XLII, he did not sound like a man who was thinking about leaving Foxborough: Like Belichick, he was in an excellent environment for a football man. There was minimal intrusion from a stable ownership, as well as a solid working relationship with the coaching staff.

"This is a good situation. We're winning. Because of what my title is, people have a perception. I know how things go inside. I'm happy with the situation and the way things are right now," Pioli said. "It's a pretty good situation.

"There've been questions and temptations, but so far, this is where that I wanted to be."

"Scott and I have a great working relationship," Belichick said. "Even though there are times we disagree, we are always able to work it out and be honest. It doesn't matter who is right or who is wrong, it's important that we get it right at the end. That's one of the things I really appreciate with Scott. He works very hard. He's well prepared. Nobody spends more time and diligence at his job than Scott Pioli does."

And at the top is Kraft, who appears happy with the balance, and maintains that running a football team is like running any business.

"It is the same principles. It is having a vision for what is right for your organization," he said. "Then picking good people. Whether it is picking your life partner or partners in business, it is the same principles. What works for me might not work for other people.

"In the business of professional football, having trust between ownership, the head coach, and their personnel people is very important."

"Ownership is smart enough to realize that Belichick and Pioli are football-wise people, and they put the football fortunes into the hands of the football people. That's a credit to Robert Kraft, that he's allowing the football people to function, and that's why they've had so much success," said veteran personnel man Charley Armey, who worked for several teams. "He's relied and depended on their judgment about players and player moves and roster adjustments and so on and so forth, and it's paid off for them, because Robert Kraft has had confidence in the fact that they know what they're doing and he allows them to do it.

"It's a real difficult situation, because if you don't allow your football people, the people who are responsible for putting the product on the field in the end, your coaching and your personnel people to run the personnel department and get you the right players, it usually leads to mistakes. They've done a very good job of knowing their needs and knowing who fits and who doesn't fit. And Robert Kraft has been remarkable in that he's allowed them to do that. He understands how to get a franchise going and how to get it off the ground. And they've done it successfully."

The last two seasons, the Patriots missed out on a Super Bowl title, but that doesn't diminish what they've been able to accomplish when it comes to building their overall brand. According to Andrew Zimbalist, one of the nation's top sports economists, their off-field financial sustainability in an economic environment that's so inherently socialist is worth marveling at.

"The Patriots share 70 to 75 percent of all of their revenues. The NFL has a salary cap. They have an imbalanced schedule so that strong teams play strong teams and weak teams play weak teams. They have a reverse order draft. They play a season of only sixteen games, which makes it more subject to random outcomes, as opposed to a baseball season where they play 162 games," said Zimbalist, ticking off all the reasons why a team shouldn't be able to build a dynasty in the NFL. "They have all these things that say, 'This league is a league where everybody has an equal chance.'

"It's not like the Yankees or Red Sox in baseball, where you can have a payroll of $210 million or $150 million and the other teams are all down at $70 or $80 million," he adds. "You don't have that starting advantage in football, so it's really all got to be in the organization and in the brains. And frankly, I'm surprised the Patriots been able to sustain it as long as they have. In this kind of a world, in the NFL's world, to be able to do that, I think you have to infer from that that there's something very, very special happening on the management end."

Off the field, there's no reason to think the Patriots won't be able to enjoy the same financial success. Despite the negative publicity the franchise suffered through with Spygate, the team and stadium remains extremely valuable—in 2007, *Forbes* ranked them as the third most valuable football team, worth over $1 billion. And Kraft is consistently listed by *Forbes* as one of the world's richest people. But despite Kraft's deep pockets, long-term success in the NFL can often be a double-edged sword: There's no great financial gain to be made with extra playoff games—quite often, according to Zimbalist, sustained on-field success in the NFL's current economic climate can be a money-losing proposition. In the locker room, it can breed a me-first culture that means higher contracts and extended holdouts. Off the field, the simple cost of an extra month of games can run into the tens of millions of dollars in extra expenses.

How can a franchise make that money back? Zimbalist says one of the secrets to the Krafts' financial success around the Patriots lies in the fact that they use nontraditional thinking when it comes to maximizing the revenue streams that are available to them. Like the Red Sox, the relatively low capacity of Gillette Stadium (it seats roughly 68,000, which puts it in the middle of the pack) combined with the overall success of the team allows the Patriots to maintain a "scarcity value" on each ticket, which remains the highest average price in the NFL. Then, there's the signage.

"Instead of adding more and more seats, they used the extra

space that could have been seating, they used it for signage. And signage is revenue they don't have to share with their fellow owners. Gate revenue is revenue they have to share. And this way, they get to create a scarcity value," Zimbalist said. "One of the values of having fewer seats rather than more seats is that it always maintains a scarcity value. You get that benefit. You get the benefit of substituting signage revenue for gate revenue, and that means you don't have to share it.

"They have found little niches where they can exercise entrepreneurial behavior, and get some return for it."

Another area where they've been able to exercise some entrepreneurial behavior is with the creation of Patriot Place, a $350 million retail and entertainment complex being built on the land around Gillette Stadium. Five years after the stadium was completed, construction began on a series of outlets—including a four-star hotel—that Zimbalist believes will ultimately make Foxborough a destination spot: When football fans used to fly into New England for games, they would stay in Boston or Providence and spend their money in those big cities, only going to Foxborough for an afternoon of football. With the completion of Patriot Place, fans will fly into New England and spend the entire weekend—as well as their money—in Foxborough.

And the Krafts won't have to share any of it with the NFL.

"One of the things that I think inspired Patriot Place, is that there are two individuals in Robert and Jonathan Kraft who are bursting all over with entrepreneurial ideas and instincts and they can't really implement them in the NFL system. Patriot Place is a place where they can actually be entrepreneurs, and the NFL can't stop them."

It's one of the great mysteries of the sports world, right there with Isiah Thomas's ability to continuously find employment and the

Cubs' run of postseason failure. Year after year, the team that loses the Super Bowl inevitably suffers through a miserable campaign the following season. There are different reasons for different teams—injuries, team dissension, coaching change, losing primary focus, etc. But the combined consistency of the struggles the following year remains puzzling: Entering the 2008 season, just three of the last ten teams that lost the Super Bowl made the playoffs the following year, and only two teams even reached double digits in wins. In all, Super Bowl losing teams averaged just fewer than eight wins the following season.

During the off-season, the Patriots spent their time doing their best to avoid the same pitfalls that befell other teams that came up short the year after a Super Bowl loss. There were setbacks, most notably in the secondary: All-Pro cornerback Asante Samuel, feeling wronged by the way he was franchised by the team the year before, was the first one to leave, and he tore out of New England so fast he left skidmarks in the parking lot. He was holding his introductory press conference with the Eagles less than eighteen hours after the start of free agency. Safety Eugene Wilson, Samuel's partner in crime who came in with him as part of the 2003 draft haul, signed with Tampa Bay. And New Orleans overpaid to bring nickelback and native son Randall Gay back home to Louisiana. (However, it's worth noting here that defensive backs in the Belichick system have always been somewhat fungible. While much is placed on the shoulders of the linebackers—many of who end up sticking with Belichick for great lengths of time—defensive backs are treated mostly like impulse items at a supermarket. With precious few exceptions—Ty Law, for one—safeties and cornerbacks have always been relatively interchangeable, coming and going at such a rapid rate that they're often difficult to keep track of.)

But at the same time—after a few anxious days—they were able to re-sign wide receiver Randy Moss to a three-year deal. And while there were no splashy headlines like the previous off-season when the landed Moss, Adalius Thomas, and Wes Welker, they were able to keep most of the rest of the core of a team that went unbeaten through the regular season. And when you consider that the Patriots entered the 2008 season preparing to face the easiest schedule in the league—including six games against a collection of AFC East teams that could make up one of the weakest divisions in the history of football—barring injury, you would have to be foolish to consider the idea they might fall victim to the usual post–Super Bowl hangover.

"I think they're still the team to beat," said NFL Network analyst Brian Baldinger as the 2008 season drew near. "They play in an awful division, and for six games a year, they can try new things and escape with easy wins."

"Trying new things" was certainly the phrase for the Patriots through the first stages of the off-season. The Patriots' team-building model that was crafted by Belichick and Pioli in the early days of the twenty-first century heralded a new era in pro football management—namely, focus on acquiring veteran linebackers while spending wisely, stocking up on draft picks, and always keeping an eye on the bottom line. But in the early days of 2008, it was clear the model had been tweaked a bit, altered to reflect the changing and evolving nature of the NFL. After drafting just one linebacker before the fifth round in their eight previous drafts—preferring instead to go with veteran linebackers like Thomas, Rosevelt Colvin, Mike Vrabel, Roman Phifer, Junior Seau, and Bryan Cox, all of whom arrived via free agency—Belichick and Pioli selected linebacker Jerod Mayo out of Tennessee in the first round. There appeared to be other changes: missing was the traditional multiple selections of down linemen on both sides of the ball. In addition, it was just the second draft in New England where he didn't take at least one tight end. Belichick poked fun at himself after the draft: "Who would have ever thought you would be covering a Bill Belichick draft with no offensive linemen, defensive linemen, or tight ends taken, right?" he asked the media with a smile. Despite the levity, the selection of Mayo did appear to be a break from the Patriots usual approach on a number of levels: an early draft pick spent on a linebacker out of a school where the coach wasn't a Belichick confidant. But for a team that saw its defense fail when the season was on the line two straight seasons, getting younger on defense was a necessary maneuver if they wanted to keep their edge.

"The one play that exemplified their age and lack of speed on defense was the screen pass that Indianapolis running back Joseph Addai took for a touchdown in a midseason game—the players had angles in open field, and they couldn't get a glove on him. They need speed on defense, and in a limited draft, they addressed that," Baldinger said of the Patriots, who ended up taking six players with defensive experience out of a possible seven draft picks, one of the highest ratios in franchise history. "I liked the Mayo pick. They picked the smartest defensive back in the draft in Colorado's Terrence Wheatley, and got a quarterback to replace Matt Cassel, which was on Belichick's mind ever since Cassel threw that interception versus the Dolphins and then was pulled by the head coach."

(However, while there were things that appeared out of character with their style, there was another part of the selection that was to be right in line with their approach: They were able to trade down three spots to get Mayo at No. 10, and, if history is any indication, that would mean a real savings when it comes to negotiating a contract. The No. 7 pick in the 2007 draft, running back Adrian Peterson, signed a deal with the Vikings that was for a guaranteed $17 million after options. The No. 10 pick, defensive tackle Amobi Okoye, inked a contract with the Texans worth $12.8 million guaranteed.)

Another signal of change can be seen with a quick glance around the locker room. Players who were high school underclassmen the night Adam Vinatieri's kick split the uprights in New Orleans are now joining a team they watched while growing up—Mayo was just a sophomore in high school when Tom Brady managed to tuck the ball away that snowy night against the Raiders. As 2008 spring minicamp began, just eight of the players on the roster were with the Patriots at the start of the 2001 season: Tom Brady, Tedy Bruschi, Kevin Faulk, Larry Izzo, Matt Light, Lonie Paxton, Richard Seymour, and Mike Vrabel. For the NFL, it represents a remarkable run of stability, but at the same time, many of the veterans who helped the franchise achieve much of its early success are gone, either retired, released, or traded. In their place is a new generation of Patriots, a second generation who is well aware of the situation they are entering into. "I never thought I'd be on a team that lost only one game last year. I'm excited to learn from some of the great vets and become as good as those guys are," said Mayo in his first visit to Gillette Stadium that spring. "I'm just going to sit back and learn from the greats. Guys who have been winning championships before me. Hopefully, they'll be winning them with me."

As the 2008 season looms, Belichick, Pioli, and Kraft are set to begin their ninth season together, and Brady will be in his eighth season as a starter and ninth year in the NFL. While the Patriots have been able to achieve great things since those four first came together, it may take years to measure their ultimate impact of their blueprint for success. However, good or bad, it's undeniable that their style and success has changed the game of professional football forever: Their effects can be seen everywhere. It's seen in ownership, where millionaires and billionaires sometimes must realize that they simply need to trust in the men they've hired, and give them a wide berth when it comes to making the right decisions. It's seen in front offices, as more and more teams raid the Patriots' coaching staff and front office for the next great young coaching or personnel mind. It's seen in front offices, where coaches and general managers agree to work together in the team-building process and realize that the most successful franchises consist of a series of complimentary parts instead of an Pro Bowl roster of players from one to fifty-three. It's seen in the locker rooms, as players start to realize that sometimes, if you want to win, money must come second. It's seen in coaching staffs, where the realization that a smart, well-prepared team will beat a physically superior team nine times out of ten. And it's seen in the lessons of Spygate, which will impact game preparation, scouting, and NFL security.

But will anyone be able to truly emulate the Patriots' blueprint and create the next great dynasty? In this current economic climate—with planned parity, balanced scheduling and the salary cap—it doesn't seem likely.

"I think that everybody will *try* to emulate what they're doing. Whether they're able to execute it the way the Krafts and Belichick have executed it is another question," Zimbalist said. "There are no great mysteries. I don't think you have to be a rocket scientist to design a spread offense. You don't have to be a rocket scientist to be able to read other teams' offenses and set up your defense accordingly. You don't need to be from Wesleyan or Williams or Harvard to do those things.

"But you do have to have a certain power of perception and interpretation so that when something is being thrown at you, you adjust properly, and as quickly as possible. I think that it's very easy to say, 'We want to adopt the Belichick system.' But to implement it as effectively as he has and be able to evaluate talent as effectively as he's been able to do, it's questionable."

# INDEX

Richardson, Mike, 249
Rison, Andre, 86–87, 124
Roberts, William, 72
Robinson-Randall, Greg, 110, 189, 192
Rogers, Carlos, 247
Rolle, Antrel, 247
Rolle, Derrick, 127
Romer, David, 257–59
Romo, Tony, 279
Rooney family, 261
Rowland, John, 103
Rucci, Todd, 110
Ruddy, Tim, 127
Runyan, John, 107
Rush, Clive, 50, 170
  firing of, 27
  on media, 15
  reputation of, 24–25
Russell, Bill, 227
Russell, Leonard, 58
Rust, Rod, 45
Rutledge, Rod, 110, 196
Ruud, Barrett, 248
Ryan, Bob, 200
Ryan, Buddy, 74

Saban, Lou, 20
Saban, Nick, 249, 250–51, 253
Sackrowitz, Harold, 259
Samuel, Asante, 209, 246, 269, 273, 308
Sanders, Deion, 84, 224, 275
Sanders, James, 248
Santos, Gil, 27, 155
  on Belichick, 114–15
  on Coates, 205
  Sullivan, Billy, and, 37–38
  Super Bowl XXXVI and, 170
  on Vrabel, 119
Saturday, Jeff, 271
Savage, Phil, 250
Scarnecchia, Dante, 108
Schatz, Aaron
  on Belichick, 97
  on draft strategy, 262–63
  on Grier, Bobby, 105
  on Hill, Pat, 250
  statistics and, 261
  on Vrabel, 119
  on West Coast offense, 191–92
Schiano, Mike, 259–60
Schwedes, Gerhardt, 20
Scott, Chad, 158
Scroggins, Tracy, 123
Seals, Ray, 117
Seau, Junior, 269, 309

Seely, Brad, 157
Sehorn, Jason, 178
Seymour, Richard, 114, 157, 235, 276–77, 300, 311
  2003 AFC Championship and, 237–38
  on Branch, 267
  evolution of, 4
  Pioli on, 11
  signing of, 125–26, 246, 280–1
  on Super Bowl XLII, 300
Shackleton, Ernest, 226, 289
Shanahan, Mike, 105
Sharpe, Shannon, 107
Shaughnessy, Dan, 59, 102, 155
Shaw, Willie, 74
Shula, Don, 89, 303
Shurmur, Fritz, 80
Sidwell, Steve, 74
Simmons, Jason, 158
Simms, Phil, 87, 151
Simpson, O. J., 177
Sims, Kenneth, 42
Sisson, Scott, 56
Slade, Chris, 56, 69, 122
Slusher, Howard, 36
Smith, Antowain, 124–25, 141
Smith, Emmitt, 5
Smith, Kate, 18
Smith, L. J., 240
Smith, Otis, 6–7, 72, 108, 137
  on Belichick, 149
  release of, 209
  Super Bowl XXXVI and, 167, 170
Smith, Rod, 127
Smith, Steve, 222–23
Specter, Arlen, 297–8
Spygate, 286–90, 297, 312
  Belichick on, 290
  Brady on, 286–7
  media and, 288–9
Stabler, Ken, 35, 224
Stachelski, Dave, 189, 191
Stallworth, Donte, 272, 292
Starks, Duane, 270
Starr, Bart, 31, 181, 187
Starring, Stephen, 42
Steinbach, Eric, 293
Stevenson, Dan, 249
Stewart, Jon, 298
Stewart, Kordell, 157, 188
Stingley, Darryl, 33, 37
Stone, Ron, 127
Stover, Matt, 127
Stram, Hank, 22
Stringer, Korey, 127